Like Father, Like Daughter

SUZANNE FIELDS

Like Father, Like Daughter

How Father Shapes the Woman His Daughter Becomes

Little, Brown and Company   Boston — Toronto

Third Printing

LIBRARY OF CONGRESS CATALOGING IN PUBLICATION DATA

Fields, Suzanne.
  Like father, like daughter.

  Bibliography: p. 291
  1. Fathers and daughters. I Title.
HQ756.F53   1983   306.8'742   83-7953
ISBN 0-316-28169-7

Excerpt from SOMETHING HAPPENED by Joseph Heller.
Copyright © 1966, 1974 Scapegoat Productions,
Inc. Reprinted by permission of Alfred A. Knopf, Inc.

Excerpt from "I Knew a Woman" by Theodore Roethke,
copyright 1954 by Theodore Roethke, from the book
THE COLLECTED POEMS OF THEODORE ROETHKE.
Reprinted by permission of Doubleday & Company, Inc.

"Visiting Rights" (p. 64) by Gretchen Van Ness, 1982

BP

Book designed by Patricia Girvin Dunbar

*Published simultaneously in Canada
by Little, Brown & Company (Canada) Limited*

PRINTED IN THE UNITED STATES OF AMERICA

For Sadie Hurwitz Bregman, my mother, whose love and nurturing made my relationship with my father, this book, and all other good things possible.

Acknowledgments

To those several hundred fathers and daughters who told me their secrets, frustrations, and triumphs, and whose appearances here are, as promised, carefully disguised; to my husband, Ted, and to our children, Alexandra, Miriamne, and Tobias, whose love, confidence, and forbearance were my sustaining encouragement; to Wesley Pruden, who taught me how to write; and for Barbara Ellen Friedman Chambers (1941–1982), whose ideas and insights inspired so many of my own; my heartfelt thanks.

Contents

SIX Driving into the Future

P A R T   O N E

An Electrical Connection

"If you want to know more about femininity, en-
quire from your own experiences of life, or turn to the poets, or wait
until science can give you deeper and more coherent information."
— Sigmund Freud
"Femininity," 1933

Daddies, Daughters, and Dilemmas

"**B**ring the big car, Daddy."
I giggled into the telephone. The big car was the Detroit definition of Big Car, a maroon Cadillac with lush white sidewalls and creamy white carpets, with seats so thick and soft that a little girl could get lost in them, snuggled down deep in the leather next to her daddy. I was waiting to be picked up at Ginger's birthday party and I wanted to show off the maroon Cadillac. Most of all, I wanted to show off Daddy.

The year was 1941. I was five years old.

Daddy was Mr. Magic, a big man with a big car. He peeled big bills from a roll he kept under a money clip of solid gold, fashioned in the sign of the dollar, and he wore wide silk cravats painted by Countess Mara in the patterns and colors of the rainbow. Expensive, like the car. His coat was a blend of cashmere and vicuna, his gloves were suede and soft. I knew vaguely that he was something called a "sports promoter," that his good friend Billy Conn was a famous prizefighter. Billy Conn, whoever he was, was not as big and as strong as my daddy. Nobody was.

When he drove up a few minutes later and tooted the horn, I ran out in a hurry, anxious for the other girls to follow me with their eyes but just as anxious not to make him wait. He wouldn't come in after me, not like the mothers coming in after the other girls. Daddy was too important to spend *his* time on chitchat.

I slipped eagerly across the leather seat, tucking little baby legs under me because they wouldn't reach the floor, and watched, entranced, as his big strong legs worked the clutch, the brakes, the accelerator. We glided smoothly and confidently away from the curb into busy uptown traffic.

He let me help him shift the gears, his hand on top of mine, giving me the fleeting illusion that I was actually working the stick in the side of the steering column, leaving all those other cars trailing in our wake.

I loved it, helping him make the big car move along, feeling both powerful and weak. In control of the maroon monster, I was helpless to make it do anything unless he wanted it to, too. My feelings were mixed, but very nice.

My emotions were always mixed when I was with my father. That big maroon Cadillac seemed almost as powerful as he was, and it was I who was making it run. Almost. I decided then that when I grew up I would drive just like he did — or find someone to drive me around, like he did. Dr. Freud would have explained some of those mixed feelings easily: "I'll find a man who drives like Daddy." The brutal symbolism of that gear-shift stalk, the father's hand on mine, the need to grow up and find another driver like Daddy; all that would have been obvious enough.

Some feminists cry foul. They focus on the implications of those feelings and say: "I'll grow up and drive that monster as hard as any man!" Such resolve is the seedbed of revolution.

Like many of the women of my generation, I wanted to be *like* him as much as to be *with* him. Mom's was a cozy world of hot bread and Cream of Wheat with lots of sweet-cream butter, warm feet in the rain because she reminded me to wear galoshes, and loving admonitions to look both ways when crossing the street. "Don't talk to strangers, and never take candy from anyone you don't know." The do's and don't's to insure a safe passage through childhood nearly all came from my mother.

Daddy's world was the unknown, exotic and deliciously terrifying, filled with colorful strangers with lots of candy, the bizarre and unpredictable, the tumult and the mystery of "out there." I resolved to get some of that "out there" for my own life. It was conflict and female desire that Freud barely considered.

Growing up on the cutting edge of a sexual revolution, like so many women of my generation, I was trapped in a velvet dilemma. Nurtured on the pleasures of being Daddy's Little Girl, I nevertheless saw enough of the "out there" to want to become one of the boys, and identification with my father fell somewhere between interpretations of the Freudians and the feminists.

Even those of us who were not trapped in a velvet dilemma of a father's own making were nevertheless put in a dilemma fashioned by the demands and expectations of society itself. Ten years ago, says Gloria Steinem, women were trained to marry a doctor, not to be one. "Now we are becoming the men we wanted to marry."[1]

Marrying a doctor — or lawyer, merchant chief, or any man with a good income and good prospects — assured us of the plush comfort and security that paternal love represents to a child. But such comfort and security inevitably exact a price. Terrified of being kept forever as Daddy's Little Girls, even if as the little girls of new and younger Daddies, many of us could not pay the price. Yet few of us wanted to become, in Gloria Steinem's formulation, "the man we wanted to marry."

It was a true dilemma, a Hobson's choice: neither alternative pleased.

Because parents are the first models for everything, the parent of the opposite sex carries a special responsibility: the child's first guide to dealing with the opposite half of the human race is the crucial one. How carefully a little girl is taught by her father, and how thoroughly she learns his lessons, may well determine how she enjoys the rewards of bedroom and, for the women who reach it, boardroom.

Freudians, with their emphasis on sharply drawn differences between the sexes, stress the father's impact on a daughter's future love relationships. Feminists, emphasizing sexual similarities, concentrate on identifying Daddy's influence on a woman's ability to work. Neither Freudian nor feminist offers ultimate insight into the complexity of a father-daughter relationship.

Why were my feelings always mixed when I was with my father? What significance did these feelings have in the forming of an adult? I was interested in exploring these questions personally, to find answers to the most fascinating questions about ourselves. The exploration of what fathers actually mean to us has been much neglected.

Forgotten Parents

Fathers have long been the forgotten parents, daughters the forgotten offspring, says Dr. Michael Lamb of the University of Utah, one of the most important researchers in the field of father-daughter relationships.[2]

And yet, a girl's first perception of the opposite sex comes through her daddy: he forever colors the eye through which a woman sees men. He shapes her expectations of male behavior. Did he hold our hands when we took our first faltering steps? Did he care when he watched us struggle through the multiplication tables? Was he comfortable showing us affection? Did he hold us close when we needed to be hugged, roughhouse with us when we wanted to play, punish us when we secretly yearned to be disciplined? Did he care how we looked? When our bodies began to change did he notice — or pretend not to? Was he pleased when we appeared in the living room all dressed up for a boyfriend?

Whether at school, with our mothers, or with our first boyfriends, could we count on him to see us through those early, agonizing crises? As we got interested in the world around us, did he freely share his knowledge and perceptions?

When I set out to find the answers to these and other questions,

I determined to start, as my father would have, at home plate. Three years ago I began to meet my father for lunch, with the tape recorder between a bottle of steak sauce and the salt and pepper shakers, and we started to talk about "the old days." My mother and my older brother, Stanley, recalled their own versions of those days. I could have written a psychological *Gulliver's Travels.*

I then moved outside my family, comparing my experiences with those of other fathers and daughters. To better understand the complexities of what I was discovering about this relationship, I talked to experts in psychiatry, psychology, sociology, theology, and anthropology, searching for clues to understand why humans act the way we do.

Invitations were extended in several national magazines to fathers and daughters to participate in a questionnaire about this relationship, heretofore not closely nor systematically examined. In interviews with hundreds of men and women, from all the fifty states, women talked eagerly about the figure all women have in common: a father.

I was not prepared for the enormous response. Hundreds of women wrote for the questionnaire, and nearly 92 percent of those who wrote for the questionnaire returned it, many enclosing the names and addresses of friends to be included in the survey. They came from every state and every faith (and many of no faith) and from city, town, and farm. A thirty-one-year-old farm woman in Idaho told me that I had touched the vital nerve: "Thank God! Someone is finally looking at what I have not dared examine."

A twenty-six-year-old Charleston, South Carolina, woman named Regina described her relationship with her father as "a dance": "Neither of us understands or knows who the other really is. Our dance is born from our need to know each other in order to know ourselves."

Regina and her father are different: he is a doctor, she an abortion counselor. "We disagree on the abortion question, which is my line of work. We disagree on political candidates: my father is a hard-core Republican, and I am not. He defends his life-style

and the economic inequity that he sees all around him. We disagree about whether women should be physicians. We disagree
about the importance of expressing anger. He fails to understand
the importance of my job and how well suited I am for what I am
doing. He does not understand that I want to get more out of life
than he did."

Yet the ties that bind them grow stronger, and continue to
change. "The most generous thing he ever did for me was to tell
me he loved me. That's so rare. He was always generous with
money, but not with verbal love. I think giving things or money
meant love to him, and that's changing as we both mellow. He
continues to influence my emotional life, if not my practical, professional life. I'm still trying to please him."

Yearning for More

Daughters open a window on their memories more readily than their fathers, who, consciously or not, talk about their
daughters only with the greatest of restraint. Even the most admiring of them are generally unwilling to speculate about why
they were close to their daughters, or if not, why not. If the typical
daughter wonders why this special relationship has never been
carefully examined, the typical father wonders why it should be
examined at all.

Women interpret the relationship in the most clarifying detail,
living again every phase of life with father: the thrill of his brawny
arms tossing them high in the air, the glorious wonder of dancing
on his shoe tops, fighting with him in the throes of adolescence,
walking down the aisle on his arm on the way to a life with another
man, and the final vigil at the side of a sickbed, saying a last, inadequate goodbye.

But in most of these female recollections there persists a
brooding, elegiac lyricism of yearning — yearning always for
more, more, more, a hunger for something never quite captured
in that secret place in the heart. Instead, there is a terrible sad-

ness, an emptiness, or an overwhelming and destructive anger.

Jackie, thirty-eight, a bank teller in a small town in North Dakota, rues the fact that her father never truly acknowledged her. "He never asked about *me,* and I realize now that I have no idea who he really is. What were his dreams and his fears, and who were the devils that seduced him with whiskey and work, keeping him away from us? When I cut my long, straight hair, changing it to short and curly, he never even noticed."

Evelyn, forty-four, an office supervisor in Nashville, Tennessee, will never understand the seeming indifference of her father, a retired army colonel, who was only at ease in the robust camaraderie of barracks and parade ground. The easy explanation doesn't satisfy her. "Deep down, I know he cared about me," she recalls, bitterly. "But I wish more than anything he had been able to express some of that caring to me directly, verbally if not physically. If only he had just said the words!"

This is a female fury psychologists know well. A frequent rage of women in therapy is that their fathers never allowed them to express love. Over and over again, women talk endlessly about the inability of their fathers to break through the public facade, to reach out to a daughter with the tender touch of affection.

In style and content, this central thesis emerges from hundreds of interviews and questionnaires: *Daddy hides, and we forever seek him, only occasionally flushing him out of his hiding places.* We know where he hides. He hides behind his newspaper; he hides behind his wife; he hides behind his work; he hides behind his public image; he hides behind his authority. Most of all, he hides behind his fear of intimacy.

For many women, the only authentic closeness occurred just after a family tragedy, such as the death of a parent or a grandparent.

"When Grandma died, that's the only time I ever saw my father cry," recalls Melanie, thirty-four, a librarian in Tulsa, Oklahoma. "He poured out the stories of his childhood, finally giving me a glimpse of the little boy he was, and a sense of his hard times. He was like a medieval knight without his armor: he let me see beneath the chain mail, all the rips and tears he had mended clumsily." Melanie was filled with compassion, and realized that many of his restrictions were attempts to spare her the pain of his own wounds. How sorry she was that it took a tragedy for him to become a man of flesh and feelings, and even then the intimacy did not last. "The tenderness was only fleeting, and he put aside his mourning, and the closeness that was so special was forgotten, as if it had occurred only in a dream."

Other women told me that they got a glimmer of intimacy and insight when their fathers were ill, and aware as if for the first time that they were not immortal. Even then, it was usually only temporary. As a father recovered, he took refuge again behind restored health, as though the closeness belonged to the disease.

Shortly after her father's heart attack, Beverly, thirty, a secretary in Flagstaff, Arizona, had her only heart-to-heart talk with her father. "We had a long conversation early one crack of dawn, down by a lake where my father had gone to recuperate. This was the only time we ever had a truly intimate conversation. We talked about how he felt as a father."

Beverly learned that her father believed he had failed her and sensed that his other children didn't like him. He talked of the things he wished he had done differently, of all the things he had hoped for his children, how unsure he had felt trying to push his family to develop their abilities. He told her of novels he wrote as a college student.

"I was astonished to hear about the novels," she says. "I never suspected that he had done anything like that." What kind of stories did he tell? She wondered. Why hadn't he let her read them? Why had he never discussed them with her? She realized that somehow the role of father didn't encompass his other selves.

We arrive in the world too late to know the man our mother fell in love with, the man who bequeathed his body to us in an act of love. By the time we get to know him he is shouldering the burdens of the world, or at least the burdens we have imposed, and his halcyon days are lost dreams, a source of frivolous nostalgia, longing, or sometimes even bitterness for things past. Though we may inherit his temperament, we have no gene coded with information about his early life. If we want to find out about it, we have to dig with a small spade, delicately.

Beverly did that. She even coaxed him to describe the silly plots of his college scribbling, and they laughed together at the earnest young mystery writer who had armed his fictional private eye with water pistols, pop guns, and rubber knives. Beverly thought their talk presaged a new kind of relationship between them, with directness and intimacy. Alas, her father's impulse toward introspection didn't last. When she later tried to joke with him about Daddy the Novelist, he brushed her aside gruffly. She was shut out, again.

Many women echoed Beverly's lament, the desire for the greater intimacy they are resigned to doing without. Helena, twenty-seven, a social-studies teacher in North Carolina, lives with the fear that her father will die and they will never have had the heart-to-heart talk she craves. "I'm terrified that when he dies I will be crushed by the weight of our unresolved feelings toward one another."

Writes Angela, a young Vermont woman who has not seen her father for five years: "I'm still trying to find the love and unconditional acceptance I never got from him."

Dangerous Love

A father's love is often more qualified than a mother's. Where a mother's love is unconditional, a father's often is given as a reward for performance. Because her love is blind, a mother confirms a child's sense of security in a general way. When the father approves, a child generally assumes that the love was earned. "Fathers cannot be taken for granted," notes psychologist David Lynn. "They love us, as Erikson says, 'more dangerously.' "[3] A mother, as if fearful of this dangerous love, often enforces the distance between father and daughter.

Often a father's love is made even more conditional than he

means it to be because he allows his wife to speak for him, to transmit emotions for him. When the mother interprets for father, both father and daughter lose; something is always lost in translation. Though the mother may occasionally say how pleased Daddy will be, more likely she delivers threats, implied or otherwise: Wait until Daddy gets home and I tell him you skipped school again; Don't tell Daddy that I bought you that new dress; Daddy works very hard, so be quiet when he comes home; Don't disturb Daddy with a lot of questions. Daddy, like the Wizard of Oz, is often a small man with a booming voice, dispensing judgment behind the skirts of the mother's contingencies. How often does a father tell a teenage daughter how much her *mother* worries when she stays out past her curfew?

A man can hide behind several barricades: his role as father, his paternal authority, his rational concern for his daughter's protection. In his desire to protect her, he often neglects his daughter's feelings as well as his own.

Carl Whitaker, a family therapist, tells of a man who, having been accused by his daughter at high-decibel level of knowing nothing about her or her wishes and needs, falls behind the barricade of authority and concern: "Damn it! Claudia, you can make fun of me but I have a right to insist that you obey the rules of the house. I'm your father and I have rights, too. They aren't unreasonable and they have your best interests at heart."

This father, unable to offer spontaneous and direct affection to his daughter, hides behind a painful, irritating reasonableness. He glimpses his own paternal ineptitude when he watches his younger daughter console Claudia: "I wish I could . . . have hugged her like that," he says, wistfully.[4]

The more women I interviewed, the more I heard about men like Claudia's father, who hide from their daughters: well-meaning men, many of them, but they are afraid to admit to being made of flesh and bone, and vulnerable to love, sadness, joy, and emotional intimacy. These men have often enjoyed the physical intimacy of the playing field with their sons, but their daughters were alien creatures, whom they could not and would not try to understand.

For many women, fathers opened their emotions only when they had had too much to drink, or were vulnerable because of an argument with a wife, or from a crisis at work.

Helga is fifty-three, a housewife in St. Paul, Minnesota. The only time she ever felt close to her father was during telephone conversations. She regrets and resents it. He was a traveling salesman, often calling in the small hours of the morning from the road when he was alone, lonely, and, more than a few times, in his cups.

"Those calls meant much to me. He was the daddy I had loved so as a child. When he was sober, he was quiet, sullen, and unapproachable, but in those telephone calls he was chatty, amiable, and fun. He talked about his accounts, the towns he visited, the funny people he had talked to during the day. He teased me and I loved it. When we met face to face he wasn't like that at all, and it was awful."

There was always a barrier of a father's making between the father and the daughter: a long-distance telephone line, a drink (or two or three), his wife, his job, painfully thought-out reasonableness. While most of these women could talk about anything with their mothers, conversations with their fathers were like censored letters from a soldier at war, with lines excised and words cut out, thoughts squeezed out and feelings extracted so that it was difficult to determine where he was or even who he was.

As I listened to the yearning of Beverly, Helga, and Claudia and others like them, I discerned patterns in their relationships with their fathers, similarities and differences around issues of sexuality at various stages of the life cycle. I began to notice a continuing theme of the father engaging in a subtle game of hide-and-seek, on *his* terms, with rules for governing a daughter's sensuality and the regulation of Daddy's sexual conduct. This game of hide-and-seek undergoes striking changes for a daughter in early childhood, adolescence, and adulthood, but the pattern for it begins in infancy, and contributes to the fundamental dilemma a daughter faces when she becomes independent and confronts work and mature love.

Rituals of childhood begin with the central fact that Daddy and daughter are of different sexes. Recent research confirms what is obvious to anyone who watches: a father holds an infant daughter more carefully than he holds a son; he speaks to her with tender deference, he plays with her more gently.[5] He lets her go with greater reluctance.

Biological, developmental, and maturational explanations for this abound, starting with the fact that girls and boys develop according to different timetables. Boy infants are more physically aggressive, display greater activity, and generally are larger than girls in the second half of their first year. A father who participates more actively with the older infant responds to these differences.

Puberty presents new conflicts of sexuality. The young girl disappears inside the young woman, and the teasing and tickling father must become the wise and authoritative adult.

Maturity brings to fruition the patterns established earlier. In adulthood, fathers and daughters either find warm compatibility through friendship as well as kinship, or their relationship disintegrates, characterized by deepening isolation and growing despair.

Before making generalizations based on these many stories, I turned back to Freud, the Big Daddy of psychoanalysis, to read again what he had said about fathers and daughters. It seems clear to me that he suffered from wearing the personal and political blinders that handicap the rest of us, blinders that some of his followers have tried to remove posthumously.

Freud's Blinders

When Freud was asked what he thought was important for a fulfilling life, he responded, *"Lieben und arbeiten"* — to love and to work. It was the aim of clinical psychoanalysis to help people achieve just those two things. But Freud was unable to examine closely the issues between fathers and daughters that affected the normal development of a daughter's ability to love and to work. Like all men before and after, he was a man of his times. He naturally saw a woman's fulfillment residing in motherhood, although he seemed happy enough to have his daughter carry on his ideas. He asked his daughter Anna to present an important essay on male and female differences to the Psycho-Analytic Congress at Hamburg in 1925, in which he once again describes a woman's envy for the penis: when she discovers she doesn't have one, she becomes aware of "a sense of inferiority."[6]

Freud developed his notions about penis envy in order to discover a reason for a woman's "Oedipus complex." This complex is nature's way, he says, for a woman to prepare psychologically for bearing a child. At best this is a convoluted argument: "She gives up her wish for a penis and puts in place of it a wish for a child: and with that purpose in view she takes her father as a love-object." Conceiving a child requires union with someone of the other sex, and her father is a daughter's first, early experience with desiring the physical being of another. This experience will be her psychological guide to sexual desire.

Freud had difficulties with his penis-envy theory because he couldn't support it with strong reasons why a woman ultimately gives up her envy, and thus gives up her unconscious wish for Daddy as lover. Sons were threatened with castration if they continued to lust for their mother, so the theory went, but daughters were already wounded. Why should a girl have to give up Daddy if he couldn't hurt her?

Freud found himself in a dilemma of his own making. If she maintains the envy, Freud said, a daughter develops a masculinity complex. Wanting what Daddy has would surely make his daughter competitive and aggressive; yet, if she gives up the envy, she is locked in an unconscious sexual duet with her father that easily leads to temptation. If she gives up wanting Daddy's penis, she can settle for Daddy himself.

The Oedipal relationship with the father provides the little girl with what Juliet Mitchell, the psychoanalyst, describes as a "love nest."[7] The daughter's lust for her father continues unless the father rejects her, and there's the rub. Fathers don't always know how to do that: to love a daughter tenderly, while rejecting her sexually, is a central conflict in the father-daughter relationship. It is a conflict Freud began to explore with his seduction theory, which placed a father's sexual abuse of his daughter at the center of female neurosis. He abandoned that theory because he could not accept the prevalence of fathers seducing daughters.[8]

As the growing incidence of father-daughter incest is documented in court proceedings (statistics suggest that it occurs as often as in 1 family in 10) it becomes clear that Freud erred in giving up his seduction theory so readily.[9] On the other hand, Vienna at the turn of the century was a very different world from the one most of us live in today.

Why Freud changed his mind has always interested psychological historians. Some say he was worried about the reaction of his Viennese colleagues who were fathers, and the impact their hostility could have on the rest of his work. He was concerned with good reason. Krafft-Ebing set the tone of its reception; he called Freud's theory a "scientific fairy tale."[10] Others speculate that Freud fretted about the hysterical symptoms he detected in his family of origin, that he was afraid his early theory implicated his own father. Freud might also have been afraid of his own impulses. About this time, he described a dream in which he felt sexual longings for Mathilde, his eleven-year-old daughter. He refused to speculate what the dream implied about himself.[11]

For whatever reason, Freud repudiated his belief in the seduction theory, concluding that reports of paternal seduction by "hysterical" women were untrue and derived from fantasies, not real occurrences.[12]

Hysterical women were as important to Freud as the Galapagos Islands were to Charles Darwin;[13] both provided an abundant source of evidence for scientific speculation — in Freud's case, for speculation about a daughter's unconscious sexual wishes, rather than those of her father.

Freud did not set out to learn who among his patients told the truth. Instead, he postulated an unprovable thesis that daughters unconsciously wanted to be seduced by their fathers. He was simply not interested in what fathers did, or why.[14]

By placing the burden on unconscious infantile perceptions of sexuality, rather than on real sexual abuse by the parent or even the unconscious sexual desire of the parent for the child, Freud overlooked the active flow of sexual energy that passes in both directions between a father and daughter. He missed an opportunity to examine closely the way a father and daughter sexualize their relationship, the titillation that propels two people toward love, respect, trust, and admiration. By missing this opportunity, he investigated neither the strengths that flow from love, respect, trust, and admiration, nor how the exploitation of love can move people in opposite directions.

Freud understated the significance of a father's participation in a daughter's life and focused instead on the daughter's drives and desires. What a father does, he seemed to say, is of considerably less importance than how a daughter reacts to what he does. There is an ancient precedent for this.

Seductive Daughters

Genesis (Chapter 19) describes filial sexual drive originating in not one, but two, daughters. Hard times had settled upon the ancient city of Sodom, and the prophet Abraham's nephew Lot, on a tip from the angels, fled with his wife and two daughters. Mrs. Lot turned into a pillar of salt when, despite her husband's warning, she turned to look one more time at their nice little house in the suburbs. Lot pressed on with the girls, who looked about their new hometown and saw that Daddy was the only man around.

The older daughter, driven by the over-thirty syndrome known even then, drew her little sister aside: "Come," she said, "let us make our father drink wine, and we will lie with him, that we may preserve seed of our father."

Led to strong drink, seduced and then abandoned in his stupor on successive nights, Lot never felt a thing: "he perceived not when she lay down, nor when she arose." The girls had stunning news for him later, and nine months thence little Moab and little Ben-am-mi arrived.

In the unembellished Biblical account, where much is left unsaid, the daughters are portrayed as the villainesses; Lot is more sinned against than sinning. He was, after all, drunk. But was he? The universal contempt and loathing for incest seems proof enough that fathers are terrified of the desire they often feel for their daughters' bodies. Large temptations require severe restraints. By drinking himself to a point just this side of alcoholic insensibility and helplessness, Lot could have his daughters and save his scruples, too. The devil made him do it. As a convenient device for passing the buck, alleging drunkenness is not unknown even today.

Freud, writing within literary and religious traditions, held that the "seductive daughter" bears the brunt of the burden of sexuality in her relationship with her father. From the stories of Lot's daughters to Vladimir Nabokov's thirteen-year-old nymphet Lolita, incestuous fathers have often tried to excuse themselves as not really responsible.

Freud, who questioned many of the shibboleths of his time, nevertheless theorized that the incest taboo was developed primarily to control sexual rivalry between fathers and sons, without so much as looking at the "other half" of the incest problem.

To Freud's credit, he was never satisfied with his theories about women, and encouraged others to go where he declined to tread. As early as 1905, the year he articulated his penis-envy theory, he complained that the sexual life of women was "veiled in an impenetrable obscurity," and twenty-one years later he conceded that "we know less about the sexual life of little girls than boys. . . . After all, the sexual life of adult women is a 'dark continent' for psychology." [15]

Illuminating the Dark Continent

That continent is still dark, though not as mysterious as it was to Freud, and much remains unexplored. We can flash a beam of light on that dark continent by reconsidering the father-daughter bond as an active relationship, showing how cultural and psychological forces work on both of them in different ways and at different times.

Like most of life's complex issues, the father-daughter relationship cannot be explained in a single theory of human behavior. Did Anna Freud become a psychoanalyst like her father because or in spite of his theories? The father-daughter relationship is an expression of the unique formulation of each family, inevitably influenced by the patterns of male-female relationships in the larger world, changing as the cultural context changes, differing for different generations of women and men.

In only three generations, such change can astonish. My own mother stood in awe of her father. "He ruled the roost," she says. He was a man of dark, forbidding mystery, with a short gray beard, quiet blue eyes, and the stentorian voice of a rabbi. When he was sick with influenza in the epidemic of 1918, he liked nothing so much as to lie upon his bed and listen to my mother, who was eight years old, read to him from the *Book of Knowledge.*

When I was eight years old, that same man treated me with gentleness and affection. When I danced my first solo in Miss Adelaide Courtenay's Dance Recital, he bought a nosegay of yellow roses and lilies of the valley and tried to come up on the stage to present them to me when the dance was over. I was embarrassed, but pleased, too: an eight-year-old girl is woman enough to be touched by a courtly male gesture.

I both feared and adored my own father. I tiptoed around his bad moods, and stood on the tops of his shoes when he danced me around the room to a Judy Garland recording on the Zenith phonograph. My two daughters share two views of their own father, first as "authority" and then as "buddy." They hang out with him, laughing at his jokes and joshing at his expense in a way that my mother and I would never have dared with our fathers.

The father-daughter relationship is a reflection of both nature and nurture — the play of genetic inheritance and biological forces on the one hand, and psychological and social forces on the other. Neo-Freudians, or what came to be called "the cultural school" of psychoanalysis, expanded Freud's theories of personality as they bear on the psychology of women. Clara Thompson, Karen Horney, Harry Stack Sullivan, and Erich Fromm emphasized the need to examine the environmental influences and the interpersonal relationships that shape personality and behavior, and were thus able to suggest new perspectives on the father-daughter relationship.

Family therapists, whose discipline emphasizes the need to understand psychological forces within each nuclear family and the extended family of kin, give us recent insights into the cross-currents that pass between father and daughter.

Sociologists, studying the ways different families are structured, offer still newer models of analysis of how rapport between father and daughter is changing. Talcott Parsons, a sociologist who studied the structure of the family between 1942 and 1964, identified the father role as "instrumental," a mediating influence between family and community.[16] Women, he said, were "expressive," charged with the emotional, nurturing side of life. At the period of time under analysis, the division of labor inside the house was not yet blurred. Today 44.6 million women work, almost a 50 percent increase in a decade; nearly half the women with children under the age of six work; 19.3 million women are now solely responsible for supporting their families; 43 percent of all workers are women.[17] Fewer than 1 in 5 families are organized along the structure that was once the American standard, when Daddy worked and paid the bills and Mom reigned absolute over kitchen, hearth, and nursery. A two-career family with different demands creates different identities, and such changes dramatically affect both father and daughter roles.

More than two hundred theories and therapies have been applied to the problems of personality and growth over the past two decades, and bits and pieces of the evidence of a father's influence on his daughter are found in many of these theories. But no comprehensive survey has identified the crucial links in that relationship. Not until now has there been a systematic study of how fathers and daughters behave with each other at different stages of their life cycles, bringing psychological and sociological theory in line with personal experiences of the father-daughter relationship, as viewed in three major phases of development: early childhood, adolescence, and maturity. In each of these broad periods, clusters of connection and disaffection are rooted in the heterosexual nature of that bond, in the conscious and unconscious male and female desires that form the basis for a game that is nothing short of sexual hide-and-seek.

A family brings up a child and is also brought up by that child. Her growth provides a series of challenges, and the family changes in reaction to her needs for encouragement and protection.[18] Much has been written about each successive step between mother and child, but little about father and child, even less about father and daughter.

New research indicates that babies attach themselves to fathers as well as mothers,[19] but what does this research mean for Daddy's daughter? In what ways is a father a different attachment figure for a girl than for a boy? How do the childhood rituals between father and daughter influence the adult woman? How can a father prepare his daughter for her first relationships with other men? How does she make the transition from filial dependency to mature give-and-take of erotic love? What is good and what is bad about being a Daddy's Little Girl? These are among the important questions explored in the complexity of the father-daughter bond, and many of the answers are rooted in the earliest experiences of that bond, the way in which the love flows.

Love Affair with Daddy

In the beginning, father and daughter have a mini–love affair with each other. Daddy is the admiring suitor, taking pleasure in the way his daughter wears her hair or a new dress or a new pair of shoes. She gets admiration from her mother, too, but the mother takes a parental pleasure in making the daughter "look pretty for Daddy." He is no less a crucial audience for his little girl's first steps, new words, and other developmental milestones. Because a father is rarely present as often as the mother is in those early years, he makes admiration, approval, and encouragement an important occasion, validating each new success, enhancing capability with additional security and support. If a father offers his daughter loving appreciation for her abilities, she will develop early self-esteem on which to build self-confidence. She will then easily and confidently seek the friendship of men who appreciate her as a competent person as well as an attractive female.

Leon I. Hammer, a psychotherapist who deals with frigidity in women, stresses the ways a father should conduct his little love affair: "This man must see, feel, appreciate, and respond to every aspect of the little girl's femininity — her hair, her body, her clothes, her laughter, her voice, her walk, her gestures. He must show his pleasure by holding her, kissing her, tickling her, cuddling her, and playing with her. The pleasure he gets and the pleasure he gives in open response will determine how far the little girl can be pleased by the presence and existence of a man. . . ." [20]

If she does not suppress her creativity and intelligence in the vain hope of maintaining her little-girl relationship with this man she has lived with since birth, if the love affair also includes respect and encouragement for her competencies, she can develop a woman's femininity and a woman's sensuality in a mature relationship with a man who is prepared to indulge those appetites that her father had always concealed and restrained.

Fathers and daughters, like mothers and daughters, have to work at changing the patterns of the early years. They have to learn how to walk through a minefield of possibilities.

The early love affair must transform itself from titillation into admiration. Daddy's Little Girl must in the best of all adult lives become Father's Special Friend, a woman supported by his appreciation and respect. Both father and daughter must give up the easy thrills of an innocent but seductive flirtation, replacing youthful mythologies with realistic appraisals of each other, knowledge informed with the deepening but wiser understanding of their special bond. This is not easy to do. Just as a mother has to let her baby go, gradually to let her walk toward independence, a father has to calibrate his authority and affection sensitively in ways that allow his baby girl to grow into a healthy, independent woman. Many fathers and daughters get stuck in the Daddy's Little Girl syndrome, never able to adjust themselves to the scales of change. Instead they remain trapped in a perpetual psychological dependency, which tantalizes as it restricts. Sex compounds the problem.

Terrible Teens

If anatomy is not destiny, it nevertheless makes for dramatic differences at puberty. How a father acknowledges the almost-daily changes in his daughter's body, and how she accepts his admiration, how he responds to her boyfriends and her developing sexuality, how she reacts to him during these hectic changes, becomes the crucible of adolescence.

"You begin to worry," says the father of two teenage daughters, as he tries to hide a sheepish grin, "when your daughter's friends and your friends' daughters begin to tempt you."

No books guide fathers or daughters through these sexual shifts in the relationship. "I miss sitting on my daddy's lap," says one wistful adolescent girl, becoming curvaceous with her twelfth birthday. "He almost acts as though he's afraid to hug me now. I don't expect him to carry me on his shoulders like he did when I was little, but I don't see anything wrong with holding his hand when we walk down the street."

Many adult women recall that turning thirteen was something like being expelled from the Garden of Eden. "Things were never the same again with my father," explains an investment broker who sighs with the pensive recollection of wrestling with her father. "But that kind of play stopped abruptly when I left elementary school. I distinctly remember my father buying me a beautiful dress for graduation. It was as if he said, 'It's time to put the tomboy away.' That particular graduation felt like a graduation from childhood."

These feelings can be no less troubling to Daddy. "I never felt actual lust for my daughter," says the father of a young woman in an affluent western suburb of Philadelphia. "But I wouldn't be a man if I didn't notice that she is turning into a beautiful woman, with the curves and the imaginatively sculptured flesh that makes a beautiful woman such a joy to behold. I've walked down the street with her and fantasized that people were thinking that she was 'my girl' instead of my daughter. Those thoughts troubled me. I suppose I even became distant with her, in a way, and what she felt as rejection was what I considered only the proper way for me to behave." These unstated, often unacknowledged, feelings between father and daughter can hurt on both sides.

The daughter of a physicist in California's Silicon Valley looks back at her rejection of her father, and regrets that it was she who set the terms for the lack of expressed affection between them.

"My strongest memory of my father is probably the last occasion on which he hugged me and kissed me as a child. I was twelve years old, and feeling the stirrings of my female nature. He leaned over to hug me as he had always done when I went off to school, and I pushed him away. With great deliberation he straightened his tie and tucked in his collar, that defensive gesture men make, and said to me: 'I won't ever kiss you and hug you again.' And he didn't."

Most of her memories focus on this image. She keeps thinking of what a good relationship they might have had if they both hadn't been so stubborn, pulling farther away from each other. The memory looms large in a daughter's mind, but her father was actually responding equally to something in himself.

"I was embarrassed when I hugged my fourteen-year-old daughter," concedes a Denver businessman whose two grown daughters are married now with children of their own. "Elizabeth told me when she was eleven that I shouldn't hug her quite so hard because it hurt her chest, which was just beginning to bud. I realized then that it was time to put some physical distance between us."

This Denver businessman was frightened for his daughter, ashamed of himself for noticing. His own teenage years informed

his memories — all those lustful thoughts he had had as a growing boy. "Were young boys now having those same wishes and
desires about my daughter?" he asked. "Those pimply-faced
drugstore cowboys who took her to the movies? Do they want to
do with her — and to her — what I wanted to do with and to
every young girl I furtively watched when I was a high-school hot-
shot?"

Suspicious of his own nature and motives, a father sets up restrictions to protect his daughter from falling prey to selfish and
powerful lusts like his own. His power is greater than even he
knows. Fathers and daughters walk a high wire, a wire pulsing
with electricity. This electricity, particularly in a daughter's teenage years, can shock.

"I dated only one boy while I lived at home," recalls Doreen, a
pretty Louisville waitress in her late twenties. "After two double
dates at the age of sixteen, Dad screamed that he hated the boy,
that I couldn't see him anymore. Dad even checked my underwear
for blood stains, and [when he found menstrual blood] he swore I
had had sex with the boy. Little did Dad know that he had made
me too afraid of men, his 'animals,' to let a boy even hold my
hand."

More often than we once thought, a man surrenders to selfish
and powerful lusts of his own and breaks the most basic taboo of
civilization. He descends to the making of a secret so terrible that
he must hide it from everyone.

Such fathers are not necessarily the slum-dwellers of smug
middle-class imagination. "I was robbed of almost everything I
needed in a father," recalls one such daughter, Nadine, now
forty-seven, whose father sang in the choir of the church he attended with the family and who first molested his daughter when
she was nine. "I was robbed of a father's sensitivity, his caring, his
communication, and his real love."

Every visit to the park, every ride to the grocery store, every
adventure to his office, doing the things that most young girls
thrill to do alone with their fathers, became scenes of terror. Her
father never took her anywhere with him except to molest her. "I

remember the first time he asked me to go with him to the shop where he worked," she says. "It was a Saturday and no one else was there. I thought it was going to be fun, but as soon as we got there he got down on the floor with me and began to touch me all over. I was afraid to be alone with him, then and forever after."

The supportive father abides by the rules and customs that preserve a daughter's sexual innocence; they are, after all, *his* rules and *his* customs. When he gives his daughter away to another man in a public ceremony, he announces to the world that he has done his job well: "How but in custom and in ceremony are innocence and beauty born," wrote the poet William Butler Yeats in "A Prayer for My Daughter."

Mutual Mellowing

A daughter's early adult years and a father's late middle years can mellow their relationship in such a way as to offer a calmer course after the turbulence of the teenage years. Patty, twenty-six, a woman who remembers a stormy adolescence with her father, describes how her problems with authority are muted now, eased by the religious faith and ethical standards inculcated by her father. She sees her father as human, his values enduring. She finds solace in religious faith after deviating from it during her teens.

"I need spiritual food and I know this is because of certain attitudes Dad passed on to me," she says. It was her father who showed her that one has to move inward first, and a realization of self-worth is the fuel for the journey. He taught her this without words. "All I had to do was to watch him struggle."

Patty's father taught her to use her own judgment. He was proud of her when she marched for women's rights.

"His greatest gift of all was his letting me love him. I realize now how crucial it is for women to have a healthy, loving relationship with their fathers. Alas, few do."

Women older than Patty offer a retrospective range of perceptions as they reflect on the changes in their father-daughter relationship. As adult women describe their memories, they touch on the key issues of adult sexual and psychological maturity. Women see father-daughter parallels in their marriages and love relationships as father casts a lengthening shadow over sexuality, work, procreation, and recreation.

Competency and *femininity* are the twin values most of the women I interviewed stressed as the values strongly influenced by their father, the positive qualities that feed their self-esteem, their work, and love. "We used to take walks to a brook which ran in a park behind our house," one woman recalls. "My father inscribed my name next to his in a small white-wooden railing on a bridge that crossed the bubbling water. He said it showed anyone who came there that it was ours."

When she was with him at *their* brook, she felt like a special girlfriend. But the moments went deeper than that. "In our talks at the brook he always told me that I had to work hard at whatever I did. 'No one will hand you anything — you must earn what you get,' he always said. He developed my curiosity in nature, and he gave me the time and space to formulate my ideas and concepts about life and to see them through."

This woman, and women like her, describe their budding love affairs with Daddy as the root and branch on which a mature relationship with him flowers. Affection ripens into mutual respect, and when they are adults father and daughter can meet each other as two competent people, exploring the world and exchanging admiration and affection.

One such woman, a landscape architect, cannot separate the pleasure of her work and the pleasure of being female. "There was always a kick in my experiences with Daddy, in the things he taught me about the world. If someone were to tell me that I 'think like a woman,' I'd know it was meant as an insult, but I consider it a compliment. My father encouraged my interests in science and art, but he never forgot to tell me that he thought I was beautiful, too."

Planting Seeds for Her Future

When a father does not value a daughter's developing competencies, when he does not respond to her femininity, she must seek for herself, and with greater difficulty, what should have been hers by inheritance.

Women with autocratic fathers, men who criticized their every move and imposed harsh limits on their developing independence, complain of problems in the workplace, an inability to deal with any kind of authority without expressing overwhelming anger. The childhood response of these women forged a debilitating personality trait for the adult.

"If we experience something too strongly in the past, we may anticipate it where we ought not and perceive it where it does not exist," says Willard Gaylin, the psychoanalyst author of *Feelings*. "If, for example, we were intimidated by a punitive father who terrified us, we may approach all authority figures with the bias of that early dominant memory. The memory of that authority may possess a greater reality to us than the actual authority figure with whom we were involved. Regardless of how gentle and unchallenging the authority figure is, we may approach each teacher, each employer as though he had both the power and the personality of that dominant father who once ruled our life." [21]

Problems of authority are easy to pinpoint. Of greater complexity, and a more persistent theme recurring throughout my interviews and reading is a daughter's fear of her father's abandonment, a fear that seems to have primitive psychological roots going back to the days when a father was required to protect his daughter from outside physical harm. Though protection takes a different form today, it is no less important, and it is less available as divorce rates continue to rise and single-parent families increase, usually with an absent father. In many cases the fear of abandonment has become prophecy, with a daughter experiencing her absent father as a rejection of her.

Even when abandonment does not actually occur, the fear lingers, deep in a daughter's consciousness. Because it knows no age boundaries, this fear spreads throughout the life cycle with varying effects depending on the cause. For this reason it must be examined across the spectrum of life cycles, from early childhood through maturity, beginning with the love — or loveless — affair the tiny girl has with her father. This fear can persist in various forms through the teenage years, often reappearing after a woman marries. Eventually the fear of abandonment becomes symbolic of life's journey and of her recognition of age and death.

Most women whose experiences make up the core of this book are the progeny of men who guarded their daughters' physical security carefully, in hopes this care would insure emotional security; the ways they accomplished this made a lasting impact on their daughters' sense of self, self-esteem, and sense of accomplishment. Because the father role is ultimately more cultural than biological (it is, after all, impossible to prove to an absolute certainty that a given man is the biological parent of a given child), paternal love is fragile and contains for the daughter the seeds of adult love, with all its complexity and vulnerability.

The magic of the sexual differences, as we all learn well, is born in mystery. Such mystery can never be diminished, nor should it be, if, as many of us believe, it is the animation of the ceaseless fascination and attraction of one sex to the other.

But this mystery can be better understood. Often the misunderstood differences are the source of the debilitating games men and women play, all too often ending in numbing disappointment and withering ruin. Her father's imprint marks a woman's identity for all time — her sense of self, her work, her love relationships, her understanding of the sexual differences. His effect varies at different stages of her life, but the important qualities of psychological development are strongly influenced by the first man in a woman's life.

These qualities include trust, autonomy, ambition, initiative, creativity, and an expanding capacity for intimacy. A father's absence, coldness, or cruelty is no less crucial as an adverse effect, fostering mistrust of others, dependency, self-doubt, and a sense of inferiority in the marketplace, and a contracting capacity for intimacy, love, and, ultimately, happiness in marriage.

Not all of these elements of feminine character and emotional and intellectual development can be fairly charged against the father, just as all cannot be charged against the mother. Most women, having moved beyond the myth of blaming their mothers, yearn now to stop ignoring their fathers and their influence, putting an end at last to the destructive father-daughter game of hide-and-seek.

With the two-career family in ascendency, it becomes doubly important to examine the changing role of fathers. I grew up in the house of a strong father, a man who represented the unequivocal values of an earlier time, when America had just won World War II and was proceeding to clean up the wreckage and rebuild the shattered world. American confidence and certitude were at flood tide. Big Daddy wrote his own mythology, and it was a mythology that served its time well enough.

But the times, as the lyricist noted, the times they are a-changing. What does the new family organization presage for father and daughter? Though Margaret Mead calls fatherhood a "social invention," it is nevertheless true that fathers, *daddies* if you will, continue like the wheel to reinvent themselves, exerting a critical influence on their daughters' lives from birth through childhood, marriage, parenthood, and beyond, as we learn, over and over, that our fathers are in more ways than one *the* seminal influence.

PART TWO

Fear of Abandonment

My life closed twice before its close —
It yet remains to see
If Immortality unveil
A third event to me

So huge, so hopeless to conceive
As these that twice befell.
Parting is all we know of heaven,
And all we need of hell.

—Emily Dickinson

Daddy the Protector

Florence was the teacher's pet.

She always got to choose the Psalm, and got to read it to the class; it was Florence who distributed the milk and graham crackers after the afternoon recess. Florence was the class representative on the student council. When the teacher was called out of the room, Florence was always the one who was called to the front of the class to preside as the surrogate authority.

One muggy spring afternoon just after the last of the graham crackers disappeared, the fire bell rang. The fifth graders scurried outside to safety, rescued from tedium, and lined up on the playground to wait until the teacher called the roll.

Florence took a place at the head of the line, as she had been asked to do. A boy stepped out of the line and without a word knocked her down.

"I was in a fearful fury," recalls Florence, who twenty years later remembers the incident vividly in an instant emotional replay. "Aggression and confrontation were the way of life in our school, but I was floored by that little boy in more ways than one. When I got up I ran to a telephone to call Daddy."

Ten minutes later, her father drove up with her mother seated next to him.

"The boy had run away with his friends, and Daddy lit out after him. He found him leaning against the front of the local diner. Daddy told my mother and me to stay put. I'll never forget the look on that boy's face. Daddy grabbed his collar, pinned him against the wall, and screamed for everyone to hear: 'If you ever touch my daughter again, I'll kill you, and you can count on it.' "

Florence's father converted the experience into a practical mission. Though he could hardly afford it, he enrolled Florence in a private school. She was grateful for his financial sacrifice, but her pride swells with the remembrance of that moment when her father walked through the crowd of bullies: "And I still feel that if anything happens that I can't handle, he can take care of it for me."

Rather than allow such feelings to inhibit her development, however, Florence has used her schooling to enable her to take care of herself and others. She is one of the first black women appointed to administer a public-health program in a large city.

When she was growing up, friends and relatives often remarked how close Florence was to her mother, who was privy to all her secrets. Nevertheless, Florence believes now that emotional security was a gift from her father. Says she: "I have a powerful fear of his death in the same sense that I fear losing my protector."

Making the World Safe for His Daughter

For many women like Florence, a father is first a protector, guardian, custodian, champion. The world is a safer place because a strong and loving male figure stands between vulnerability and the dangers that lurk in the dark crevices of every girlhood. Children's fairy tales give these fears dramatic form.

The father-as-hunter is a protector-figure, says Bruno Bettelheim, the psychoanalyst, who has studied methods and messages in these tales. "On a deeper level [the father] represents the sub-jugation of the animal, asocial, violent tendencies in man. Since he seeks out, tracks down, and defeats what are viewed as lower aspects of man — the world — the hunter is an eminently pro-tective figure who can and does save us from the dangers of our violent emotions and those of others." [1]

By turning his bow and arrow against ravenous animals, the fa-ther saves himself from his own violent emotions as well. He busies himself with foreign prey; he sublimates his own animal de-sires. He makes the world safe for his daughter and thus safe for himself.

A girl's early love affair with her daddy is determined by the nature of his protection. He must provide his little girl with the sense of security that enables her to grow up trusting both him and herself. He must endow her with strength and support she can count on until that time when she will look for those qualities in an adult love relationship with another man.

Even as Florence continues to think of her father as protector, she has incorporated his values into her own, to use the education he gave her to undertake a tough and challenging career, and to seek and find a man with her father's positive qualities with whom to create and nurture children. She dreads the day when her fa-ther will not be her ultimate protector, but credits him for be-queathing her a strong sense of self-protection.

An underlying fear of abandonment is the mature recognition of the tragic element in the nature of life, rather than a reflection of personal insecurity. No father can offer lifetime guarantees of protection; what he can offer is help through the emotional pas-sage into adulthood. By encouraging the development of skills a daughter will need to get along in an unforgiving world, his strength will always be there for her.

The Father Who Fails

Men who fail to protect their daughters, who offer no shield of paternal strength, are judged harshly by society. Caspar

J. Milquetoast has a long history in folklore, and daughters of such men work hard to compensate for their fathers' weakness.

The fairy tale father of Snow White is such an allegorical father. He is married to the queen, Snow White's stepmother, who insists that he kill his daughter and bring her the lungs and liver for an evening's meal. Too timid to follow the queen's order directly, he nevertheless lacks the courage to save his daughter. Rather than kill Snow White himself, he abandons her deep in the forest, expecting wild animals to accomplish what he cannot, and he takes his wife the lungs and liver of an animal instead.

Mr. White is unable to meet his moral obligation to make Snow White safe and secure, and thus fails as father. Observes Dr. Bettelheim: "In the typical nuclear family setting, it is the father's duty to protect the child against the dangers of the outside world, and those that originate in the child's asocial tendencies."[2]

A father's traditional responsibility includes the obligation to introduce his daughter to the larger world, to help her meet and learn to know others in a safe environment beyond the family.

The father has been his daughter's protector since men first established themselves as the figures of authority in society, and our perception of the father in this role is most dramatic when he abuses this trust. When King Lear banishes his daughter Cordelia for not loving him enough, he betrays the bonds of closest kinship. He pays for it dearly with his kingdom, his daughter's life, and ultimately his own.

Ancient Greek audiences were horrified when Agamemnon sacrificed his daughter, Iphigenia. Iphigenia, as the playwright Euripedes saw her, is sacrificed to political expediency, "a doomed victim of my father's villainy." Agamemnon offers her to the gods, trying both to appease his mutinous crew and to call forth good sailing weather. He succeeds, and his crew's grumbling fades into sullen silence. Fresh winds fill his sails, blowing the ship toward a rendezvous with Troy. But Agamemnon's sacrifice also calls down a curse that destroys root, branch, and flower of the royal house. Before the deed is done, Iphigenia recalls her childish love for her father, a gesture rendering his abandonment all the more cruel:

"The times I stretched my hand to touch
My father's beard, [clinging] to his knees . . ."

With the sacrifice, Agamemnon violates a fundamental strain of paternal love, and his wife kills him for that deed.

Changing Heroes

The idealized man of the eighties' pop culture is the man who cares, and who shows it by hurting, crying, bleeding, and suffering in public. Alan Alda, the actor, portrays this man with such skill that it is readily apparent that he sees himself as such a man in real life. In a succession of movies he shows us that the father-daughter relationship lies heavily upon his mind.

Alda the actor portrays a wickedly ambitious senator in *The Seduction of Joe Tynan,* sacrificing the love of a daughter to pursue the Presidency. When she reproaches him with a wistful and tinny echo of the wail of Iphigenia ("You weren't at home very much, were you?"), he presses on, driven, only to rue his failure as a father. In his later *Four Seasons,* he portrays a more benign father who works at being close to his two daughters. And in real life, Alda the guru sums up the role of the modern father, his role having been diminished to the dispensing of bread and cautious advice, in a remark to his daughter's college class: "If you get into any trouble, don't forget that you can always call me at the office." [3]

Thus has the protection of the father, once rooted in authority, become devalued currency with strings attached. But the giving of financial support, passive enough as it is, often conceals deeper, less accessible bonds of emotional attachment that make for another kind of problem: the unearned "easy life" that camouflages psychological deprivation, and an ignorance of practical information, undercuts a daughter's developing independence.

An example: "Tuition and living expenses were completely accounted for when I went away to the university," says Ellen, twenty-five, a recent graduate from a Big Ten law school. "My father had set up a modest trust fund for me to make my early career years comfortable, so I never felt I'd have to worry about my next meal. But on the day I boarded the train for my freshman year, I cried tears of fear that he would die before I saw him again.

"I fantasized that his recent flu had been cancer. I punished myself in the horrible thought that he was dying, that he had decided not to tell me about it so that I could go off to school in a happy frame of mind. It was only after my sophomore year, and a long summer vacation at home, that I realized that my mind had truly run away with me."

A therapist helped Ellen to realize that she was afraid of being emotionally and financially on her own. Rather than face up to her own fears, she unconsciously projected them onto her father, seeing him ill and abandoning her when in reality it was she who was leaving him. But she was leaving him, unprepared for the world beyond his house.

Therapy for adolescents like Ellen who are troubled by separating from their parents can be a coming-of-age ceremony, as they put aside the terrors and fears of childhood. But this means giving up those special feelings that come from being Daddy's Little Girl, and to consider this is a dread that many women know only too well. Becoming an adult is as inevitable as the turning of the autumn leaves and as natural as the snow that flies before the harvest moon. But easy it is not. A thoughtfully protective father can help smooth transitions by offering loving care and useful information. Ellen's father fulfilled only half of the equation.

When a father is overprotective, he inhibits his daughter's independent development, much like the overprotective mother who is the familiar target of Jewish humor. It is not enough for a truly responsible father to offer his daughter love and comfortable financial supports: he must also initiate her into family secrets, explaining to her the financial procedures, teaching her the ways of the world by passing on his savvy, expertise, and hard-won experience. In doing this he takes her seriously as a woman who is growing up and becoming capable of taking care of herself. Many fathers hide behind the "mysteries" of money as if afraid that explaining and identifying the family's financial resources would reduce their power in a daughter's eyes. This infantilizes a daughter, rendering her powerless in a way that few fathers would render their sons. He keeps her his little girl.

A daughter's fear of abandonment grows out of this kind of powerlessness, a response that is appropriate enough in a child who depends on her father for survival, but not in an adult woman. Thus money becomes a very effective way for a father to maintain his daughter's dependency on him.

Ellen's father considered himself a responsible father, and in many ways he was, but his financial support did not erase her sense of psychological abandonment. He was a traditional man who saw his role of protector as one who provided care rather than imparting useful knowledge gained from his life experience. Both are essential.

Care and responsibility are constituent elements of love, says Erich Fromm, "but without *respect* for and *knowledge* of the beloved person, love deteriorates into domination and possessiveness."[4]

A daughter can get stuck in the love-affair stage with her father, just as a woman can get stuck in an adult love affair in which she is powerless. Women thus pay a high price for protection if they do not also learn to protect themselves. A father's love and admiration for his daughter must be accompanied by his confidence in her ability to make use of practical information, which is to him second nature.

Striking the Delicate Balance

A father has to strike a balance between protecting his daughter and helping her go unafraid into the world with the knowledge in which he has armed her. When a child is young, Daddy feels powerful, as every little girl who has ever thrilled to jumping into his arms well understands. But life is too large even for a daddy to guarantee perpetual safety, and a daughter has to learn that no one else will ever catch her like that again.

Many women today have been thrown on their own unaware of

having had any psychological preparation. But in looking inside themselves, they find resources they never knew they had, and discover that their "old-fashioned" fathers gave them more than they realized. Fortunate are those who have internalized or assimilated positive images of their father's authority. With a little help from their friends, they can learn to use that authority to take care of themselves when Daddy is not around. Carlos Sluzki, a psychiatrist at the Mental Research Institute in Palo Alto, California, told me how one woman, whose father was a benign protector, was able to find her father's voice inside her during her first trip away from home; she was then able to use it in her own behalf, awkwardly at first, but then to her advantage.

"A 19-year-old Guatemalan woman . . . came to the hospital complaining of bursitis in her shoulder, which would not respond to medication. She was in the United States to train as an executive secretary. Not only was it the first time she had left her country, but the first time she had been separated from her family. She described the pain as diminishing with rest and increasing with movement, so she went to bed early every night and stayed inside on weekends to 'alleviate the pain.'

"I said, 'It sounds like the pain is telling you to stay home at night and not to go out during the weekend.' She looked at me, frowning. I asked, 'Who is this person in your home who would tell you not to go out at night without a chaperone?'

"She answered quietly. 'My dad.'

"I said: 'Well, you are an ingenious young lady. You have managed to bring your father along to America with you. Here you are, in a strange country, with no friends and feeling very isolated, and you carry your father's representative on your shoulder, telling you what to do. You are also a responsible woman. Do you really think you need to carry around your father's representative, who has turned out to be such a pain?'

" 'But my father only advises me. He doesn't punish me.'

" 'Then I advise you to establish a dialogue with that pain in your shoulder. Talk to it when you are lonely in your room. Be respectful. Remember that it is your father's representative. Try to convince it that you are a responsible woman without it.'

"She became very angry with me, but when she returned to the hospital two weeks later she had listened to my advice. She had made several friends, she was happier, and the bursitis was no longer a problem."

The young woman from Guatemala was reacting to her conscience, that overpowering restraint on initiative that helps us make personal and moral choices. A child listens to this inner voice that proffers guidance and inflicts punishment as well, often leading a child to obey parental strictures with far greater fidelity than the parent either wished or expected. For Dr. Sluzki's patient, it provided a mildly painful transition toward independence. As she developed self-confidence away from home, she was able to trust herself without needing debilitating controls. She was able to take over the reins from her father. His loving discipline of her became her strength to take care of herself. His safeguards became her stability. Many women with protective fathers spoke to me about the ways they expected to flaunt their freedom when finally they left their father's house and his "constricting" authority, but without his roof and his protection they discovered they were much more cautious than they ever expected to be.

Sins of the Father

How a daughter separates from her protective father may depend on how he separates from her. Sometimes the sins of the father's family can be visited upon the daughter, and it is Daddy who cannot abide separation.

Ava, thirty-three, teaches advanced biology classes in a high school in a small town in Indiana. "I realize that my loving and overly solicitous father had a problem when he helped me move the last of my furniture out of the house, *his* house, into an apartment. I had left home a year earlier, and the furniture had been stored in an unused storeroom. When I wanted the furniture he was busy, so I hired a moving truck on my own.

"When Daddy found out what I had done, he exploded. I was inconsiderate and had disregarded his feelings and needs. He said he would close his business, load up my stuff, and meet me at my new apartment. I canceled all my other arrangements, losing my deposit with the truck driver, and met my father as he was *leaving* my apartment. He had arrived early and didn't intend to stay around."

Though Ava's father disguised his power in the act of helping her, it was *power* that he was asserting. His anger was irrational.

"He lit into me with scolding and lectures as soon as he saw me at my new apartment. He ranted and raved, working himself into a fine rage, calling me an ungrateful leech, a moocher, and worse. Then he disowned me! This was more than I could handle. For years Mom and my brother tried to heal the breach between us, but they never could. Mom knew I was declaring my independence by moving out, and she was sympathetic. Dad forever saw it as my abandoning him."

Years later Ava learned that the way her father had separated from his parents had influenced his actions toward her. He poured out the sad story of his life after Ava's mother died. He had been abandoned by *his* parents when he was quite young, and left to grow up as an unwanted relative among aunts and uncles who resented the burden of an extra child who wasn't theirs. He had never told Ava about his parents, so acute was his humiliation. Instead he had always hidden behind the "strong man" image. When Ava moved into her own place, he felt again the vulnerability to being abandoned by someone he loved.

"Though most men prefer sons, a large number would rather have daughters, because they don't want to relive their childhoods in a son," Sue Rosenberg Zalk, a psychologist who teaches at Hunter College and who writes about "expectant" fathers, told me in an interview. "They are fearful that they will repeat their original relationship with a son, and they will become a father like their own fathers. It is as though they sense they have a better chance at being a father to a daughter, though that may not happen." Having grown up unprotected themselves, they feel inadequate as a protector.

Family patterns repeat themselves in unusual ways. Just as

Ava's father's abandonment by his own parents carried over into his relationship with his daughter, so the patterns of leaving behind a life with her father have a powerful impact on the way a woman in Ava's position matures. Attachment and separation from a parent have been the subject of extensive examination among psychological researchers.

Separation Anxiety

Attachment theorists believe the need to be close to a loving parent as important as food and drink — an essential ingredient for survival. Stressing attachment and loss as the two poles of experience profoundly consequential in the shaping of personality, they have until recently focused primarily on the mother-child relationship.[5]

"The dread of loss of the mother," says Dr. Margaret Mahler, the New York psychoanalyst, is the infant's first deep trauma. Dr. Mahler reasons, like others who have studied separation anxiety, that the baby fears this separation when it first realizes that its body is indeed separate from the mother's. Separation anxiety created the first market for security blankets, teddy bears, and cuddly dolls. These totems remind us of the familiar world of our mothers, and even when she is not there we have something familiarly soft and reassuring, and when she leaves us and returns we learn to trust: if, after leaving us, she returns once, and then twice, three times, she will return again and again.[6] Gradually, we test the chilly waters of separation when we first begin to crawl and then to walk, always looking back to make sure that "home base" is secure. We return to our mothers for "emotional recharging."

New research suggests strongly that fathers are such attachment figures, too, offering renewable reserves of emotional energy. "As attachment figures and sources of security, the two parents play similar roles in their children's development," says researcher Michael Lamb, whose infant studies were among the first to discriminate between the ways a child attaches to each parent.[7]

Attachment begins in the first six or eight months of life, when the baby has formed a primitive conception of the independent existence of self and of others, and continues to build slowly during the years of immaturity — infancy, childhood, and adolescence. The patterns of expectations developed during those years persist well into adulthood. Psychological theorists differ in interpretation of how and at what age the patterns are fixed, and at what age they become irreversible. Some hold with Freudians, who believe the first five years to be the most crucial; others that the personality remains flexible and adaptive through adolescence, and even after. Whether fixed or not, most psychologists concur that early years with both mother and father, in the best of circumstances, exert a powerful influence on the perception of self: put simply, the availability of those who love us is what influences our development of self-esteem, our expectations of how others will see us, and the degree to which we can place trust in the people we love. "A child's security," says Bruno Bettelheim, "relies on his conviction that his parents are powerful protectors." [8]

A mother is nearly always there, at least in the beginning, and a child learns not to worry. It is her responsibility to see that we are cared for, if not always her responsibility to provide the actual "hands-on" care herself. A father comes and goes at odd hours, but it is the father who spreads over the household a renewed sense of physical security when he returns. Often our feelings about fathers are rooted in primitive origins, when a man's size and strength dictated that it was he who must be the protector.

The complicated demands of a changing society and technology that relies more on skilled fingers to press buttons and pull levers than on muscle and brawn to tame enemies and the elements have abraded the role of the father. But the all-powerful image of the father-as-protector persists, often in the subconscious of women who are astonished to find it there. The price of that omnipotent image is a little girl's fear of her father abandoning her.

Most of us remember an occasion when a father was away on a trip, ill, or didn't come home. Our mothers reassured us; his separation was only temporary. Most of the times she was right. Still, the little girl was never quite sure. "When is he coming back? Why did he go away without telling us?" We devised strategies to cope with the change. Some of us pestered our mothers with questions. Others said extra prayers at night.

The anxiety we feel during separations, such as vacations, going away to college, or moving from one place to another, is often rooted in childhood experiences we think we have forgotten, or that we believe are no longer important but revive in us a sense of powerlessness.

The most ordinary absences sow the seeds of fear of abandonment. In countless examples of positive father-daughter relationships, where daddy is a benign protector who shows concern for his daughter's day-to-day well-being, women grow up worrying about their father leaving them. An unspoken ache in a catalogue of childhood pains, this worry is often rooted in an otherwise insignificant event. How each woman deals with this fear of the ordinary determines the degree of independence she wants for herself.

Down on the Farm

Marjorie, a forty-four-year-old Idaho farm woman, decided to handle her "crisis" by staying home, or close to it. She lives today down the road from her mother and father. When she was three, her father went into the hospital for back surgery.

"I was terrified that he had gone away forever. There was only my mother and me, bumping into each other in a big lonely farmhouse. When I looked out at the tractor I longed to see Daddy high up on the seat, riding out to the wheat and corn. Happiness was in limbo until he came home, and things got back to normal."

But forever after, what was normal had changed. Marjorie had experienced fear, and fear could reappear. Separation from her father had made the world feel less safe. When her father was again strong enough to climb on the tractor, all seemed fine, but only as long as she could actually see him working at his chores. Time was measured against a new standard. The first time he got into his pickup to drive into town, she fell into panic. Surely this time he was going away for good. She screamed and hung on to him. "Don't go! Don't go!" This went on for nearly a year.

Marjorie married a small-town boy, so that she could stay on the land, to live close enough to keep an eye on her father. "It makes me feel secure to have him down the road in that familiar gray frame house. My brother moved on to Boise, where he sells insurance, but I want that sense that 'all's right with the world' when I look out at the fields and see Daddy, high up on that tractor."

Marjorie's father is pleased that she stayed on the land, but scoffs at the notion that it was for him that she did it. His recollections of their early years are not hers.

"Marjorie was always a farm girl," he says. "She liked to ride on the tractor with me, taking a close interest in what I was doing, and preferred the farming with me to the cooking with her mother. When she was a little thing she wouldn't let me out of her sight, but I don't remember her being afraid I would leave her. Her mother and I have been married for fifty-one years, and I guess it's fairly clear by now that I'm not and never was going anywhere. The only time I left was when I had back surgery. Marjorie was so tiny then. I doubt if she even remembers it. She cried a lot when I went off to the hospital, but she was so little then it couldn't have made much of an impression on her."

Both Marjorie and her father no doubt remember it "like it was," and the differences in their recollections illustrate how difficult it is for a parent to perceive the significance of an event in a child's small and troubled mind. So much of what an infant learns is through repetition: Marjorie's father's back surgery broke a pattern in a routine presence and planted the first tiny doubts of a father's infinite power.

Because the harsh and unforgiving nature of the land can make the traditional organization of family life seem essential and inevitable, when Marjorie's father went away to a hospital in a nearby town a little girl could logically conclude that half of her protection and well-being had been stripped from her. By a child's unformed lights, she was wise to worry, having learned early that to lose a father is fully as disastrous as losing a mother. Who would feed her? Where nature dictates choices with brutal certitude, the father's protection is the first law of survival, and debates about the proper role for male and female are rendered meaningless. From life, that most effective of teachers, Marjorie was learning that roles are born of necessity, and out of necessity emerges pride.

Though Marjorie still articulates her fear of loss, she knows that such feelings are natural for an adult woman who sees her father growing old. Today, instead of struggling with forebodings of abandonment, she is comfortable with the knowledge that her father's teaching and example are responsible for her secure values, her love of the land, her love of family.

Fear in the Big City

Marjorie's childish nightmare struck an echo of a similar terror in my own life. I was barely four. Daddy had taken the three of us — Mom, my older brother, Stanley, and me — on a weekend in New York City. Jakie and Tessie, my parents' best friends, went with us. The holiday turned to terror when my father was struck with sudden illness.

The hotel doctor suggested that Daddy ought to be taken to the hospital, and soon my world was filled with wailing sirens and strange men in white coats rolling a long narrow bed toward my father. With my father lying deathly still and silent ahead of us, we followed the men in white coats into the elevator, down to the lobby and past gawking kibitzers, and into the ambulance.

"But why couldn't they take Jakie?" I asked my brother, sobbing through tears that I remember as if that day were only yesterday. "Why don't they take Jakie instead?"

Stanley, who was eight, looked at me with an older brother's total contempt. "Because Jakie's not sick, dummy. Daddy is."

The hotel doctor thought Daddy had come down with typhoid fever. I didn't know what that was, but it sounded dreadful enough to spoil the entire weekend. There would be no more strawberry cheesecake at Lindy's, no more visits to the Automat where the milk poured out of the mouths of brass birds, no more standing in Times Square counting the smoke rings popping out of the mouth of the man in the Camel sign, and worst of all, no more Daddy. I felt abandoned. I was sure I would never see him again.

New Jersey never looked so gloomy as on the long train ride back to Washington. The grime and soot of the factories hunched up to the Pennsylvania Railroad right-of-way never looked so oppressive. My stomach was knotted with fright and panic.

Then, on a sunny afternoon five days later, Daddy appeared once more at our front door, dapper as ever in the familiar dove-gray fedora folded softly to shade his eyes, and as fit as on the day he had taken me to watch the Rockettes at Radio City Music Hall. He had only had a touch of food poisoning, and all was well again.

But not for me. I never again felt perfectly secure: it was not enough that he had come back. If he could abandon me once, he could do it again. He had demonstrated that he, too, was capable of dying when I had been safe in a little girl's certitude that nothing could touch or harm her father, a giant who was bigger and stronger and more powerful than any force on earth. In the labyrinth of my own childish emotions, from that moment on there dwelled a monstrous fear of abandonment, one that I have converted to my own advantage by maintaining a close relationship with my father.

Her father remains a girl's first buffer against the world even as the world around them changes. The demands of contemporary life have altered the pattern of family organization, perhaps beyond recall, as women move in increasing numbers into the work force. Yet, psychological needs change at a rate much slower than sociological change dictates.

"I do much more actual hands-in-the-soil farming than my

mother did," says Marjorie in Idaho. "I like to drive a tractor, to watch the earth opening up behind me in perfect furrows. A woman is as capable as a man for doing hard work. But I can't imagine running this farm without my husband, or of raising my children without him. I was right to fear my father's departures. I knew even then what I know now. A child ought to grow up with both parents."

Though it is more unusual than it once was for women to stay as close to home as Marjorie has done, her convictions about the importance of both parents to a child is borne out by recent psychological studies of the personal experiences of women who were actually abandoned by their fathers. Such experiences can condition girls to expect to be abandoned when they become women and forge alliances with men. The experiences of the child thus create a perverse and destructive self-fulfilling prophecy.

CHAPTER THREE

Daddy the Defector

My friend Shirley Silverman was trying to fake an answer to Miss Bunn's question about the position of the midday sun in the Belgian Congo, and it was hard going. Bees darted in and out of the azaleas just beyond the window, and wasps, waking from the long winter, bounced in lazy confusion against the windowpanes.

Shirley's father was coming for us in just ten more minutes to take us to our dancing lessons. Good things stretched ahead endlessly.

Shirley's father had a new car, a pea-green Nash, and he had promised that we could stop at the Hot Shoppe on the way downtown for a root-beer float, a slice of hot-fudge cake with chocolate-chip ice cream on the side — and if we were very, very careful we each could work the Recline-o button on the front seat to turn it into a bed and pretend to sleep until the car-hop arrived. Only the Nash had the seat that turned into a bed, and Mr. Silverman was pleased.

Having a real bed in a car seemed to a sixth-grade sensibility the absolute height of worldliness and sophistication; on the John Greenleaf Whittier Elementary School playground, the boxy Nash, with its bed and a peculiarly shaped body, exuded an ambiguous air of furtive and wicked sex.

"That thing looks like a pregnant turtle," Buddy Porter, whose father drove a Chevy, told Shirley. She affected taking offense, but then collapsed in giggles with the rest of us.

The classroom door opened and a secretary from the principal's office, distress on her face, whispered something into Miss Bunn's ear. She asked Shirley to step outside with her. We were puzzled: Shirley's answer about the midday sun in the Belgian Congo was vague, but it wasn't *that* bad.

Shirley did not come back, not that day; nor was there hotfudge cake that afternoon, or ever again. Mr. Silverman was on his way to school to collect us when he collapsed against the steering wheel with a heart attack and drove into a telephone pole on Sheridan Street. Shirley's father was dead.

I never rode in a Nash again, and years later, when I read that the Nash had joined the Lincoln-Zephyr, the Packard, and the Studebaker in automotive Valhalla, I still thought of Mr. Silverman in a final resting place somewhere beyond the stars on that fold-down bed. Shirley's mother never bought another car, and things were never quite the same between Shirley and me again. She wouldn't leave her mother very much, and six years later, two months before we graduated from Calvin Coolidge High, Shirley married a man almost old enough to be her father. Her diploma was inscribed with her new married name.

I think Shirley never forgave her father for driving his new car to his death, for making her half an orphan when life was sweetest and just beginning to require her full attention, for choosing the big sleep when she had just begun to share her dreams with the first man in her life.

I lost all touch with Shirley after high school, but I never forgot the sad transformation of vivacious child to bittersweet adolescent, the cruel way she was cheated out of happiness on the threshold of her teenage years. She was my first friend to whom life was so visibly unfair, and for years afterward, I prayed to be forgiven for having envied her that pea-green Nash.

Ghosts of Little Girls

Fear of paternal abandonment haunts the psyches of most females; for some, like Shirley, the fear becomes grim reality, the ultimate game of hide-and-seek, with no "time outs." Daddy does, in fact, leave. Whether in death or through divorce, even when a daughter's parents separate with the most sensitive consideration of the child's fears and feelings, the effects reverberate through the years, pursuing the woman through all her adult relationships.

Anaïs Nin, the writer, was separated from her father when she was twelve and her parents dissolved their marriage. Miss Nin recalls being driven to frenzies of anxiety that her husband would abandon her when their first child was born. She became so obsessed with this notion that she heard herself actually talking to the child growing inside her belly:

Inside of this woman there is a child; there is still the ghost of a little girl forever wailing inside, wailing the loss of a father. Will you go about, as I did, knocking on windows, watching every caress and protective love given to other children? For as soon as you will be born, as just as soon as I was born, man the husband, [man the] lover, [man the] friend will leave as my father did. . . . He will hate your wailing and your slobbering, and your sickness, and my feeding you rather than his work, his creation. He might cast you aside for this love of his work, which brings him praise and power. He might run away, as my father ran away from his wife and children, and you would be abandoned as I was. . . . It would be better to die than to be abandoned, for you would spend your life haunting the world for this lost father, this fragment of your body and soul, this lost fragment of your very self. . . .[1]

The death of either parent is a crippling wound that a child must overcome; the early death of a father can drive a sensitive daughter to thoughts of suicide. Sylvia Plath, the poet and novelist, never got over the yearning to join her father, who died when she was eight. "I'll never speak to God again!" she cried, on being told of his death.[2] Red-eyed, angry, demanding her mother's fidelity to her father's memory in the way that she herself determined to pay fealty to it, she returns from school to thrust a paper into her mother's hands for a signature on a promise: "I promise never to marry again." (Years later, Sylvia would ask if the signature had bound her mother to widowhood; her mother said it had not, though it is a fact that she did not marry again.)

Suicide haunted Sylvia Plath's life and work. The autobiographical heroine of *The Bell Jar* weeps at the grave of her father, and tries to follow him into his sepulcher by swallowing fifty sleeping pills. She described a similar incident in her poem "Daddy," when she cries out that she had tried to die in an attempt to get back to the bones of her father.[3]

A. Alvarez, Sylvia Plath's critic and friend, suspects that when she actually did kill herself, years later, she was only rekindling the anguish she felt at her father's death. Her husband had left her for another woman; she felt forsaken again. Her husband had been the fulfillment of the father she had lost, a man she described in her journals as "my savior," "my perfect male counterpart," "the buried male muse and god-creator risen to be my mate." [4] Her husband was a reincarnation of her father, the buried man whom she had years before tried to join. When he left her she could not go on. Concludes Alvarez: "Despite herself, she felt abandoned, injured, enraged, and bereaved as purely and defenselessly as she had as a child twenty years before. As a result, the pain that had built up steadily inside her all that time came flooding out." [5]

Greater Than Life Size

When a father leaves a daughter during infancy, she is likely to have an exalted and idealized image of him, which drives her to search for him constantly, to long for the love affair she never had. She often is tormented by thoughts of suicide.

Dr. Marjorie Leonard, a psychiatrist, tells the story of Rita, an adolescent girl whose father disappeared when she was born. When, in high school, Rita nursed a long and idolizing crush on a teacher-priest, she was referred to Dr. Leonard. In therapy she unraveled her fantasy: because he was a representative of the realm of God, the priest became in Rita's mind a man with connections with the dead, a magician close to heaven where her father lived.

Without treatment Rita would have been repeatedly disappointed in her love affairs, where all men were doomed to fall short of the father she never knew, and there would have been a strong possibility of suicide as "an unconscious attempt at union with her father." [6]

Laura Cunningham, the writer, who was not born until 1948, tells how she grew up thinking her father, whom she would never meet, was far away across the sea fighting the Axis in World War II. She carried the double burden of never knowing her father and knowing nothing about him. She filled in the gaps with melodramatic fantasy: wearing all white and in a slouch hat, she would, typically, run into his office to surprise him, or standing between the columns shading a Tara-like gallery, wait to be hugged and kissed in a frenzy of regret and reunion. In train stations and airports in new cities, she always went first to the bank of telephone booths to rummage through the directories, hoping against all hope that she would find his name and number there.

She finally came to terms with reality: "If my early life is a fiction, well, then fiction is my trade." [7] Not all women find such sublimation for their personal tragedy. Idealization is a dangerous psychological defense, and a daughter must mourn that which she missed. Thus psychologists stress the importance of talking about a little girl's father, even when he is not around.

Keeping Daddy Alive

Judy Blume, the author of many children's books, lost her father when she was twenty-one. She thought that by writing about the effects of a father's death on an adolescent daughter she could help teenagers understand separation and loss. The protagonist in *Tiger Eyes* expresses frustration and disbelief when her father dies: "Don't be dead, Daddy. Please let it be a big mistake. I need you and I want you."

No matter at what age a father dies, Miss Blume says, "you never really get over that. It's my theory that you keep someone alive by not being afraid to talk about [him]." [8]

Adolescents, who are so dependent on their friends, often find it difficult to discuss the loss of a parent. "Their peers can't really bear to listen to them and they are fearful of burdening [the remaining parent]," says Barbara Kaplan, a psychologist who operates a self-help group for teenagers who are mourning the loss of a parent. Theirs is a tragic, lonely, isolating, and alienating experience, and often the effective therapy is in offering and receiving mutual support with others like them. [9]

Lisa, seventeen, isn't conscious of thinking of her father at all times. But when she is alone she talks to him. "I play the flute in several bands and he enjoyed marches. So when I'm playing in a band, I instinctively see my father, and when I feel really alone, I talk to him."

Amy, who is also seventeen, continues to watch football games on television because that is how she spent time with her father. "I watch by myself, as if it's up to me to keep it up."

A Harvard coed, whose father had only recently died, told me of her need to punish herself, to make some kind of sacrifice, when she heard of her father's death in a plane crash. "He was only forty-nine and I needed a ritual to confront the reality that I would never see him again. I had long blond hair which I used to playfully wrap around my father's bald head when I was younger, helping him pretend he had lots of hair, too. The day after he died I chopped off my hair, and I don't think I'll ever let it grow out again."

The younger the child at the time of her father's death or separation from him, the greater is the likelihood of her repressing her mourning. Children younger than five often perceive of death as reversible.

All young children struggle with a frustrating sense of their own powerlessness over those on whom they depend. How wrenching then is the death of a father who signifies the protective life, and who offers the little girl her first experiences of admiration from the opposite sex. Young girls without fathers often create fantasy fathers: "If he cannot be there for me in real life," this fantasy says to a little girl, "I'll make him be there for me in my imagination."

Preschoolers especially, those whose fathers left them before the age of three, idealize the departed parent in their imaginations. "The . . . father they create is rooted in early-attachment images, which find satisfaction in nurturing and caretaking activities," says Carol S. Michaels, a psychologist who studies these fantasies among black, white, and Hispanic children.[10] However, their fantasies pose a problem for the future: it is unlikely that the child who suppresses negative and painful feelings will be able to integrate a realistic father into her own concept of herself and of others. Other men will suffer the consequences of a fantasy father.

As an adult mourner becomes for a time an infant crying in the night, the loss of a parent intensifies a child's feelings of helplessness. Martha Wolfenstein, a psychoanalyst who works with grieving children, says this feeling persists if the child continues to elevate the lost father as a way of mitigating the bad feelings she had about him when he was alive.[11]

Feelings of helplessness in relation to Daddy erupt in other kinds of separations when a daughter feels rejected by her father. Daughters of divorced parents, of psychologically absent fathers, of workaholic fathers often experience a spiraling effect in their anger and anxiety, which stays with them, accelerating as they grow older.

Repeat Performance

The nature of a daughter's separation from her father determines the way the woman relates to men. Consider the paralyzing anger of a young child after her parents have left for a vacation or a weekend holiday alone: love, anxiety, anger, frustrated possessiveness, even hatred become mixed up in a child's mind and vicious circles are born. The child wants to reproach the parents for leaving, but at the same time she wants to prevent a future separation. She makes herself so unpleasant that only exceedingly understanding parents can deal with her tantrums and moodiness.

Rejection, like loss, brings out a child's anger and anxiety, and is often replayed over and over again in adult relationships, frequently forming the basic pattern in marital quarrels. "Fearing rejection, we build up all sorts of hostility, which increases the likelihood that we will indeed be rejected," writes Martin Goldberg, a psychiatrist, discussing the problems of marital intimacy.[12]

A daughter who sees her father depart after a divorce, and sees the departure as a rejection of her, may too easily anticipate a similar kind of rejection from her husband. Consequently, she brings about that very disappointment she fears. She starts a fight when he comes home late. His tardiness unconsciously reminds her of her father's tardiness on those occasions he collected her from school, church, and childhood outings. Her anger is disproportionate to her present situation; her husband storms out of the room, slamming the door in her face. Hostility courts rejection, fear incubates fear: the perfect vicious circle is born.

Cynthia, thirty-two, offers a variation on Dr. Goldberg's theme. Cynthia had been married for ten years when she discovered that Eric, her husband, was having an affair. She confronted him with the evidence, a Holiday Inn receipt that he had left on his desk. She shrieked at him in a voice she had not heard since she was a little girl; she now felt as helpless as a child buffeted by forces stronger than her power to resist. What was happening to her had happened before, when her mother discovered that her father was having an affair, and he moved out of the house. Cynthia was eleven, and life was forever altered. Was this to be a second tragic alteration of a happy life?

Fortunately, Cynthia and Eric worked their way out of their difficulties, learning for the first time who they were. In her own fear of abandonment, Cynthia had become overly possessive, smothering Eric with *haute cuisine,* frequent telephone calls to his office, a constant counting of all the ways she loved him. She wanted to please him, and she came close to accomplishing the opposite, bringing about the very calamity she wished to avoid, abandonment.

Cynthia was acting as though her husband were her father, and was therefore likely to leave her as her father had left her mother. She was experiencing what psychoanalysts call transference, a process by which a person transfers her feelings, fears, and frustrations onto another person as though he were one of the parents. It is an illusion psychiatrists know well, but it doesn't occur only in a psychoanalyst's office.

"Transference occurs in every marriage, but when there is a significant trauma or difficulty in the family of origin, seeing the partner as parent can seriously interfere with the marriage," says August Napier, a family therapist.[13] When a father leaves after a divorce, a daughter is likely to cling to her mother for "dear life." With only one parent left, the fear of abandonment looms larger than ever. A father's departure often revives those earliest feelings when mother and child were as one. With all eggs again in one basket, desperation ensues.

A young girl cannot know why a father leaves her mother, and she is likely to think it has something to do with her mother being an inadequate female. Without a father in the house, making crucial male distinctions so that his daughter learns the complicated ways of the opposite sex, almost all of what she absorbs about intimate behavior between men and women is guesswork, images pieced together from the popular culture and painful memories of what she observed between her father and her mother.

Daughters of divorce, women who are left alone with a mother after their father leaves, often create adult relationships that are too close for comfort.[14] Such women become stifling for both husband and lover. If a child overidentifies with the mother who is left behind, she thinks of herself as victim, too. Later she will have difficulty remaining open to a man both in bed and out. Neither stifler nor victim is likely to forge a satisfactory relationship with a man.

Getting Back

Many of the women who talked to me, women who felt rejected by their fathers, said they look constantly for sexual outlets for their anger, even years later. The greater the hurt, the greater the expression of it. Some women find it impossible to trust any man, others escape deciding which men to mistrust by embracing promiscuity. Still others find it impossible to make any commitment through love.

"My father destroyed my trust in men," says Miranda, twenty-four, a lesbian whose father disappeared when she was twelve. She has not heard of him or from him since.

"Did he love me? Then how could he leave me? He always said he loved me. He had to; he was my father. But he left, anyway. What was wrong with me? I blamed my mother and warred with her for three years afterward and attempted suicide twice. I had absolutely no self-esteem until I allowed my mother to help me to see that I was still a person."

Miranda lives with uncertainty. All the grief she could have felt if he had died is locked in the mystery of his disappearance. Before he disappeared her father always made her feel that she was his favorite — she had three brothers — making his sudden disappearance doubly difficult. "My relationship was special because I was his only daughter. He always brought me candy on Valentine's Day. I still have the heart-shaped red candy boxes. He was the first man who ever treated me like a special lady, and then he went away without a word. Sometimes I hate him. I hate him for making me wonder where he is every day of my life, for hurting every day of my life. He never tried to understand how much I'd need him when I was growing up. I hate him most of all for not leaving me a grave to put flowers on."

A grave to put flowers on can be important, but more important still is a mother's continued chatter about a child's father. What he looked like, how he wore his hat cocked to one side, the sound of his laughter when they drank wine together, how he loved to play with his daughter when she was a baby. A woman needs to recall to the daughter those qualities both good and irritating that made her fall in love with him in the first place. It would be unreal for a mother to talk about him as if he had no faults, and it is no less important to make him a man of flesh, blood, and bone with positive qualities to imitate, with negative ones to beware.

One of the most difficult aspects of a divorce a child must deal with occurs in the bitter wake a father leaves behind. If his wife continues to criticize him to her daughter, she runs the risk of severely damaging the daughter's self-esteem — that part of the father a daughter carries within herself. The daughter may become destructive to herself later, as she takes revenge on men.

Maxine Schnall, a social psychologist, describes Amanda, who indulges in kinky sexual promiscuity with a special taste for sado-masochistic games for three. Amanda persuades her boyfriend to watch. At sixteen, she put an illegitimate child up for adoption, and at about that same time found several devastating letters her father had written to her mother on the occasion of their divorce: "You can take those kids and do anything you want with them. . . . You can go to hell — I don't care."

Amanda never spoke to her father after she read the letters. Says Dr. Schnall: "If Amanda could work through her hate of her father in therapy, she might be able to accept [a] boyfriend in a relationship with greater depth and stability." [15]

Just as a man who as a boy was abandoned by his mother may feel compelled to make conquests of women, to seduce and abandon them, a woman who feels abandoned by her father may become promiscuous or a femme fatale.

"I have always attracted men," says Erika, a tall, willowy blond Manhattan model, who at twenty-seven has a history of bad relationships. "But I've established a terrible pattern that I'm trying to break. As soon as a man makes himself vulnerable to me, I attack. My psychiatrist told me that I was punishing my father for moving across country after my mother divorced him, that I'm still angry with him because I never got to see him. But why can't I let other men be nice to me?

"I feel great sexual passion only with a man who is obviously not a kind person, and make mincemeat of nice guys."

Women like Erika build a barrier around their emotions, warding off vulnerable longings to trust a man. By choosing men who are bad for her, she maintains a solitary existence, making sure that no man who matters to her will ever leave her as her father did. She will show *them*.

Paternal Deprivation

Do girls who are raised in fatherless homes relate to men differently than girls who grow up with their fathers? Does the reason for the father's absence make a difference to the daughter? A major study conducted by Mavis Hetherington, a psychologist, concludes that young girls raised without fathers are more likely to have problems relating to men than girls raised in intact families, and that the cause of the father's absence affects the nature of those problems.

Dr. Hetherington observed and interviewed white, lower middle-class adolescent girls between the ages of thirteen and seventeen who were regulars at a community recreation center. All were firstborn children without brothers, and formed three distinct groups: 1) those whose fathers were absent because of divorce, and whom the daughters seldom saw; 2) girls whose fathers had died and who had had no father substitute; and 3) girls who lived in intact families.

The girls were interviewed in a room with three chairs; each would choose where to sit. One chair was close to the interviewer, one directly across from the interviewer, and one still farther away. A woman interviewer seemed to have no bearing on the choice of the chair, but on the occasions the interviewer was male the girls made marked distinctions.

Daughters of divorcées generally chose the chair closest to the male interviewer and daughters of widows sat as far away from the man as possible. Girls who lived with their mothers and fathers usually chose the middle chair.

Body posture revealed striking differences, too. The daughters of divorcées were more likely to sprawl with arms and legs in an open position, often leaning forward while hooking arms over the backs of chairs. Daughters of widows usually sat stiffly upright or leaned away from the interviewer, sometimes turning their backs, hands folded primly with legs together.

Facial expressions also offered insight. Daughters of widows looked at the interviewer less often than daughters of divorcées, who made eye contact more frequently and smiled more often. Girls whose fathers had died when they were quite young talked and smiled the least, avoiding eye contact when the male interviewer was talking.

Dr. Hetherington concluded that the adolescent girls growing up without fathers felt less personal control over their lives, and had more difficulty dealing with boys and men. Confidence in their own femininity and competency were missing. They were compelled to project images of how they thought a woman ought to appear, or they went into emotional hiding, afraid to show themselves, afraid to be spontaneous. In the presence of men, they suffered, and resorted to extremes of behavior.[16]

The decline of paternal authority, as in the family with an absent father, makes it difficult for a child to develop self-discipline and self-restraint. Christopher Lasch, the sociologist, takes note of this in *The Culture of Narcissism.* So does Mary Gordon, with the novelist's eye and ear, in *The Company of Women:* "I suspect that being fatherless leaves a woman with a taste for the fanatical," she writes, in the voice of her character Felicitas, whose father had died when she was an infant and who takes as her first lover an amoral 1960s guru whose irresponsible radical politics is surpassed only by his sexual depravity. "Having grown unsheltered, having never seen in the familiar flesh the embodiment of the ancient image of authority, a girl can be satisfied only with the heroic, the desperate, the extreme. A fatherless girl thinks all things possible and nothing safe."

Felicitas wants something different for her own daughter, for her "to know the silent protection of a good and ordinary man. I missed that; it was a grief and a loss. . . . I want her to feel safe, because somehow I can't bear the thought of my frail child loose in a world of danger."

The Legacy of Loss

More than 19 percent (about twelve million) of the children of America live in fatherless homes at any given moment; an even higher percentage is fatherless for a significant part of their childhood. In some city slums more than half of the children are fatherless. These fatherless homes have special consequences for girls. Girls growing up without fathers suffer more drug addiction, alcoholism, reactive depression, and suicide attempts.[17]

Many women addicts carry fantasy images of their fathers, says Penny Pearlman, director of Family House, a rehabilitation center for drug and alcohol abusers in Norristown, Pennsylvania. "You frequently hear them say, 'my father could have saved me; he could have protected me from my mother.' "[18]

Paternal deprivation often is paid for by society at large. One British study of the population of women's prisons found that more than a third of the prisoners were fatherless. Says psychologist Felix Brown of these findings: "It is hardly an exaggeration to say that women's prisons are institutions for the aftercare of fatherless girls." [19]

Judith S. Wallerstein and Joan B. Kelly, researchers in a children-of-divorce project, found that only 30 percent of the children they studied had an emotionally nourishing relationship with their fathers five years after separation. They describe Lea as typical; she is a quiet girl who believes that she cannot succeed at anything. Interviewed at her home, Lea brings out a box of letters from her father, received over the previous years. The letters were dog-eared, folded, and refolded like a precious collection of love letters, read and reread until stained with tears. Lea's father had visited her once in two years.[20]

Although joint custody cases are on the increase, most divorces still decree father visiting rights only, and experts disagree about what post-divorce arrangement is most beneficial to the child. But few fail to notice the profound sense of loss both sons and daughters experience when their father leaves home. A respondent to my questionnaire, whose father left her house when she was sixteen, wrote a poem she calls "Visiting Rights," translating her loss and anguish into bitter images:

> We meet at the dinette set
> once a month for chicken from a cardboard box
> barrel or chinese food from a cardboard box
> he's our father you know and has visiting
> rights as often as he chooses
> and he chooses Sunday nights for take-out
> food in his grimy kitchen and rerun
> movies at the corner theatre he's our father
> you know and sometimes looking at his white
> hands and sweaty tee shirts
> and sometimes listening to his droning voice
> and his rerun stories there is no blood
> between us my flesh was never his

The high rate of divorce that involves children effectively disposes of the myth that Americans have created a child-centered society. Ever since the beginning of the "human-potential movement," with its slogans emphasizing "self-realization," and catch phrases like "creative divorce" and "open marriage," couples talk less about staying together "for the sake of the children." And yet children, the true victims of divorce, pay a heavy price.

In a study to explore generational differences between children of divorce and children of intact families, social psychologist Richard Kulka and Helen Weingarten examined the results of two random national surveys of 240,000 Americans, one conducted in 1957, the other in 1976. They conclude that although much of society has changed in the decades since the first survey, children's reactions to their parents' divorce have not. Young adults in their twenties, whose parents had divorced when they were young, were those least likely to be happy, exhibiting more symptoms of poor physical health than those of the same age from intact families. Of all ages, children of divorce remembered their childhoods as unhappy times, and were likely to say they had been "on the verge of a nervous breakdown." [21]

Most studies of divorce focus on the effect of the absent father on boys because boys lack the parent they need for identification. Girls, constantly seeking the "hiding father," suffer his absence in another way.

A daughter in a father-absent family is often given too much responsibility while she is still quite small and incapable of handling it. Family therapists call this the "parentification" of the child, and it usually happens when parents abdicate their emotional responsibility. If there are younger children a daughter may be pressured to assume a mother role when she still needs a mother herself. Or she may be thrust into the role of companion to her mother, privy to adult confidences and anxieties she cannot fully understand. [22] A father's separation from the family not only means the loss of a father for the child, but for the mother it means the loss of a husband.

Social legislation may help the mother provide for her child, but it rarely can keep a man around to be a father. In Sweden, where social programs provide day care and both maternity and paternity leave, the divorce rate is 60 percent higher than the United States; illegitimacy is 300 percent higher than in the United States, with one of every three Swedish children born out of wedlock. [23] Though single-parent homes and the pressures of inflation and the consciousness-raising of feminism have heightened the American woman's awareness that she is well-advised to learn how to take care of herself, illusions die hard.

"My mother did a heroic job, raising me alone," says Eloise, fifty-three, a black psychologist in Baltimore, "but she couldn't make up for the mixed messages I was getting all around me." On the one hand Eloise knew that her father had left her as a baby, and that she shouldn't ever rely on any man to take care of her. She nevertheless yearned for a family of her own.

"I hankered for a cottage, a doll house, and a breadwinner," she says. "The black culture taught us that we have to work for everything we get, but the larger culture kept saying that a woman's place was in the home. An alcoholic husband assisted in the development of my sense of independence by leaving me when our daughter was five years old."

What Eloise realizes now is that women have consciously left men out of the parenting role. "We have denied them child-care responsibilities," she says. "When I meet a man today, I'm interested in knowing what kind of relationship he has with his parents and with his children. That can tell you a lot about him.

"We have colluded in supporting the absentee father. We have let them lose touch with their children. I like men who care passionately about those children."

PART THREE

The Impact of the Early Years

".. . and the thoughts of youth are long, long thoughts."

— Henry Wadsworth Longfellow
"My Lost Youth"

CHAPTER FOUR

Rituals of Childhood: For Better and Worse

I became a bride for the first time when I was five. I married Daddy in the den. Mom was my matron of honor, my older brother Stanley doubled as my father's best man and as the rabbi who recited the vows, such as the vows were.

I wore my favorite party dress and my father gave me a corsage of pink roses, which he cut from a vine curling around the window of the stucco apartment house on Yucca Street in downtown Hollywood. We had gone to Southern California to live for a few weeks while Daddy helped Billy Conn, the number-one heavyweight contender, make a movie.

"The best thing about marrying your daddy, Suzie," my brother Stanley said, "you won't have to change your name."

We all laughed. Even then, light-years ahead of the feminist revolution, I thought Stanley's reason made good sense. The injustice of discarding my father's good name was something I felt even as a child. Stanley, who became a lawyer, was already a stickler for custom and usage. He insisted that my father break the ritual glass under his heel with the pronouncement that my father and I were man and wife.

"Let's do it this way, then," my father said, picking up a whiskey jigger from the sideboard. He wrapped it in one of Mom's handkerchiefs for the traditional conclusion of the Jewish nuptial rite. When the moment came we listened in vain for the tinkle and crunch of the broken glass. The jigger rolled out of the handkerchief, bounced across the floor, and came to rest against the sofa with a soft thud.

"Well, that's all right," my father said. "When you marry your daughter, the glass isn't supposed to break."

Any grade-B psychologist could spin all sorts of speculation today about that ceremony: that I was resolving my Electra complex by officially turning to Daddy, or that I was getting trapped in it, "till death do us part." But for us it was only a lighthearted way of entertaining ourselves, making dramatic what seemed to be a natural love affair between my daddy and me in a time when whimsy and sentiment were the buffers against the grim war reality that children knew well. The streets beyond the bougainvillaea framing my bedroom window reverberated with the shouts and chatter of sailors, soldiers, and marines from all over America: the men at arms gathering in California to ship out to Guadalcanal, Tarawa, Saipan, Iwo Jima — even an *island* called Bougainville. My daddy was too old to go to war, but I didn't know that then, and like most women and little girls living during that fearful juncture of history, I knew that men, and only men, were going to keep the death and destruction away from my doorstep, that daddies, brothers, boyfriends, and husbands had to fight in faraway places to protect us at home.

I also know now that I never felt as close to my father as I did the day we got married. Later, after I started to school and my world grew larger than the house where Daddy lived, I grew shy with him, embarrassed about the "wedding." But I never forgot the thrill of that attraction, my touchstone for schoolgirl crushes and later for adult love.

When Her Heart Belonged to Daddy

Such little girl crushes on Daddy are not unusual, and they begin very early. "The first memories of my father were having him hold me, rock me, and sing to me," says Anna, sixty-five, a St. Paul, Minnesota, woman whose own children are now in their forties. "I was old enough to run and crawl up in his lap. He had a wonderful voice, deep and rich like Mario Lanza in *The Great Caruso,* and I felt warm and comfortable in his arms, very similar to the security I've felt in a lover's arms."

Jessica, twenty-five, a Hollywood actress whose eyes take on a genuine sparkle when she talks about her father, remembers how his touch taught her what she could expect from a man. "He might run his hand through my hair, tousling it, or squeeze my hand, and I recall vividly the innocent sensuous sense of excitement. When I feel loved by a man, really loved and cherished, it is very much like the feeling of love I used to have with my father."

For many of us, life with father is the dress rehearsal for love and marriage.[1] Between three and five, many little girls pretend to marry their fathers, or begin to think and sometimes speak of their fathers as husbands. At that point in a girl's development, any other love object, even in playacting, is unacceptable. Fortunately, little girls learn to change their minds.

Our feelings are never again as intense as in childhood, and the secret rituals of affection take on an importance to us beyond our father's wildest imaginings. "The last thing Daddy did before he left the house for work was to kiss me goodbye," recalls a Mississippi woman. "I'll never forget the first morning he forgot." Her mouth comes together in a pout as she relives the event.

"I was furious, stomping through the house like a little wet pullet. My rage frightened my mother to the point that she put me into the car and carried me off to Daddy's office, just so he could give me the goodbye kiss he forgot."

Psychological theorists might debate whether the mother was

right to humor a little girl so, but few underestimate the significance of such a disappointment in a girl's life. It is precisely because a child's feelings are so strong, argues Dr. Alice Miller, a Swiss psychoanalyst, that they cannot be repressed without serious consequences.[2]

Early childhood years can set the pattern for Daddy's Little Girl for years to come, depending on how a father responds to his young daughter, how he admires her winning ways and developing capabilities. Because her mother traditionally is associated with the ambivalence of the first months of dependency, a father, if he wishes, can be what the psychoanalyst Margaret Mahler calls the famous "knight in shining armor." For two decades her research has emphasized the early importance of the father: "Beyond the 18-month mark and even earlier, the stable image of a father . . . is perhaps . . . necessary to . . . counteract . . . the threat of re-engulfment by the mother." [3] He is her insurance policy for independence of her mother.

But if her infantile wishes, longings, and fantasies remain at a little girl's level in relation to her father, if she becomes independent of her mother only by becoming dependent on her father, a woman will develop a mature relation with a mature man only with difficulty. Wanting to live with Daddy as a little girl, and even to fantasize marrying him is natural; to play out any part of that fantasy as an adult is a regressive act.

Mona, twenty-six, single, tried to live out a romance with her father after she was old enough to know better. "As a young girl," she recalls from her home in Wheeling, West Virginia, "I had pretended to be Daddy's wife, and when my mother died a month before I finished college I thought I had got my chance.

"I went home to spend my summer vacation taking care of him. What a shock I got! I cooked, I cleaned, I talked, I argued — and no matter what I did or said I discovered it simply wasn't possible for me to make my father happy."

Mona always thought she was number one in her father's life, and it was tough realizing that such feelings belonged in a little girl's fantasy. She simply didn't want to grow up; she wanted her father to protect her from all the things in the world that were frightening and unpleasant, to succeed in all the ways she thought her mother had failed.

When he remarried a few years later Mona resented her father's new wife because she got the role Mona mistakenly took to be hers. She is just now beginning to face the world as an adult, discovering that her father is there if she wants to talk over problems with him, but not to take care of her.

Lena Horne, whose parents divorced when she was three, always wanted to marry her father, a romantic, adventurous gambler and racketeer, who was made even more attractive because he wasn't around much. When she was sixteen she ran away from her mother "because I wanted to marry my daddy. Of course I couldn't do *that*. So I wound up marrying the closest thing, this fellow that my dad knew. I made a lousy wife." [4]

Giving Up the Bottle, and Daddy, Too

Most of us give up the baby bottle naturally, if sometimes reluctantly, and most of us come to terms with the fact that we can't actually marry our fathers. For many women, playful fantasy is a cherished memory of childhood, an intimation of adult love.

Dolly, thirty-nine, fell in love with her father, a Baptist preacher in Arkansas, when she was very young. "One day, when I was about six and just starting to school, my father asked me if I ever intended to marry. 'Of course not,' I told him fiercely. 'I want to stay with you at least until I'm fifty-nine years old.' How I came up with the magic number of fifty-nine, I have no idea."

Her father went into his study for a piece of his stationery and a pen and came back to the kitchen table, where he and her mother were having their morning coffee. "Let's put that in writing," he said. Dolly was thrilled that he was taking her vow seriously, and she never forgot how excited she was watching him write out her promise. He helped her to sign her name, taking her hand in his and guiding the pen through the signature. Then her mother witnessed the letter, very solemnly, trying not to smile.

"I forgot all about it after a week or so," she says, "and it never came to mind until years later on the night before my wedding. When I came in from the rehearsal dinner, my father called me into the living room where he and my mother were once again having a cup of coffee. 'I have a wedding present for you,' he said, his eyes twinkling.

"He brought out a folded sheet of paper. 'I've had this in my files for a long time, and this seems a good time to give it back to you,' he said. 'I could hold you to it, but since you seem to be so much in love with someone else now it wouldn't seem quite fair.' "

Dolly opened the paper, and there it was, her old promise not to marry until she was fifty-nine. "All of that wonderful excitement came flooding back, and I think I never loved Pop more than I did at that moment."

The playful exchange between Dolly and her father occurred in a strong marriage of two loving parents, where the open play of father-daughter affection in no way threatened the bond of mother and father. The first childish "love affair" must take place in the context of a reasonably good marriage. Psychosexual satisfaction, therapists remind us, is a learned experience and we develop it in one of two directions: for a little girl to develop in the direction of sexual pleasure, she must elicit from her father, through her very nature as a girl, an appreciation and pleasure that is distinctively hers.

We have been blinded to the importance of sexuality between father and daughter, argues Leon Hammer, a psychotherapist who treats frigid women, because we fear incest, which is a power struggle between mother and daughter over her father's attention. There is no motivation for incest, however, when the parents have a strong marriage.[5] Except for the authentic psychotic, no man wants to seduce a little girl when he can satisfy his appetite with a woman.

Keeping Mother in Sight

The rituals of childhood, however, can foreshadow a more possessive bond as the daughter grows older. A father who spends special time with his daughter *instead* of with his wife is courting trouble. Many women told me of the pleasures they had with their fathers when he wanted to take them fishing, camping, things mother didn't want to do. They loved the private time with their fathers. But as they grew older and wanted to build a social life around their friends, their father's entertainment still centered on them because his wife hadn't changed her interests.

"When I was nine, my father frequently went to the races at Saratoga," recalls Edith, now sixty-seven, reminiscing about her good old days, days when her mother stayed home. "In the mornings we read the Racing Form together and he showed me how to pick our afternoon bets. Then we'd go to the bookie. All bets were taken by the bookies, who gathered in the infield in front of the grandstand."

Edith felt very grown up. Her father showed her how to give the bookie two dollars and he took her back to cash her winnings. She loved watching the bookie peel the bills away to pay off her bet, and she always gave the money to her father to keep. When they won they went to the cigar store and her father let her pick his cigar. It was a glorious ritual.

"I always picked an El Producto, Daddy's favorite. He carefully slipped the paper ring away from the tobacco and onto my finger. I don't remember whether I pretended to be his wife, but I was thrilled to wear Daddy's ring."

If the ring did not a marriage make, even for a few innocent minutes, it symbolized an intimate bond, and because he was locked into an unhappy real marriage, the bond of father and daughter would cause problems later. When Edith began to go out with boys, none was good enough. The bright ones didn't look good enough, and the good-looking ones weren't smart enough. He never gave her fatherly advice because he secretly hoped she would never marry and he did his best to prevent it. Edith had become a "surrogate" wife.

The happy days at Saratoga would have been harmless if her father had eventually let Edith go. But he turned the pleasure into possession, and when it came time to let Edith move on to men her own age, he confused past with present. He turned a ritual of childhood into an inhibiting rite of passage, holding her too close. It was difficult for Edith to find boys who would compete with her father.

When the father becomes the all-loving hero of childhood, he makes it difficult for adult men to take his place. He remains the titillation of girlish dreams. "I've had two husbands and three live-in lovers, and I've lived alone with my kids and my cats, and I've always been looking for a man who would cherish me come hell or high water," says Anabel, who is still stuck on her father. "But when they made my daddy they threw away the mold."

At forty-seven, Anabel is a little old to idealize her father still, but that idealization reflects a strong and continuing dislike for her mother. Dr. Mahler and her co-workers describe the father in terms of the "awakener" of the child, the one who can help an infant separate from a clinging reliance on the mother. The daughter who sees her father as an Adonis merely replaces the fantasy of the all-giving mother with the fantasy of the all-enticing father.

For this reason it is particularly important for the early father-daughter love affair to be more than titillation, more than a superficial appreciation of the opposite sex. The father must understand that he has a special responsibility to respond to his daughter with love, admiration, and guidance. He is a loving escort to the larger world. The ties that bind a girl to her father must be fastened with a slipknot that moves as she moves, that does not constrict to impede growth, that accepts the sexual attraction as natural and enhancing, but one that can easily be loosened at the appropriate time.

"The father image comes toward the child," according to Dr. Mahler, ". . . from outer space as it were . . . as something gloriously new and exciting, at just the same time when the toddler is experiencing a feverish quest for expansion." [6] He provides a daughter with a sense of adventure and knowledge of sexual difference. If he spends a lot of time with her he will humanize the opposite sex rather than cause her to idealize it. A father helps a daughter strengthen her sense of being female by providing a male self to see in contrast, but she must see this male affection in relation to her mother as well as having it directly expressed to her.

In the best of circumstances, a daughter develops with two parents who love her *and* each other, and she enjoys positive sexual distinctions. From the beginning, from touching, laughing, and playing with her parents, she learns that there is a difference between father and mother. Father and mother are neither better nor worse than each other, just different.

Parents pick up their babies for different reasons. Mothers are more likely to perform caretaking chores and to impose disciplinary restrictions, fathers more likely to play. They also play differently: mothers are more likely to initiate conventional play with toys, while fathers prefer physically stimulating idiosyncratic play, tickling and teasing that infants respond to eagerly.

A father also brings to the crib of a little girl a mighty awareness that he is different. He holds his girl child more gently and plays with her more gingerly than with a son.

For his daughter, a father uses a "full stroking and lilting language," says Willard Gaylin, the psychiatrist. By contrast, his son hears a staccato, withholding verbiage, an "infantile version of the punch in the ribs and the sock on the arm." [7] Girls receive more affection than boys do.

How a Girl Is Not a Boy

A father has different expectations for his daughter, and girls build on these messages when quite young. Such messages are not necessarily one-sided. Since the personalities of female babies differ from those of male babies, the nature of their attachments to their fathers may well grow out of their biological differences.

For example, researchers have found that girl babies smile more often, and form animated jabbering sounds when they see a human face more readily than boy babies do. Girls at three months show "sociable" responses to a face in a photograph, while boys of this early age usually do not discriminate between a face in a photograph and a simple line drawing.

Does this suggest a difference in sociability? Maggie Scarf, whose book *Unfinished Business* describes how women are more vulnerable to depression when there is a breakdown in close relationships, thinks so. Her findings "suggest an innately greater level of sociability, attachment to others, interpersonal sensitivity that may, in fact, be part of the female's biological heritage. . . ." [8] Fathers inevitably react to this sociability in a way that reinforces the fundamental sexual attraction between male and female.

"Mirroring" between mother and child is a well-known phenomenon: each looks into the other's eyes for admiration and confirmation of desirability, and this healthy interplay is crucial to the way the baby defines herself in relation to her mother. The child's father cannot offer a mirror image. He is a shadow dancer, a figure who first steps from behind the mirror to take her by the hand to lead her into another world of greater variety, complexity, and hence excitement. His is a complementary world, where she learns to develop her sense of self within a wider perspective. Because what he teaches also titillates, he carries a special responsibility rooted in a seductive power beyond conscious recognition, alerting her to the existence and presence of a sexual nature within her self.

Seductive flirtatiousness begins between father and daughter at an unconscious level where neither is aware of it. At nine months, Kathy had learned to strike a coy pose, tilting her head toward her father, lying on her back stretching her tiny arms to offer herself to him. Researchers at the Masters Children's Clinic in New York City observed Kathy with her father over a three-year period, tracing the beginning of her "vamping" behavior to this very gesture. At eighteen months, Kathy was an outrageous flirt, once beguiling a male stranger to hug, kiss her, and smile at her, all the while calling out: "Da, da, da." With her father, she learned to alternate smiles and pouts in a precocious game of "hard-to-get."

She went through subsequent stages of rejecting her father for the attentions of her mother, but by the end of the third year she had rediscovered her father with enthusiasm. As if cued by Dr. Freud himself, Kathy could say clearly: "Daddy nice, Mummy mean." She effectively understood the differences between her parents and shrewdly exploited those differences. The earlier "passive-receptive" aspects of her relationship with her mother were transferred to the more powerful image of her father.

In a study with four girls, these researchers observed that between the ages of fourteen and sixteen months a child would climb onto the lap of a male observer, an *ad hoc* surrogate father, hugging and kissing him, flattering the pleased male object of their self-conscious feminine attention.[9]

Men occasionally discover this phenomenon in unsuspected ways. A man who married a woman with a three-month-old daughter recalls how it was he who could most easily quiet the infant's crying. "Laurie suffered with the colic. My wife, try as she might, never could get her to go back to sleep after we gave her the prescribed medication. So I started getting up with the baby. Desperate for a little silence, I once tucked Laurie under my pajama shirt and pressed her firmly against my bare belly.

"It was magic: instant silence, followed by the even breathing of deep, contented baby sleep. My wife tried it, but it rarely worked. It worked for me long after the colic disappeared. Did that little girl, at some infantile level, feel a pleasurable sexual difference, and respond to it? I've always wondered."

For Freud, the infant that father held was much too young to make sexual distinctions. Freud saw girl babies and boy babies as similar in their sexuality; they were both like little boys, without significant differences occurring until the phallic stage, age three to six. Before the phallic stage, Freud said, "We are obliged to recognize that the little girl is a little man." [10] It was Melanie Klein who postulated the essential "femininity" of the little girl, arguing that an infant girl had an early awareness of her vagina and a *conscious* and *feminine* awareness of her father's penis. For the Kleinians, the little girl knows from the beginning that mother is an "inadequate sexual object" for her in contrast to father, who has the real thing.[11]

Recent research in biology and genetics suggests the existence of an original feminine identity, though *recognition* of the penis is irrelevant to this identity.[12]

Gender is firmly established between eighteen months and three years, and it is likely that self-images for the little girl are built on biology and enhanced by parental and cultural interplay in infancy.[13]

Cross-Cultural Coquetry

Flirtatious behavior, for example, may be culturally determined but rooted in sexuality, and it may be universal. Margaret Mead writes that men among the Arapesh tribe in New Guinea often sit entranced by the coquettishness of a girl-baby whose mother, for her own amusement, has dressed her daughter in a seductive grass skirt. Because a girl child is betrothed when she is seven or eight years old, fathers relish romantic notions about their daughters. The little girls know it.

"Young men will comment with enthusiasm upon the feminine charm of a five-year-old," says Dr. Mead, and ". . . when mothers occasionally deck out their tiny daughters . . . the conversation of a group of big boys is hushed for a moment as a small girl flips by, rustling her stiff little skirts." [14]

Arapesh life is hard, resources scant. Male children are greatly prized. Girls are sometimes killed soon after they are born.[15] Since the father decides whether a newly born child lives or dies, enhancing the prospective sexuality of a girl can be a powerful reminder to a father that a daughter has her uses, too.

An American man, who wouldn't think of betrothing his little girl before puberty, is no less susceptible to the temptation of a tiny rustling skirt. Americans have formalized flirtatiousness and satirized little-girl coquetry. Beauty contests commemorate everything from Miss Drumsticks of the Ozarks (a contest in which everything but the contestants' legs are hidden by a screen) to Miss America.[16] Some beauty contests measure the physical charms of girls as young as eighteen months.

Christy was four when her father took her to Washington, D.C., to try to become Tiny Miss United States. She was a tyke but not a tyro: she had already been Miss Land of the Sky, Our Little Miss, Miss La Petite, even judged by a presumably awed Las Vegas tribune to be the World's Best Three-Year-Old. Her father gave up his taste for fifteen-year-old Scotch whisky and sold his golf clubs to support Christy's appetite for handmade dresses, sports outfits, makeup, and professional hair styling.

"I guess I could put her through college for what I've already spent on her," her father told a newspaper interviewer with no real trace of regret. "But everyone likes a hobby, and this is one the whole family can enjoy." [17] (Papa most of all?)

Few girls become Daddy's pets in the way Christy did, and it may be difficult for most women to remember such dramatic events in the first few years of their lives, but Freud, like Masters and Johnson after him, stressed his belief that such early experiences have a powerful impact on later sexual development.

Changing the Message

A one-sided appeal to femininity is likely to cause an imbalance in a woman's development, an overemphasis on vanity rather than capability. A child's interior life suffers if she is only concerned with the impact of her image. A father can help straighten out the conflicting sexual messages of the popular culture — and those of his own making, too.

"I was five and precocious," recalls a thirty-one-year-old wife in Providence, Rhode Island, "and I overheard my mother and father discuss a striptease dancer they had seen in a nightclub.

"I had seen some of Daddy's photography magazines and concluded that he appreciated the 'cheesecake' look, so I decided to provide it for him. I took two of his hankies and fashioned a very effective bikini. I couldn't wait to hear his compliments, and in a five-year-old way I was feeling very sexy and pleased with myself.

"Daddy took one look at me, and frowned. He told me with a

stern voice I can hear yet: 'Put your clothes back on. That's not *nice!*' "

A father as well as a mother helps a child become a fully formed, complete person; but a father especially helps the child bring together a coherent sense of his or her sexuality, because as a boy learns about sex by imitating his father, so a girl learns by observing how her father responds to her feminine mannerisms.

Because parents are so much bigger than their children, and what they do often seems greater-than-life size, children exaggerate their parents' exploits. That includes their sexual prowess, too, and little boys embellish in a way that is different than little girls.

I recall two earnest young boys having what they thought was a private discussion in my kitchen one day, comparing the size of their fathers' penises. "My daddy's goes down to his knees," one of them boasted. "Well," said the other, "my daddy's goes all the way down to his ankles." Such dialogue is unthinkable among little girls, two of whom were found giggling with mortification when they overheard this young male conversation.

Little girls exaggerate the romantic rather than the sexual. For my generation the romantic ideal was Clark Gable as Rhett Butler, fearless man of adventure, love, and Lost Causes, or Humphrey Bogart as the world-weary Casablanca innkeeper whose tough exterior masked a heart of enduring tenderness, subject to melting at a low temperature when confronted with female distress. Many of us thought of our fathers in such terms, too.

Such innocent fantasies are harmless enough if Daddy doesn't join in them. When he does, the wife and mother suffers, and consequently, the daughter does, too.

And Baby Makes Three

Many women remember making mischief that makes Mother mad, and Daddy becomes either a coconspirator or at least his daughter's defender, with Mom left on the short side of a scalene triangle. Emma, a New York City woman, has such recollections, but at age sixty-five, with grown daughters and granddaughters, she is less sympathetic with her father than she once was. A train ride with her parents when she was two stands out in vivid memory:

"We were riding to Long Island to visit my aunt, and I decided to throw my new bonnet away. I untied the ribbons and tossed it through the open window with glee. My mother screamed at me and then at my father to stop the train.

"I must have screamed, too, because I remember laughing at her while he held me in his arms, and I remember a joyous feeling of power that I had managed to get her in 'trouble' with my father. He had a round little face and every time I see the man in the moon I think of him and remember that strange, wonderful, and slightly unsettling feeling."

A man in the moon the father may have been, to a little girl; to that little girl's mother he was an all-too-flawed mortal. Short of stopping the train, how could he have satisfied his wife's anger and distress? How much easier to surrender himself to the worshipful seductiveness of his daughter, who was eager to leap into his arms with no complaints. Thus little girls learn to apply the squeeze play with effortless skill.

Lillian, sixty, a psychologist, recalls with pleasure and rue the way she and her father allied themselves against her mother.

"My mother yelled at both Daddy and me, particularly during meals. 'Take your elbows off the table, finish your peas, drink your milk, don't eat so fast.'

"When she started in on me, Daddy reached across the table to put his hand over my tiny fist, letting her know that *he* was with *me.*" This gesture frightened little Lillian because she knew it would inflame her mother, but she cared more for her father's feelings than for her mother's. He was a weak but kindly man, and better to have him as ally than no ally at all.

As she grew older, she learned that it was easy to manipulate the situation: "A wounded expression on my face brought my father's hand over mine, and my mother was vanquished — again."

The father who draws his daughter into an unholy alliance against her mother is playing a dangerous game. While a little girl may take pleasure in her connection with the powerful man, she is liable to feel guilt and fear for betraying her mother. It is also likely that her father is less powerful than she at first presumes, a fact to which she is undoubtedly a witness when her parents argue. A man who feels powerful in the family need not enlist the support of a girl.

Daddy Now/Jealousy Later

The danger of the family triangle, with father and daughter against mother, is that a daughter may feel omnipotent, but this may mask self-contempt and deepen insecurity.[18] By siding with Daddy, a daughter undercuts that part of herself that identifies with her mother. She is likely to suffer wounds to her self-esteem and she is a candidate for extreme jealousy as she gets older and chooses a man for herself. Even in a casual relationship, how can she possibly trust her man with another woman when she knows how treacherous an "other woman" can be, having seen at an early age the threat she was to her mother?

One theory of jealousy is that it is an unconscious impulse toward infidelity, projected onto the object of affection. A girl who competes against her mother for her father's affections, and wins, may come to believe unconsciously, when she is a woman, that no woman is safe. Won't there be women like herself, setting traps for her husband? And if her husband is a man like her father, isn't he likely to be trapped, too?

A father who lines up a daughter against her mother dramatically illustrates the dangerous zone of a father's love. This experience is not unique to our culture.

When Margaret Mead studied the Mundugumor of New Guinea, she saw family jealousies institutionalized within a social organization based on the theory that members of the same sex feel a natural hostility to one another. The little Mundugumor girl, who is much closer to her father than to her mother, exploits this advantage whenever she can and has little trouble winning her father over with a "pert smile" and kinship terms he has taught her. "Often after the mother has carried up an especially tasty dish for the father's evening meal," observes Dr. Mead, "it is the daughter, not the mother, who is *bidden* to creep into the father's sleeping-bag for the night." [19]

Blurring Family Boundaries

Such activity, as we know, is hardly restricted to the Mundugumor. Incest is the growing ugly secret in our own society. The origins of incestuous episodes often can be traced to the years before puberty, when a guilty father first separates his young daughter from the rest of the family. Special favors, typically accompanied by fondling and touching, as we shall see later, slip seductively into episodes of physical eroticism.

In her book *Father-Daughter Incest,* Judith Herman describes how easily sexual messages between fathers, father-figures, and little girls can get mixed up, and must be guarded against.[20]

Maya Angelou illustrates this problem poignantly in her autobiography, *I Know Why the Caged Bird Sings.* She nourished an eight-year-old's crush on Mr. Freeman, one of her mother's beaux. She craves his attention, longs for him to hold her, for him to wrap his big arms around her, to listen to his heart beating against hers.

One evening, when I couldn't concentrate on anything, I went over to him and sat quickly on his lap. At first Mr. Freeman sat still, not holding me or anything, when I felt a soft lump under my thigh begin to move. It twitched against me and started to harden. Then he pulled me to his chest. He smelled of coal dust and grease and he was so close I buried my face in his shirt and listened to his heart, it was beating just for me. Only I could hear the thud, only I could feel the jumping in my face. He said, 'Sit still, stop squirming.' But all the time, he pushed me around on his lap, then suddenly he stood up and I slipped down to the floor. He ran to the bathroom.

For months he stopped speaking to me again. I was hurt and for a time felt lonelier than ever. But then I forgot about him, and even the memory of his holding me precious melted into the general darkness just beyond the great blinkers of childhood.[21]

Miss Angelou recognizes the part she played in what happened, but as Dr. Herman observes: "She clearly depicts the utter incongruity between her childish longings and adult sexuality."

Incest is actually child abuse, an adult taking advantage of something that a child does not understand. The incest taboo insures the physical and emotional survival of the young. Sexuality itself is the root of the problem of the father-daughter relationship, as witnessed in this taboo.

"The protection of the children from the parents, once established as desirable, involves the need of protecting the parents from the children also," says Margaret Mead. "The protection of a ten-year-old girl from her father's advances is a necessary condition of social order, but the protection of the father from temptation is a necessary condition of his social adjustment." [22]

The Cinderella legend dramatizes the need for reciprocal protection of both father and daughter. Though the most popular version tells us what happens when a father marries a wicked stepmother, others address the danger for Cinderella, who is left alone with a widowed father. In some, the father attempts to extract an exaggerated declaration of love from his daughter. When he finds her expressions too pale for his purposes he banishes her. It is not difficult to read the father's anger as one arising from sexual desires thwarted by his daughter's innocence, and it is but a small literary step to make the daughter inconspicuous, drab among the cinders, hiding her beauty from her father to avoid banishment. When a mean stepmother becomes the instrument of punishment, Cinderella falls victim to jealousy. Her father still loves her too much for her own good. In other versions, the widowed father wants to marry his daughter and she runs away from him.

This same story has a tragic twist when it is translated into a parable of Christian saintliness. Dympna, a Christian princess who is the young daughter of a pagan Irish king, is elevated to martyrdom when, after her mother dies, she refuses to marry her father. She tries to escape with her priest and confessor, and the king beheads her. Dympna today is the patron saint of the mentally ill.

Father-daughter love rests upon a delicate fulcrum with an exquisite balance. The balance between the father's taking his child's love and returning it without damaging it with eroticism is a delicate one, lest his love be transformed into what one family therapist calls "emotional incest." A father must treasure his little girl's need for him, and work to impart the reassurance and confidence that comes with her understanding of his high opinion of her. With this, she can choose a mate with whom to make a good life, and with whom she may forge a happy sex life. Her choices flow from self-esteem.

Is it so far-fetched to suggest that modern fathers and daughters often conspire to protect one another? One of the positive ways they do this is by maintaining clear-cut generational boundaries. Those fathers who do not so conspire with their daughters are inviting trouble.

Another way they can conspire is for both to idealize the other's role, and to romanticize rather than eroticize the way the other plays that role. Even this conspiracy is fraught with danger if they are not wary. Romanticizing her father is a girl's sweetest dream of childhood, but if she and her father persist in the conspiracy beyond the time when a girl must put away childish things, Big Daddy and Daddy's Little Girl run the risk of procreating the biggest myth of all.

Mythologies from Childhood:
Beyond the Shadow of a Dad

The dark-blue thunderclouds that ruined our morning were gone now, barely visible on the far side of the sea, and the Atlantic beach was coming alive again. One by one and in groups of twos and threes, clutching umbrellas and newspapers and children with tiny buckets and rubber ducks in their hands, the bathers reclaimed their places in the sun and on the sand.

"Come on, Suzie," cried Daddy. "Let's see if we're big enough to stand up to the waves."

I was willing to follow Daddy anywhere, even though the waves were big ones, towering high into my limited horizon like monsters, and the thunderheads that seemed so far at sea were suddenly dark and menacing again, considerably larger than they had appeared to be from the security of our hotel on the boardwalk at Atlantic City.

But if Daddy said it was a good idea, it *was*. Soon we were leaping into the swells together, laughing at the difficulty we were having trying to stay on our feet, my hand clutched tightly in his.

Suddenly, the familiar grip was gone. Water in my face was water in my throat, and with it the taste of salt, surprise, terror. I thrashed about violently, my heart pounding in my ears. Small stones rubbed against my flesh as I settled on the bottom of the sea. I was certain that I would never breathe air again, never feel the sun on my face, never feel the comforting rough planks of the boardwalk beneath my feet.

Then, as suddenly as I had lost Daddy's familiar grip, familiar arms were about me, and then my head bobbed above the sea. Once again my father's beautiful familiar laughing face was before mine, and I felt aglow with the exhilaration and titillation of an ocean subdued and at peace at my feet, safe in my father's embrace.

I never thought to question, not then, that perhaps Daddy ought not to have taken his eight-year-old daughter into such a sea. I never considered the danger that lurked there, the possibility that Daddy had waived prudence for a moment of pleasure. I felt only the rush of assurance that Daddy had been there when I needed him, demonstrating once more that I could depend on him to make everything come out right — that Daddy had the power to make all things perfect.

Of such trusting affection and intimacy are spun the illusions that make life sweet. But as a girl grows into a woman, illusions inhibit independence. For many women, the father is the first in a line of illusory men who fog our vision with roses, men with the power to make us see things not so clearly.

A strong, admiring, protective father can enchant a little girl, making her passages in the world feel safe and more secure than they really are. For many of us the father of the fantasy is rooted in reality, and as we grow older we learn to make realistic distinctions. Daddy gets shorter as we get taller. But when a father remains magic in memory, others suffer by comparison, and so do we.

The father that Eleanor Roosevelt remembered was the man who drove her frantic with joy on the occasions that he took her places with him; actually, he was an irresponsible alcoholic who often made dates to take her to lunch and never showed up.

"My father was always devoted to me," she recalled to her biographer. "I even danced for him, intoxicated by the pure joy of motion, twisting around and around until he would pick me up and throw me into the air and tell me I made him dizzy."

He made Eleanor feel wonderful in the way that her mother made her feel plain and unattractive, and she felt the warmth of his devotion even on the occasions that he failed to come through for her. Such idolization exacted a price, observed Joseph P. Lash in *Eleanor and Franklin.* By repressing the memory of the selfish side of her father's personality, she impaired her own sense of reality. "She tended to overestimate and misjudge people, especially those who seemed to need her and who satisfied her need for self-sacrifice and affection and [who] gave her the admiration and loyalty she craved. Just as her response to being disappointed by her father had been silence and depression because she did not dare see him as he really was, so in later life she would become closed, withdrawn, and moody when people she cared about disappointed her." [1]

"The Christmas-Tree Syndrome"

Seeing Daddy as the man we want him to be, rather than as the man he is, is another way we allow him to hide from us, creating problems for the future lovers of his daughter. One psychologist calls this making a myth of Daddy "the Christmas-tree syndrome." He describes a young patient who loved to talk endlessly about the way her father always bought the perfect Christmas tree.

"I thought he was a magician because he always chose the exact tree I wanted," she said. "I never had to describe the tree I wanted, or even drop a hint. Whether I wanted a pine, a spruce, a cedar, natural or silvered, tiny or tall, he always brought home the exact tree I had in mind."

Years later, her husband paid. She and her husband sparred

and bickered over their tree. He always picked one that was too small, too cheap, too green. She was amazed at the number of things she could find wrong with her husband's tree. The ritual ended, as rituals do, on a familiar note.

"All right, *you* choose the damn tree!"

"But I don't *want* to choose the tree."

One day, in therapy, she asked a rhetorical question. "Why couldn't my husband know which tree was the best, like my father did? Buying a tree with my father was an event."

Though an adult, she had not adjusted the scale of the Christmas-tree adventure to her mature life. Tree became totem. By listening closely to the arguments over the tree, she learned to detect other ways that she had allowed old images of her father to intrude upon her marriage.

"Every relationship I ever had with a man suffered because I wanted to replicate my relationship with him. The fights I picked in those first years of marriage were over things he did differently than Daddy, the way he tipped waiters, took care of the car, even the choice of books he read. My father was my point of reference for how a man should be."

He was also her point of reference for how a woman should be. Little girls learn very early what their father expects of them, and they usually play to that. When Daddy is the Big Man, and daughter is the Little Girl, when a father is "sooo big" and a daughter is "sooo small," the child feels she has little to offer. What she does have, however, she is often determined to make the most of. She plays up to her father's powerfulness by exploiting her helplessness, and Daddy usually contributes to that perception by overplaying his role as protector.

Pleasures of Weakness

Even when a daughter's helplessness begins in a relatively harmless way, repercussions can be long lasting, far beyond original intentions, setting a perilous precedent. Eva May is a seventeen-year-old Daddy's Girl in Pomona, California. By the time she was three she could wrap Daddy around her little finger. One day, when she knew he was looking, she went into the backyard, climbed onto her swing, and challenged the laws of gravity. She climbed as high as her little legs could take her until she lost her grip and fell.

That was her opportunity: "I wasn't really hurt, but because I knew Daddy was watching, I started crying, working at it as hard as I had on that swing. He came running and scooped me into his arms and held me close, stroking my hair, telling me that everything was going to be all right. I got a lot more pleasure from that than I did from learning how to control the swing."

Eva May learned the ease of achieving emotional power based on frailty and her father reinforced the pleasures of weakness. Would he have scooped up a son, showering him with kisses and soft words to dry his tears, offering him the power and pleasure of being hurt? Probably not. More than likely he would have reacted to the tears with pretended indifference to teach the boy that men "tough it out."

Masculine fathers show girl children a soft, nurturing side of themselves they would never think of showing their sons. A father and daughter can build on such affection if a father helps his daughter learn to take her lumps, too, and learn from them. Men who want sons to show a tough, hard side to adversity translate their own toughness into emotional armor around their daughters, who are expected to pay for it only with a display of vulnerable femininity.

When a man uses his protective-armor approach to impart substantive information, he can inhibit his daughter's developing into an independent woman comfortable when thinking for herself. In an experiment with fathers and children at the University of California, small children were told to arrange blocks of different shapes and sizes and colors in a certain pattern. With sons, men emphasized the principles of the pattern, demonstrating ways to work the blocks into the proper places. When the boys made mistakes, the fathers showed them where and how the mistakes were made and suggested solutions. When the girls tried the same experiments, their fathers neither explained principles nor showed the ways to solutions. Instead, they emphasized the pleasure of working together. When their daughters made mistakes, fathers quickly assuaged feminine chagrin with reassurance: "It's all right. There's nothing to worry about."

"The message being conveyed to the daughter by the father appears to be that the [affectionate] relationship is really important, that this is where her future success will be found," explains Dr. Jeanne Block, who directed the California experiments. ". . . The son is getting a message that he can create effects in the world, and I think that this fosters in boys a sense of efficacy, a sense of mastery, a sense that *I'm the person with . . . power to make things happen.*" [2]

A father looks to the future with a son — he invests him with information to serve him well in the world. A father anticipates a daughter's maturity with greater anxiety for the time she will no longer be protected by him, and thus pampers her longer. In the long run the father may serve the son better, but to a little girl the bargain of exchanging affection for immature dependency is a pleasant one.

Thus are planted the seeds of her dilemma. Just as she wants to be taken seriously, she does not want to give up the perquisites of affection that accompany the status of Daddy's Little Girl. Nor does she want to be treated as a son.

Daddy's Little "Boy"

In an analysis of the careers of twenty-five women who were frozen in mid-level management positions, Margaret Hennig, director of the management program for women at Simmons College in Boston, found that the fathers of these women had treated them as if they were sons — many had male names, such as Tommie, Jo, or Bobbie. The message received was that women must be "men" to succeed. Most never married, never reached for the "feminine" role, and grew old and embittered pursuing a style perceived by society as masculine. Instead of combining work and womanhood, such women struggled to be one of "the boys," and the "boys" ultimately turned them aside to marry girls.

Of twenty-five women in top-level management positions, women who were graduated from college in the 1930s when an educated woman was not always thought so glamorous as today, Margaret Hennig found they all suffered similar mid-life crises over finding a suitable mate. These women held strikingly similar recollections of their fathers, having grown up as "Daddy's special girl," but their shared interests and activities were those "traditionally regarded as appropriate only for fathers and sons: physical activity, the acquisition of outdoors skills, an aggressive wish to achieve, and finally a willingness to compete." These "male" qualities ran counter to strategies for finding an "opposite" to love and marry.

In their middle thirties, every successful woman in the Hennig study reined in her drive for achievement. Typically, she "did herself over" with new clothes, new makeup, and a new hairstyle to enhance her femininity. Nevertheless, only half actually married; none became mothers. Several married older men with children of previous marriages.[3]

A problem for women like these, including several whom I interviewed, is that their achievements in the workplace often are not matched by success with men, and for this they blame their fathers. Rare is the father who can fuse admiration for a daughter's femininity with pride in her other capabilities, offering affection and appreciation, giving his daughter a balanced perspective for love and work.

Women whose fathers treat them as sons, such as the women in the Simmons study, often grow up with a distorted perception of the female nature, entering into a give-and-take with a man only with difficulty. They miss a crucial stage in the development of their feminine side. Feeling driven to attempt everything the man does, such a woman often behaves in the company of a man as if to ask: "What do I need *you* for?"

Melva is such a woman. At thirty-six, she is a telephone in-
staller who broke a notable employment barrier in a small town in
northern Virginia. She gets along with men on the job, but concedes the feminine self that men would be attracted to is underdeveloped. Men respect her drive, but they don't want to take her
dancing.

"Resiliency, that's what I lack," she says. "Daddy and I did lots
of things together, but always on his turf. I can change a tire,
check the oil, splice a wire, and climb a telephone pole in an icy
wind or driving rain, but there are days when I wish I didn't know
any of that."

Though Melva has earned the respect of the men she works
with, quite a different kind of man wants to take her out. "These
want to be taken care of, and I don't want to take care of them."
When Melva meets a man who is her equal, she feels compelled to
compete. "I can be feminine with women, drinking wine and getting silly and cozy and funny, but with a man I get belligerent.
That turns them off in a hurry, and why wouldn't it? I love all the
things my father taught me to do and I'm happy that I know how
to take care of myself. But I wish just once he had told me how
pretty I was."

Melva was never able to be girlish with her father. She never
had that "love affair" in early childhood. She doesn't know how to
flirt or be feminine. She tries to find solace in women friends, but
misses men. "When I was a child everyone called me my Daddy's
girl, but Daddy never wanted me to be his girl. He wanted me to
be *like* him."

The Tyranny of Flattery

Excessive flattery can tyrannize and wound in another
way. The compliments to make a little girl feel good about herself
can, if overdone, undercut a woman's sense of control. This is
especially harmful if flattery is all she gets from her father. Just as
an affair of true love requires more than "good sex," crucial

though that is, so must a daughter experience a father's admiration beyond mere titillation. A father's compliments that embrace only her femininity are not enough.

One daughter, whose father made a point of extravagantly admiring her clothes when she was a child, told me that she dressed to please her father long after she became a mature woman, expecting to win admiration similar to her father's from other men. Her physical appearance was her only measure of self-esteem.

Extravagant praise often begins innocently. We all know the exuberant boast of the new father, usually accompanied by a deft move to hip pocket to bring out a wallet bulging with new photographs: "You ought to see her, Sam, the most beautiful baby I've ever seen!" (He has, of course, spent a lifetime observing and admiring other men's babies.) When meaningless boasting persists, however, and Daddy's Little Girl gets only the "special lady" message from her father, she inevitably pays for it with an exaggerated sense of her femininity and his masculinity. He elevates himself by idealizing his daughter; she, in turn, mythologizes him.

This man's daughter lives to be around men as she grows up, and men usually respond in kind. Because her father has courted her as a sort of surrogate mistress, admiring her hair, her clothes, her grace, she exudes sexuality. She thrives on flirtatious romance rather than the sometimes gritty reality of a day-to-day relationship, always seeking a glamorous Big Daddy to appeal to her vanity like her father did. When husband is "Daddy," too, and the romance of wine and roses gives way to the reality of unpaid bills, runny noses, and unshaved chins, the intensity of an idealized adult attraction is difficult to maintain.

"The honeymoon was over the minute we were married, and our romantic fantasies fueled our anger," says Alice, twenty-seven, divorced from her husband, Mark, an actor in New York City. "Mark was glamorous in the way I always imagined my father to be. He literally swept me off my feet. He was a great dancer, the life of the party, terrific with impersonations, and he used all of that to court me, to win my affections, to make me feel special."

After they married, Mark looked for others to entertain, and when it was time to wrap up his public image he was too drunk even to know that Alice was his wife. "I might as well have been his daughter, for all he knew or cared," she says ruefully. "I began to sympathize with Mom."

This Daddy's Girl is doomed to be disappointed because the man she inevitably chooses craves the intensity of new relationships, too; he is the kind of man who has the least to offer her. Glamour fades quickly for both of them. Flirtations make it easy for Alice to fall in love, but not to stay in love. First stages of romance recall that elusive, little-girl memory of Daddy, and because she is addicted to the good feelings that accompany "falling in love," she is likely to feed her habit with one affair after another, never gaining genuine personal growth through intimacy. She is forever dependent on her idealization of the *adoring* man.

The Dependency Drama

Dependency as an issue is more important than sexuality in understanding the Alices of the world, according to Paul Chodoff, a Washington, D.C., psychiatrist who writes extensively about patients who suffer from what psychiatrists call a "hysterical personality." Such women are extremely emotional, demanding, clinging, almost totally dependent on men for a sense of self. Bereft of a man, they feel empty, unattractive, unwanted. As a result they make the man into something he is not. They turn him into a surrogate mother.

In a highly eroticized family, women like Alice seek the nurturance from their father that they are not getting from their mother, bartering sexuality for a sense of being cared for. While their adult relationships appear to be charged with sexuality, and often are, what they are actually seeking is emotional rather than erotic nourishment. As her father becomes the mother figure, she subconsciously shrieks, "Look how attractive I am!" She is not looking for a penis, says Dr. Chodoff, so much as for a breast.

Dr. Chodoff describes a woman patient in her late thirties who was married to a man fifteen years older than she. Marriage soured as a result of her emotion mongering and temper tantrums. She had entered marriage feeling the pleasure of submissiveness, enjoying the fact that her husband, like her father, treated her as a "pussycat." But in time her husband fell short of the "perfect" image of Daddy.

Her parents had divorced when she was five, and her father became the white knight of her childhood years, the focus of her longings and summer fantasies when she had him all to herself during vacations. During these visits she often awakened to find her father standing beside her bed, his hand under her nightie, rubbing her back.

In therapy, she continued to play the helpless, obedient little girl that she had learned too well in the company of her father: ". . . The pussycat, good little girl, or the wilful bad girl, seemed to be the only two ways in her [armament] for dealing with life's problems and relationships." She wanted guidance from a therapist in the same way she sought care from her father, by attempting to please and beguile. "If I allowed her to manipulate me," says Dr. Chodoff, "we would simply be continuing the charade whereby she becomes a 'nigger,' a female acting out compliance to the master male." In a therapeutic confrontation, he was able to change her from relating to him as an unapproachable father-professor to relating to him as the clinician whom she had come to consult. (Therapists characteristically discuss the difficulty of dealing with this type of patient, because such women flatter the therapist in the same way they flatter men in their personal lives.)[4]

Masters and Johnson describe such women as victims of "father-daughter syndrome," or pseudo-incest. The father typically singles out one daughter, if there is more than one, and isolates her for himself, much as a cowboy cuts a chosen heifer from the herd. She becomes the Daddy's girl: spoiled, pampered, immature. Such girls are severely handicapped in developing relationships with boys and, later, with men. They are forever seeking someone to play the role of Daddy. They grow up "sexually dysfunctional," say Masters and Johnson, and are as psychologically crippled as girls who have actually been sexually seduced by their fathers.[5]

Working It Out

A father's seductive admiration haunts a woman far into maturity and can affect her work as well as her love life. Anaïs Nin describes in her diaries how her father, a Spanish composer-pianist who took his family with him on his concert tours of Europe, photographed her as she sat nude in her bath. Their most intimate times together were the photographic sittings.

When she was older, she once stopped in the middle of one of her own dance concerts because she thought she saw her father in the audience. She turned out to have been mistaken, and when she told her father about it later he shook his head, disapproving. "If I had been there, I would have disapproved absolutely. I do not approve of a lady being a dancer. Dancing is for prostitutes and professionals. I would not have allowed you [to go] on stage."

An old-fashioned reaction for a man who had so openly admired his daughter's naked body, perhaps, but one the daughter might have expected. She had wished him to be there, her psychoanalyst told her years after she quit the concert stage, and when she saw that he was not in the audience she tried to *will* him to be.

"You must have wanted to dance for him to charm him, to seduce him unconsciously," said the doctor, "and when you became aware that the dancing was an act of seduction you felt guilty and it was guilt which made you give up dancing. Dancing became synonymous with seducing the father. You must have felt guilt for his admiration of you as a child. His admiration may have awakened your feminine desire to please your father, to hold him away from his mistresses." [6]

The psychoanalyst's interpretation, fashioned from early Freudian theory, draws attention to Miss Nin's ambivalence about a dancing career. Once she realized her father was not watching, performing with her body gave no kick. She went on to be a successful writer because she had greater gifts for writing than for dancing, and writing freed her from obsessively seeking a limited admiration from her father. Dancing carried the displaced hurts of a childhood flaw — the wounds of a very constricted father-daughter relationship. Craving his attentions kept her from becoming critical of the nature of those attentions. Such patterns are often difficult to disengage. A wise father does not create them.

Performing for Papa

When a child develops a skill — dancing, singing, playing the piano — only to please a parent, the self-esteem produced by that skill can be precarious. Anaïs Nin unconsciously craved her father's admiration, but not until she won the praise of others did she overcome a neurotic dependence on her father.

Sorting out what is good for Daddy and what is good for herself can confuse a little girl, and maintaining the myth of her daddy as her all-powerful prince may depend on how well the daughter performs in her part of the fantasy. This can be a heavy burden. One performing daughter, now a professor of English at a large Midwestern college, explained how she wanted to be a dancer until her adolescence. Because her father had put all of his savings into her dance lessons, there was no greater thrill than to bask in his appreciation of each pirouette and glissade. Her mother was there only as a passive spectator.

Beth was barely old enough to realize that she was the embodiment of her father's dream, born in the ashes of his own ambition, when the Great Depression and the arrival of his children snuffed out his vaudeville career. He determined that his daughter the ballerina would succeed where the old song-and-dance man had not. She shared the dream until she was sixteen, when she began to have the same nightmare over and over again: "I was the prima ballerina in front of a huge *corps de ballet*," she says. "The chorus was all in colored costumes, and I always wore white, the shining star. Then I went backstage, where I turned into Raggedy Ann with my every movement determined by whoever carried me around."

The dream helped Beth to understand that her desire to be a dancer was really only a wish to please her father. She turned on the wish with a vengeance. She quit dancing when she was a senior in high school and started eating, determined to get rid of her slender ballerina body. (In therapy, she learned that eating could satisfy an emotional appetite, too.)

With no genuine desire to perform, she had danced only to win her father's obsessive attention; he was the only audience that mattered in the little girl's mind. An introverted child whose considerable intellectual capabilities had been overlooked, she began to have the Raggedy Ann dream when she realized that ballet "star quality" would forever elude her. She needed other interests, beyond those of her father. Without them she would be nothing but a floppy doll whom nobody could love. The dancing that had pulled Beth close to her father gave her a fragile self-esteem; unless she could become a "star" she would lose her father's love.

Her true sense of self was in what D. W. Winnicott describes as a "state of noncommunication," and had to be protected to survive. So long as she felt dependent on Daddy's admiration it could not emerge. Only when high-school teachers recognized her abilities in English, literature, and languages could she challenge an inner censor that had kept her other talents hidden.

When a child is old enough to go off to school, options expand and teachers who have time to give personalized attention can often break through to a child who is *limited* to pleasing parents. Just as a first grader who is "mother's baby" may want to stay home with mother rather than take advantage of anything that school has to offer, Daddy's Little Girl may close off her larger potential if her father consistently encourages a more limited one.

Had Beth grown up to be a dancer, she might well have suffered a "narcissistic" disturbance, prevalent among show-business people who crave the limelight and who often confuse admiration with love. Rock musicians, movie starlets, TV anchorfolk, famous novelists, and others in the public eye often exhibit grandiosity and exaggerated delusions of greatness. Such people are occupied body and soul with winning admiration and approval, but they don't always feel successful offstage. They may be exceedingly vulnerable between performances because they are never sure they are loved for themselves. If they fail in an acting role or in a love affair, the depression that falls over them is often more acute than for other people.

Generally the mother has been blamed for creating the love-contingency game that creates a narcissistic personality, but the father contributes, too. A daughter who earns her father's attention only when she is a "star" may compulsively seek admiration from others, but usually as a substitute gratification for the love, respect, and understanding she never got — needs that are locked in her unconscious. She will envy those who experience ordinary emotions without always having to "show off."

Playing to an appreciative paternal audience, report card after report card, award after award, is also a common female experience and one that can invest a young woman with feelings of extraordinary power and fulfillment. Like all power, it can be a dangerous business unless the parent, and particularly the male parent, is careful to make it clear that his love and admiration do not rest upon her awards and accomplishments. Otherwise her positive feelings can dissolve in the ordinariness of everyday work when a daughter becomes a mature woman, to be replaced by trepidation and emptiness.

Such a woman is destined to remain emotionally underdeveloped. Alison, who has had years of psychotherapy and who is familiar with all the trendy diagnoses, is quick to tell a listener that she is "emotionally deprived." She is twenty-four, a college dropout, and works part-time in a secondhand clothing store in San Francisco. From elementary school onward through high school and two years of college, she made straight A's, every one for her father. This, she thought, was the only way she could get him to love her. Her father was usually so tired he couldn't pay any attention to anybody and certainly not to a talkative, demanding little girl, but he did understand A's, and appreciation of them didn't require much energy.

"I would have been better off spending my energy trying to please myself, because I learned only what I had to learn to get A's. To this day I don't read much. If my father had asked me only once what it was that I wanted to do, what I thought, what would please *me!* He could have so easily made my heart sing."

Alison's problems as a woman, rooted in her behavior as a child, are more serious than a stunted attention span. She married a man who abuses her; she often leaves him after a beating, only to return when he apologizes. She does not link her obsession for straight A's to her choice of husband, but she nevertheless detects a pattern that extensive therapy has not changed. She keeps going back to her husband in the way she kept going back to Daddy with those A's, thinking every time that this time she can *make* him love her. Her father never raised a hand to her, but he didn't show her love, either, and she never stopped trying to make him do it.

Those who, like Alison, successfully repressed their intense innermost feelings often try to regain, at least for a short time, that lost intensity of experience with drugs or alcohol. In Alison's case, she recovers that lost intensity at the hands of a brutal husband.

The Three P's: Perfectionism, Procrastination, Pretention

Girls who earn report-card A's just to bask in paternal admiration, who are miserable when they get anything less, often risk becoming perfectionists who write their own script for self-defeat. A spiral begins, which may end with a daughter punishing herself for any kind of performance failure.

The twin of perfectionism is procrastination. The father who always places pressure on his little girl may cause her to put things off, giving her the perfect excuse: "If only I had had more time, it would have been perfect." Procrastinators set unreasonably high standards for themselves, like those first set by a parent. When anything less than perfect displeases Daddy, any attempt to accomplish something is treacherous, and best put off.

Procrastinators, like perfectionists, must invest every challenge with significance beyond the task at hand. This is how they remember the challenges in childhood. If a daughter remembers her father as having been there only to dispense rewards, the adult woman may unconsciously perceive success in work as a means to get rewards, especially from men. Such strategy often backfires. She may try too hard to impress, and parody competence. An intellectually arrogant woman may unconsciously be seeking a man's attention in the only way she could be sure her father would respond to her, by parading her intellectual power. Such pretention can also be compensation for the intellectual encouragement her father *failed* to give her.

According to Carl Jung, the Swiss psychoanalyst, when a daughter and her father relate to each other only on a powerful emotional level, the only way she can reduce the voltage in this electrical connection is by developing her intellectual capacity. Jung tells of one such woman, an aggressive achiever, who attempted to do this through the study of philosophy.

> At the beginning of treatment the patient was quite unconscious of the fact that her relation[ship] to her father was a fixation, and that she was therefore seeking a man like her father, whom she could then meet with her intellect. This in itself would not have been a mistake if her intellect had not had that peculiarly protesting character such as is unfortunately often encountered in intellectual women. Such an intellect is always trying to point out mistakes in others; it is preeminently critical, with a disagreeably personal undertone, yet it always wants to be considered objective. This invariably makes a man bad-tempered, particularly if, as so often happens, the criticism touches on some weak spot which, in the interests of fruitful discussion, were better avoided. But far from wishing the discussion to be fruitful, it is the unfortunate peculiarity of this feminine intellect to seek out a man's weak spots, fasten on them, and exasperate him. This is not usually a conscious aim, but rather has the unconscious purpose of forcing a man into a superior position and thus making him an object of admiration.[7]

For many women who talked to me, there was no need to idealize Daddy unconsciously because he consciously did it for them.

Typical is the father holding forth, creating and hiding behind a myth of his own making. It's not long, however, before a young girl sees through *his* pretenses. Phyllis Naylor, the essayist, recalls the sharp pain of her father's bravado, boastful and hollow, but enough to keep her father always a stranger to her: "He was a top salesman whose territory covered parts of Indiana and Illinois. However vulnerable he may have been inside (and he suffered from ulcers for most of his life), he put on an outward show of self-confidence and strength. It was usually Dad who monopolized the dinner conversation — how he managed to get to see a difficult client and how, because of his ingenuity and persuasiveness, he got a larger order than expected."

How Miss Naylor wished he had focused his attention on her instead! How she yearned to get more in answer to her questions to him than mere platitudes. Only later in life could she forgive his myth-making: "I have learned over the years that one cannot give to others what one does not have oneself — whether self-esteem or affection. Acceptance of the child my father once was and the man he became comes easier as I get older." [8]

It may be easier to give up the myth of Daddy when he has created it, as Miss Naylor acknowledges, but not without pain. Much more debilitating, however, is the myth the child creates, because her sense of self is dependent on it. No parent can read a child's mind, and even those with the best of intentions cannot see through the intricate fantasies a young child may weave. But if a father respects his daughter's feelings, if he loves her for who she is and not for what he needs, her opportunity to develop into an independent person becomes much greater.

Free to Be Me

Feminine self-esteem, like male self-esteem, evolves from an authenticity of feelings based on qualities, aptitudes, and competencies that flow from what D. W. Winnicott calls "the true self." A sensitive father can elicit and encourage a daughter's "true self" if he is supportive of her capabilities, and listens to what is unique in her without imposing stereotypes.

"My father always wanted me to be me and I am," says Valerie, fifty-three, a Honolulu psychologist whose father was a Polish immigrant. "He encouraged me to take mechanical drawing and aeronautics in high school and I made straight A's. Our family did everything together, making soap, rock candy, and candlesticks, and we talked endlessly about what we learned."

Feminism was not an issue, and her father caught a lot of flak from his friends, because he wanted his girls to go to college. His friends believed that educating girls was a waste of money because they would marry and have babies. But he always argued with them: "Look, even if they do get married they'll have something to fall back on."

Valerie's father was a papercutter who understood the value of an education. On his eighteenth birthday someone in the old country had given him a one-way ticket to America, and when he got here he taught himself to speak and read English. He taught himself to do calculations in his head. "Many times I got more out of a discussion of a problem with Daddy than with my learned colleagues because he analyzed an issue so well. He passed his love and love of learning on to me."

Because Valerie's father spoke directly to *her* at different stages of her development, she was not trapped in making him more important than he was, and she could be who she truly wanted to be.

A vital personality develops with a reasonable amount of proper guidance. A child follows her own inner laws of development, laws that allow for a full development of capacities and abilities. A healthy person actively masters her environment, reflecting a unity of personality, perceiving the world and herself realistically.

A father who offers a variety of skills can help his daughter develop a strong sense of industriousness, the pleasure of producing things. This father inculcates the values of discipline and perseverence, making the connection between the self and work at an early age.[9]

Loving fathers use what they know to teach and encourage their daughters in school and out. Lou Ella, twenty-six, an actress in Broadway musicals, tells how her father helped her tap a special talent. He was a dancer who gave up the stage when he became a pharmacist. When she was just "a little thing," he coaxed her to sing for his friends at the end of the lunch hour. But unlike Beth's father, who pushed his little girl to achieve where he failed, Lou Ella's father carefully cultivated his daughter's natural abilities.

He didn't admire her only when she performed, but listened to her poetry, telling her what he liked and what she might improve. He rehearsed lines with her when she tried out for the school play, laughing with her over the male role in *Father Knows Best.* He taught her that to excel was not as important as continuing to learn, to question. "You bring everything you've got to what you do," he would say, "but you judge yourself by your own standards. You must be your best and toughest critic."

Lou Ella's father attended all her opening nights, often dropping by for the last act on other nights just to take her home. "I think I'd have gone onto the stage even if he hadn't been around to encourage me, but I don't think I'd be as good at it as I am. I know it wouldn't be as much fun."

Most women yearn for continual, simple, loving exchanges with their fathers such as those Valerie and Lou Ella had. Ideally, women integrate their fathers' strength and protection with their mothers' nurturance. Alas, life seldom offers such perfect balance. The parent a woman identifies with usually affects her perspective on the world.

Daddy's Girl/Mother's Daughter

Amy Gross, writing in *Mademoiselle* magazine, divides women into two basic categories: Daddy's girls and Mother's daughters. Where she fits into these categories is an index to a woman's opinions on feminist issues. In each category, the parent the child identifies with is seen as the heroic parent; the other parent is seen as insignificant.

A Daddy's girl is either Daddy's disciple, who relates through the intellect, submerging sexuality under other qualities, or she is

Daddy's decoration, who at an early age discovers the seductive power she holds over men. Unlike Mother's daughters, these women are not generally receptive to the rhetoric and aims of modern feminism. She wants equal pay for equal work, but she wants none of the man-is-the-enemy rhetoric. Men simply don't oppress her, she will say.

A mother's daughter, on the other hand, gets along better with women, is at home with sisterhood, and seeks confirmation from women: she was her mother's confidante and protector, particularly in mother-father disputes, and as a result she doesn't expect much from men.[10]

Because a negligent father often contributes to the poor sexual image a daughter has of herself, she is unlikely to make the distinctions necessary to distinguish between good, better, or bad among men, and seeks the more comfortable company of other women. Some researchers go so far as to argue that a woman who has had a good relationship with a man, whether father or lover or both, is not likely to become a militant feminist. Fraternizing with the enemy is forbidden in all armies, and every general knows why. Myths, both male and female, generate sexual, psychological harassment.

Until quite recently, our passages along the road to maturity have been described mostly in terms of our relationships with our mothers. Freud thought our lifelong, if diminishing, emotional dependence on our mothers to be a universal truth of human experience. Others believe the minimum essential to mastering the emotional tasks of living to be a mother who need not be perfect, but good enough.

To that bare minimum we must add a father who is good enough, to discover how our fathers, those shadowy figures we first meet standing at a certain distance from the hand rocking the cradle, cast more than a shadow over our lives. We must bring them out of their hiding places among those shadows. Yearning for that impossible idealization of our fathers, we as their daughters hide, too, and deprive ourselves of that part of him that we carry forever deep inside ourselves.

Prelude to Adolescence:
My Father and Me

Every family has secrets, skeletons, and ghosts that prowl the small dark hours. Mine had more than some. My father was a bookmaker. Almost everything he did was against the law.

I once remarked to Joe Hirshhorn, whose collection of sculpture and paintings became the magnificent national museum that bears his name in the nation's capital, that he and my father sprang from similar origins: both were Jewish immigrants from eastern Europe who arrived in America penniless, worked hard, kept an eye cocked for the risk with the right odds, and prospered.

"What does your father do?"

"He's a bookmaker. Or, rather, he was."

"Ah, he's in publishing."

"No, not exactly. He doesn't make that kind of book."

"Ah," said Mr. Hirshhorn, grinning appreciatively. "*That* kind of book."

Having toughed it out the hard way himself, he knew the

meaning of my father's favorite words to live by: "Tough times make a monkey eat red pepper."

To a little girl who didn't meet her father until he was a big man about town, Daddy's life was the stuff of melodrama and mythology: lots of good stories, and most of them easier to listen to than to live through. Making book was far more dangerous than writing one. With better reasons than most, my father needed to hide. It was a matter of survival.

I was obsessed with a need to bring him out of hiding. I had to learn who the man was who was half of me. This book grew out of mutual wishes: it became a way we could both find out about each other in ways we could never fathom when we were younger.

One night I sat down between my mother and father in a Washington restaurant, watching a cold winter's rain beat an insistent tattoo against the fogged windowpanes. My father put down his coffee cup and turned to my mother. "How can Suzanne write a book about our relationship when it was you who were always with her? I was always at work when she was growing up. How could I have seen very much of her?"

This was just my point, of course — or at least the larger part of the point. Simply because he was not there most of the time, the occasions on which he was became special. My father's work gave him a distinctive measure of mystery and excitement, no doubt, but it is every father's absence that makes him mysterious in the imaginations of little girls, and when he returns he often makes the moment magic, making it stand out in a girl's memory, tickling and pleasing like a glass of champagne.

Not until adolescence, however, could I get things down to scale. It was at that stage I became fully conscious of my father as a man as well as a father, as a person with many selves, some glamorous, some not so. It was in adolescence that I learned the true nature of my father's business; it was in my adolescence also that he left all that behind. We both were on the threshold of a new life, or so it now seems. Crises in developmental stages were, as the psychologists say, about to intersect.

"In a healthy development of the individual, at whatever stage,

what is needed is a steady progression . . . a well-graduated series
of defiant iconoclastic actions," says D. W. Winnicott, the British
psychoanalyst.[1] Adolescence most dramatically brings out iconoclastic crises for a father and daughter. It is that time in her life
when a daughter begins to ask: "Who is this person in my body,
and who will I become?" Her father asks: "Who have I already
become, and is there still time to become the person I really want
to be?"

The daughter rebels against the conformity of childhood, the
father fights back the dread of how his life will be measured. Both
are acutely aware of the accelerating tempo of time.

Both also bring a wealth of experience with them into this new
era, as her adolescence offers them the first opportunity to appreciate the other's interpretation of their individual experiences. I
felt the first stirrings of an interest in my father's stories about his
boyhood. At last we had something in common, the memory of a
childhood. As a teenager I could compare my experiences as a
small child with his, recognizing how different our worlds had
been. I entered adolescence as America began that incredible roll
of post–World War II prosperity. My father had entered his adolescence in the poverty that was the lot of new immigrants, as his
new land entered the uncertainty of the post–World War I years.

The Daddy Diet

Daddy grew up on a diet of red pepper, a taste learned
early in his life, and I grew up on orange juice, fresh milk, and occasionally prime rib. He was the fifth of seven children, all but the
last of whom were born in Pinsk, that small doomed city on the
Russian-Polish border whose population, mostly of Jews, has been
ravaged over the centuries by czars, Nazis, pogroms, hunger, political repressions of various kinds, and hard times. The family arrived in America in 1911, as poor as synagogue mice, when my
father was four. He spoke two languages. Neither of them was
English.

My grandfather was a carpenter, who amused himself by telling us over and over again how he had helped build the railway station in Pinsk. He earned a hardscrabble living with his hands in America, too, first in a lumberyard and than as a carpenter. "He probably wasn't the smartest man who ever left Russia," my father once told me, "but you should be forever grateful that he was smart enough not to miss the boat to America."

Determined to make a better life, Daddy left school in the sixth grade for his advanced degree in the university of hard knocks. Because his father couldn't afford anything else, Daddy got a pair of his sister's shoes to wear to school.

"How could I wear girls' shoes and play ball?" he asks, remembering the pain. He quit school and his father slapped him. Daddy left home at once, living in dingy poolrooms by day, running liquor and sleeping in boiler rooms by night, surviving with a little help from his friends.

"Bellyaches from missing meals hurt most," he recalls. "But occasionally a buddy on a bread truck would let me know which one of the bins would be left unlocked when he took an armful of loaves into a grocery store, or a pal on a milk wagon would wink and tell me to watch his horse while he took a hike into the next block."

Quitting school meant more time for games on the Mall, the green connecting the Capitol and the Washington Monument, and Daddy was the player everybody wanted. He was recruited as catcher for St. Dominic's in the Parochial League, and the boys winked when his name was entered on the roster as Bregmanio instead of Bregman. St. Dominic's won the city championship.

Opposing coaches started making pointed inquiries about the catcher who looked more Jewish than Italian. When the priest learned the truth he returned the trophy, and most of the team, angered, didn't speak to Daddy again. Nevertheless, he became such a popular player that his friends gave him the ultimate accolade, a nickname, Bo, after Bo McMillan, the hero of poor boys on sandlots everywhere after he quarterbacked the Prayin' Colonels of tiny Centre College of Kentucky to an upset of mighty Harvard — at that time, unlikely as it seems today, the Notre Dame of college football.

Bo's first love was baseball, and as the feisty, kibitzing catcher of the Aztecs, a popular sandlot team, he was featured in the newspapers as the city's standout amateur player. He was fourteen, and in his world this was a credential more valuable than a master's in business administration. One rainy morning soon after, Bo took his lunch money to the old Washington army barracks, long since torn down to make room for shopping centers and apartment blocks, and established his own semipermanent floating craps game. It became a fixture on soldiers' pay day.

Occasionally Bo's game floated into a poolroom, where his grin, his hustle, his eagerness to assist a man in laying down a wager attracted the attention of the bootleggers, then striving to assuage the pain of Prohibition. They ran rum and bonded spirits in long, fast cars, and there was a high turnover of cars and drivers. Bo got to know them, helping them load and occasionally delivering a bottle or two.

Bo also tried it "straight," squeezing oranges from a box on the corner, but a policeman kicked him hard in the shins and told him to move along. He went back to the poolroom and got a job running slips for a bookie — staying on the move with the coded record of the bookie's bet, damning evidence to keep out of the hands of the police. Business was good and Bo soon had a bookmaking shop of his own in a "dry-cleaning establishment" in downtown Washington. A moth-eaten green gabardine suit in the window made everything *look* kosher.

"Occasionally a rubbernecking Rotarian from Memphis walked in with a rumpled suit, wanting to get it pressed," Bo recalls. "Naturally this always happened just as we were getting the last bets down for the sixth race at Aqueduct, and when that happened I had to stop what I was doing and send somebody out with the man's suit to a legitimate cleaner's around the corner."

Occasionally a dissatisfied cop called at the shop with the green suit in the window. Fortunately a sympathetic dentist worked in chambers just above the "dry-cleaning" shop, and Bo could run up the back stairs, leap into an empty chair, quickly tie a white apron around his neck, lean back, open wide, and wait innocently while the dentist pretended to drill a cavity. (Was it only coincidence that I would one day marry a dentist?)

Bo was a poor boy who often had a little money in his pocket, and when he had it he knew how to spend it. When he didn't have it he knew how to get it. "He was the kind of fellow," an old friend of Bo's once told me, "who would and sometimes did borrow fifty bucks from a man and then take him to dinner with all of it."

So how could a beautiful seventeen-year-old girl named Sadie find the twenty-one-year-old Bo anything but irresistible, just as I would find him some years later? Sadie lived with her parents, and they liked Bo well enough, but he calculated the chances of parental approval with a professional gambler's dispassionate eye and eloped with her to Baltimore. He made up with his own father and the bridal couple moved into a front room, and Bo found the money to buy a mahogany bedstead for his bride's wedding chamber. Bo's mother was pleased and no doubt relieved that her son was finally settling down, and with a *shana madela*, a pretty *Jewish* girl, too.

Sadie learned about the family business quickly, though Bo never let her become part of it. "My trade was among the working stiffs who would have liked a day at the races but knew they never could get one," Bo recalls. "So they saved their pennies and nickels until they had a dollar and then they came to see me. I had a blackboard against one wall with the day's entries and the odds. Or they could shoot a little pool or craps, as they liked. We had three or four slot machines against another wall. Las Vegas it was not, but it was a living."

My mother found this life less glamorous than I would — her eyes were not protected from the gritty side of the business, as mine would be. One day just before I was born she took a taxi to his "office" at the rear of something called the Temple Novelty Co., where Bo kept tacky souvenirs: pencil sharpeners in the shape of the Washington Monument, paperweights shaped like the Capitol dome, and dinner plates decorated with the faces of Washington's fun couple of that year, Franklin and Eleanor.

Just as the taxi turned the corner into New York Avenue in downtown Washington, Sadie saw a paddy wagon pull up to the door of the Temple Novelty Co.

"Never mind, driver," she said. "I just remembered that I forgot something. Take me home."

She waited there for the telephone call. The telephone didn't ring. Bo himself walked into the house a few minutes later. He never explained and she knew not to ask.

Daddy never went to jail, but there were lots of raids. Only once was it close. An undercover cop had been sent in by a new police chief to lay down a dollar on the nose of a horse in the third race at Pimlico, and as soon as Bo filled out the code slip the cop pulled out the cuffs. With his one telephone call Bo employed a lawyer, John Sirica, who would become the judge — "Maximum John" — who presided over the Watergate trials decades hence.

"My advice, Bo, is that you should plead guilty," said Mr. Sirica.

"No, I'd never do that."

"If you don't you'll regret it. With a guilty plea the court will be more likely to go easy with you."

"If I do I'll regret it more because with a guilty plea I'm certain to get a little time."

Mr. Sirica shrugged, and Bo hired another attorney. He pleaded not guilty, and the new lawyer won the trial. Years later, long after he left the world of bookies, bootleggers, and high rollers, Bo ran into Judge Sirica on the boardwalk at Rehoboth Beach, a Delaware resort much favored by Washingtonians. "You did all right by not taking my advice, Bo," the judge said. "But the best advice I ever gave you was to get out of the 'life' you were leading which I understand you have done."

Though my father never went to jail, several of his associates did. During the years we were growing up, my brother, Stanley, and I were occasionally told that Uncle Sidney wouldn't be around for Thanksgiving dinner, or that Shorty and Slim were on "vacation." Neither Bo nor Sadie gave us details, but even as children we figured out that Shorty, Slim, and Uncle Sidney were not "vacationing" on Miami Beach, where we vacationed every winter.

Bo got his break when one of the high rollers in his business went to prison and sent back word that Bo was to get a piece of the man's action. To this day my father feels a debt to the man, who died years ago. This was the beginning of Bo's big business.

"What we had," he recalled to me, "was a small-change operation on a high-volume basis. If it wasn't exactly Las Vegas it was nevertheless fast. You might say it was 'the McDonald's of Vegas' for people who 'deserve a break today' but couldn't afford to go to Nevada to get it."

Years later I stood with Bo at the opening of one of the big new casinos in Atlantic City, on the Jersey shore. He shook his head, hardly believing the sight of the rows upon rows of flashing games at Bally's Park Place Casino. "I had only one craps table, one blackjack game, and four slot machines. Nothing like this." He chuckled. "And a lot of men with less than I had got ten years as a guest of Uncle Sam for their trouble." He waved his hand to encompass the cavernous room. "Now look at all this, and it's legal besides. I was just fifty years ahead of my time."

If my mother found my father's life somewhat less glamorous than I did, Daddy didn't find it glamorous at all. "I wish I could have been in another kind of business," he says now. "I did the only thing I could do that would earn a decent living. I never really had the temperament of a gambler — I never could shuffle cards all that well, to begin with. But those were tough times and I had a lot of friends who were good to me. There are only four ways to deal with money, Suzanne: get it honest, if you can, and once you get it, spend it. When you get lots of it, give some of it to charities and get respect. When you've got enough of it to hold on to some of it, get religion and ask God to show you how to keep it.

"But don't ever forget that where you stand depends on where you're sitting."

A Secret Pact

For as long as I could remember, I was sitting pretty. I didn't know exactly what my father did when he went off into his glamorous world, but I did know that whatever it was, it was different from the world of the father of my friend Barbara. Barbara's father, like the fathers of nearly everyone else in my class at John Greenleaf Whittier Elementary School, worked for the United States Government. They were the GS-4's and GS-5's, clerks one cut above the "girls" in the typing pool. They wore green plastic eyeshades to cut down the glare on their paperwork. My girl friends never saw their fathers until dinner time.

My father was at home, asleep, when I left for school and he was often there when I got home in the middle of the afternoon. If a new police chief or district attorney had recently come to power, he might be home during the day for months at a time, waiting for the outbreak of righteousness at City Hall to subside. Until the right financial arrangements were concluded, new police chiefs and district attorneys always turned to rounding up the bookies as the quickest way to establish reputations for civic virtue. "You could make book on it," Bo said.

To the straight world, as to me, my father was a sports promoter. I traded on that, particularly with boys. In late May of 1941, Daddy promoted a world-heavyweight-championship fight at Griffith Stadium in Washington. I got to meet Joe Louis and the challenger, Buddy Baer, and even if it was not quite clear to me exactly who they were, or why they were important, it was clear that the parents of my friends were impressed, and so my friends were, too. For the first time I felt the power of conferring glamour, even if it was reflected glamour.

My father was pleased enough to introduce me to his fighters, to let me see the limelight up close, tacky though the things that limelight exposed were. He didn't want me to see much of what lay just outside the circle of that light, the carefully obscured illegal details of his life; he didn't want me hurt, scared, or embarrassed by what he did to make a good life for us. The sporting life was flashy, loud, bright, and it could be fun, but it could be dangerous, too, and the shadow it threw across our house on Quackenbos Street N.W. was larger than life.

Slowly, almost imperceptibly, as I grew older, Bo and I came to share an unspoken pact to guard and atone for this family secret.

Keeping a family secret, I would learn, was not uncommon between fathers and daughters. And secrets, as I would also learn,
create a life and a power of their own.

My role was to burnish the family name with grades, goals, and
goodness. Because my father worked the shady side of the street,
I determined to stake out the most prominent place on the sunny
side of it. It was Freud, of course, who first remarked that the
child assumes the superego, the conscience, of a parent, often
with far greater ferocity than the parent intended. (Before Freud
there was Proverbs 22:6 — "Train up a child in the way he
should go: and when he is old, he will not depart from it."). I became Freud's Exhibit A.

My father, I learned since, suffered the tortures of the damned,
obsessed with his view of himself as a man perceived by others as
shameful and dishonest. He did not realize then that he was universally seen by his peers within and without "the life" as a man
of scrupulous honesty and decency. "Bo Bregman," a man with a
well-known name in Washington told me, "was recognized as one
of the few men in Washington that *everybody* trusted." I didn't
know that then, and somewhere in the deep recesses of a child's
consciousness I set out to make my parents proud of me by making outsiders proud of our family.

I became the good little girl who always found a seat on the
front row of every class, whose hand was always the first up to answer every question. Though my parents fought with my brother
over his poor grades, both signaled an unconscious approval of his
bad marks, and their underlying message, received loud and clear,
was that books and grades were the stuff to occupy girls. Real men
drank whiskey, drove fast convertibles, gambled, and talked
about the relative merits of the single wing and the split-T, sacrifice bunts, and the favorite in the Kentucky Derby.

Brother Stanley did all of that. He excelled where it counted in
a man's world. He learned who the heavyweight, middleweight,
and featherweight champions were (and who they had been since
1882, the year reliable record-keeping began); he could tell you
without hesitating that Dolph Camilli of the Brooklyn Dodgers

was the National League's Most Valuable Player in 1941; that the Dean brothers won more than half of the victories for the St. Louis Cardinals in their 1934 pennant year (and that Dizzy won 31, Paul 19); that Sir Barton was thoroughbred racing's first Triple Crown winner in 1919, and that the last bare-knuckle heavyweight championship fight was held in Richburg, Mississippi, in 1889 when John L. Sullivan whipped Jake Kilrain in seventy-five rounds. I always secretly believed that Stanley made up this last incredible statistic until I saw a commemorative plaque on U.S. 90, the Gulf Coast highway, years later. Stanley was right on the marker.

Stanley never did well in math, but he could quickly figure the odds on the Calvin Coolidge–Woodrow Wilson high-school football game and go for a big score on his own. If he lost, he knew that his younger sister saved some of her allowance each week and was an easy mark for a soft touch. When he became a man, Stanley turned his attention to politics, and could soon recite the names of the 535 members of Congress, give you a brief profile of the districts they were elected from, whom each had defeated, and why, and recall the approximate size of the winning vote. He became a near-legendary advance man in the Hubert Humphrey presidential campaign in 1968.

The message I received was loud and clear, too. I was supposed to be the consummate good little girl — not because it was intrinsically a good thing to be, but because this was the greatest gift I could offer to my father. I became the consummate little prig.

My mother fell to the task of making me good with good heart. She was the mother every teacher could count on to be class mother, den mother, or dance mother. She always accompanied us to the zoo, the library, the museum, or the botanical garden. She baked heart-shaped cookies for Valentine's Day parties, bunny-shaped cookies at Easter, pumpkin-shaped cookies for Halloween. My friends were occasionally disappointed because their mothers couldn't come to sit through class plays, but I knew Mom would always be there on the front row, applauding me even as the Virgin Mary (a role that my parents considered me, theological considerations aside, supremely qualified to play). Mom was the mother other mothers called to see whether they should let their daughters go to a hayride across the Potomac into Virginia, or to a skating rink in a shabby Maryland suburb. Naturally, since the other girls couldn't go if I couldn't go, I rightly came to be held personally responsible for being too *good*.

Memories of Camp Kenwood, deep in the forests of western Connecticut, still bring a blush of anger and humiliation. I went to Camp Kenwood every summer, returning each autumn to fib about how much fun it was and how much I looked forward to going back again. Daddy thought camp was good for me, surrounded as I was there by nothing but fresh air, clear water, rabbits, raccoons, an occasional fox, and dozens of nice little girls from nice families who lived at nice addresses in the nice suburbs of a dozen of the nicest cities in the East.

I was so good that camp was miserable, especially on Saturday nights. Satuday night was honor-roll campfire night, when the chief counselor read out the names of the week's most honored campers. Campers were honored not for swimming the most laps across Lake Pukalot, or for stealing the most bases during the week's softball games, or for mastering the hop-skip-and-jump, or even for making the most beautiful plastic lanyard to send home to Mom. Campers were honored for being *good* for an entire week.

After three consecutive weeks on the Good List, a camper was admitted to the Valhalla of righteousness, a special honor society called Aquila. Aquila was no doubt a long-dead Indian virgin who always braked for small animals. The honorees received a pin shaped like a feather, in blue and white, the colors of undefiled virtue and untempted piety, and honored campers were obliged to wear this pin on their T-shirts, announcing to all that "here walks . . . a *good* person." I always dreaded the third campfire because I knew I would once more become a surrogate for that insufferable little virgin.

I tried as hard as I could to be wicked. Once, when our cabin plotted to dump a bucket of water on a counselor, I volunteered (being the smallest camper) to climb into a crevice above the door to play bombardier. My aim was perfect, and the counselor, who unbeknownst to her cadre of obnoxious little girls was suffering severe personal problems of her own, was so distraught over the incident that she left camp a few days later. Naturally I was inconsolable, and spent the rest of the summer writing long letters of mortification, begging forgiveness and taking solemn vows never to be anything ever again but a little girl to make her daddy proud.

My father made sacrifices for me, too, of course. When I was thirteen, the rows of telephones, the stacks of yellow legal pads with names and numbers inscribed in careful tiny script, disappeared from our house as if by magic. Daddy was no longer going to be a sports promoter. He was going to be a "home" builder.

Not until years later was I told why. "You were becoming a woman," he told me, "and I didn't think it was fitting for my little girl's father to be in 'the life' or even close to it, so I left all that behind. I wasn't worried about Stanley — learning to take care of himself is what becoming a man is all about. But I owed you something special. So one day I left all that behind and I've never looked back."

And so my father and I stepped out into the mysterious and the unknown, a major change coming over our relationship. He started building houses, and I became a teenager.

Breaking Away

The drive from my house to Missie Goldman's house was not a long one, but Daddy insisted that we take it twice: once, the night before I was supposed to arrive, just to make sure we had the directions down right, and then again on the following night for the Sigma Pi Sigma rush.

"You don't want to be worried about being late, and you won't have to worry if you know exactly where you're going," he said. "We'll make a trial run."

We talked about the reasons why I wanted to join a sorority.

The girls seemed nice enough, and the teenage social life I aspired to success in revolved around sororties and fraternities. But I was frightened and anguished over the blackball system. If only one girl didn't like me she could cast a negative vote, a "blackball," and I was out. I didn't *think* I had any enemies among the Sigma Pi Sigma girls, but one could never be sure. My "talent" number would be a piano solo, a Chopin prelude, hardly something to put life into a party. Daddy listened to my fears and anxiety, but he didn't say much.

On the following night my father got us to Missie's ten minutes early. We sat in the car while he gave me a pep talk, one of our many heart-to-hearts. I was terrified that one of the girls would see me listening to a parental lecture.

"I know you are afraid that you might not get accepted," he said. "But it's important to understand that what those girls think of you is not really very important. How you see yourself is what counts. You've got to believe in yourself. If you get accepted, that's fine, but if you don't it says absolutely nothing about you, only that those girls are unable to know what's good when they see it."

It was a short speech. It moves me today on recalling it, as it moved me then, because it established our new relationship and identified the obstacles I would face as I moved out of the family and into the larger world of my peers. My father could no longer protect me as he had when I was a child. I would have to rely on the power of his values rather than the power of his physical person. He could drive me to the sorority rush, he could even get me there ten minutes early, but he couldn't determine how the other girls would judge me.

My mother had often talked to me in a similar vein, but when the message came from my father it had the force and validity of authority undiluted by sentiment. My mother's role was to protect and nurture her children's psyches; my father, who had seen the world and wrestled with it, recognized the evil that man — even another man's daughter — could do. In his way, he was trying to toughen his sheltered daughter.

When I was very young, Daddy occasionally took us to dinner in a crowded, popular restaurant without a reservation. He liked the challenge of getting a good table and he knew he could handle it. "I've got a bet for you," he would tell the captain, waving a five-dollar bill. "I'll bet you this that you can't get us the next good table." The waiter invariably grinned; in those days a five-dollar bill was not small change. Daddy always lost his bet, and we always got a good table, usually at a window between a senator and a Redskins quarterback. Nevertheless, he couldn't bet the Sigma Pi Sigma girls that they couldn't get me into their sorority. I was on my own this time and we both knew it.

At the time I was rushing a sorority, the "straight" world that my father had so idealized from where he was sitting on the other side of the tracks had begun to pall. Legitimate business did not always look so legitimate when looked at up close, and the ethics of bankers and builders, my father's new colleagues, were not always up to the standards of the bookies and hustlers he knew from the old days. Still, he worried about the residual influence his illegal life might work on me. In the immediate event, he need not have worried. The girls of Sigma Pi Sigma accepted me as a pledge and I was allowed to join their little circle of snobs.

The sorority was for me like the other side of the tracks for my father. It was my initiation into a community of young girls whose standards of judgment were not those I had been taught, where one girl's intolerance of the way another girl wore her hair, or cocked her head, could ruin her chances of becoming a doyenne of high-school society.

Both my father and I had to learn to maneuver in the world as we saw it and as it was, and not as we hoped it would be. The passage was a painful one for both of us, because we were also forced to look at each other through adult eyes at last to see our relative powerlessness in the larger scheme of things, finally shedding the illusions of Big Daddy and Daddy's Little Girl. I had begun to move out on my own, emotionally; Daddy had to reconsider what his impact might be on my life.

As infants learn to leave their parents behind for short periods of time, learning reassurance when reunited, so must adolescents learn to endure separation for ever-longer periods of time. In both stages the child grows through major physiological and psychological changes, but not until she is an adolescent must a daughter realize that the greater part of the journey is to be on her own.

Her father, like her mother, must learn how to let the daughter go. The parents must let her go first to a social life dominated mostly by other girls, to an arena of same-sex friendship, which is not so threatening to the fundamental ties to home. With the next step the daughter forges ever-more-intimate links with friends of the opposite sex, young men with their own needs, compulsions, yearnings, and obsessions. This is threatening, indeed.

The only fate worse than being an adolescent, as any mother or father knows, is being the parent of one. Pain is acute for both father and daughter. Each perceives this pain as springing from very different origins, but for both the hurt is felt in the very same place — deep within a heart that each aches to share with the other, if only they could learn how.

PART FOUR

Adolescents and Other Beasts

"She moved in circles, and those circles moved."

—Theodore Roethke

Passing through Puberty: An Emotional Investment with Big Change

When I joined the Augustus Paul Junior High School Tumbling Club in the seventh grade, my father flew into a rage. "You can tap-dance, toe-dance, even tap on your toes," he said, "but gymnastics are for boys."

Performing under a spotlight was fine, on a stage surrounded by proper teachers and proud parents, but the canvas of the trampoline was rough and abrasive, and gyms, even junior-high-school gyms, smacked too much of Stillman's, the locker room at Griffith Stadium, and coarse professional athletes, who *sweated*. Girls were permitted to *perspire*, if they insisted.

"I won't have you playing around in those places, jumping up and down like a jack-in-the-box," he said. "You're not Joe Palooka. You're a young lady now. You can dance." Dancing was for girls: it was feminine, cultivated, refined. Playing around like Joe Palooka was for my brother, Stanley, and his buddies.

By encouraging me to dance, gender theorists would say, my father was enforcing "reciprocal role learning," the dispensing of rewards and punishments from one of the opposite sex. Other ob-

servers would say he was simply responding to the natural order
of things. As I read it some thirty years later, my father was responding to a change in me that I was on the verge of discovering
for myself.

Separating the Girls and Boys

Puberty is that painful intersection of biology and culture, when the fundamental issues of masculinity and femininity
are settled for life. Fashions change. Today boys and girls must
have equal time on the playing field, where the Duke of Welling-
ton said all wars are won. But my own interest in active sports disappeared in adolescence, and I think more than culture accounted
for that. The last burst of my tomboy energies was spent on that
trampoline, and then pubescent hormones drove me in other directions; that was the last year I wanted to climb atop a human
pyramid on the playground, yell "Crash!" and fall flat on my face,
with no worries about a bosom to absorb the fall.

It was also the last year I envied my brother the camaraderie of
the playing field. When my father organized a baseball team to
play games on the sandlot every Sunday in spring and summer,
my brother got to be the first baseman, and I thought he was the
luckiest kid in the world. I got to watch the "Bregman Wildcats"
from behind home plate.

Times and tastes changed when I entered the eighth grade.
Daddy brought home T-shirts emblazoned BREGMAN'S KITTENS.
"There's one here for you and for every one of your friends, and if
you want to have a softball team I'll help you organize it."

But he knew that by then I was no more interested in learning
to hit curve balls than I was in tumbling, so we became cheerleaders. Years ahead of the Dallas Cowboys Cheerleaders, we bought
short white shorts, short white boots, and pranced along the base
lines, fetching soda pop, keeping score, and taking pleasure in the
pleasure of the older Wildcats as they watched our T-shirts take
interesting shape.

"Pubescent change or the state of sexual maturation influences the rise and decline of certain interests and attitudes," says Peter Blos, the psychoanalyst who studies adolescence. He cites studies comparing the differences between girls before and after the start of menstruation. After puberty girls generally are more interested in boys and in developing a personal sense of style than in games requiring strenuous exertion. "Imagination and daydreaming are preferred to sports." [1]

It is this phase that most readily lends itself to the romantic "crush," which psychologists describe as "a naturally midway point in the progression of self-love to the love of another." [2]

When I entered my teens I quit sports as a participant but not as a fan, and I chose my heroes from the stars on professional baseball teams. When a favorite player came to town I fantasized that he had picked me out of the crowd to dedicate his game to me: Joe DiMaggio walked to home plate, waved, and said, "Suzie, this home run is for you." Or Bobby Feller confided to the sports-writers that he pitched a no-hitter especially for me. When I met Lou Boudreau, the all-star, all-handsome shortstop for the Cleveland Indians, I wouldn't wash my hand that he had grasped in his. I could recite batting averages, home runs, and shutouts as a teeny-bopper of today mouths the lyrics of the Grateful Dead or the Rolling Stones.

"During a phase when adolescents are still self-conscious and tentative in approaching each other, crushes may be suitable substitutes for burgeoning heterosexual interest," says Barry Farber, the psychologist.[3] These are emotional rehearsals, small, sensual dramas that carry none of the risks of real-life relationships. It is at this stage that a father and daughter change places in their game of hide-and-seek: by moving away from her father in tentative first steps to her own sexual identity, a girl begins to squirrel away a secret part of her life in a way that she learned by observing her father.

The hard task of adolescence is to break the childhood ties to parents and to move into successful relationships outside the family, learning to express sexual and affectional desires.[4] Before adolescence, a child wages an uphill battle against sinking back into the all-encompassing care of her family, and adolescent sexual excitement makes the move away from the family more enticing, more dangerous.

Crushes from the Culture

The crush is often the adolescent daughter's first sexual test of her father. How he responds to her new hero is likely to indicate how he will react when she brings home authentic boyfriends. Whom she chooses can indicate how willing she is to court her parents' disapproval. Robert Redford, Mick Jagger, and Ché Guevara all have sexy hero qualities, but why one girl chooses an actor, another a rock star, and another a revolutionary may show how determined she is to move away from her family, and at what cost. My choice of sports hero made it clear that I wasn't roving too far from my father's interests. I chose men that I thought he could admire too.

The hero crush is something like an alter ego. He becomes the complementary male side of the self with whom a young girl can fantasize conversations, consider values, and analyze changing perspectives. The women who spoke to me of their popular heroes all said that heroes helped them to crystallize and to criticize the "givens" they had grown up with.

"I was in love with James Dean," says Natalie, forty, a Chicago social worker whose young daughter now also hangs his picture in her room. "Because I had the same first name as Natalie Wood, I spent hours dreaming that I was her, that he held *my* hand, and agonized over *me* in *Rebel Without a Cause*. He was the most sensitive man I had ever seen, and sensitivity was what I wanted. The boys I went to school with were afraid to be vulnerable; they had his toughness but with nothing to redeem it. But I *knew* James Dean could understand my feelings."

Natalie began having fights with her father as Natalie Wood had with her father in the movie, and she made up conversations between herself and James Dean, asking him why their respective parents couldn't ever understand. Jimmy didn't say much in her fantasies, but the way he shrugged his shoulders — "I still thrill when I think about it."

Natalie's father didn't pay much attention to her crush, but he did pay attention to her values. They argued about the importance of hard work and discipline, qualities James Dean did not represent. "Kids these days are too soft, they have too much time to think about themselves," he would say. His lectures were always the same and it was through fantasies about James Dean that Natalie felt able to question the values of her father's generation. James was a new kind of fantasy knight. He didn't run to the rescue, but he stayed behind with the girl, sharing her bewilderment.

The young movie star was a perfect first hero for a young girl of the so-called Silent Generation of the 1950s, an inarticulate generation fond of remembering itself as tender and in search of significance, made up of saints whom Barbara Grizutti Harrison calls "lovers of unsuccess." [5] The generation that followed would find causes and heroes in protest politics, revolutionaries, assassins, and terrorists, but Natalie's decade was a more contemplative time. Natalie and the children of her time still felt their parents' remembered pain of the Great Depression. They did not trust their own innocence, nor were they so sure they could build a better world overnight.

"James Dean and Holden Caufield — those were heroes who allowed us to feel who we were before we felt we had the answers to save the world," says Natalie. "Ours was a quiet, inner rebellion. Nowadays sixth graders read *Catcher in the Rye*, but when I brought that book home in my freshman year of college, my father almost had a heart attack. Was he spending all that tuition money so I could read four-letter words?"

Natalie's father had come of age in the 1930s and worked hard to make life secure for his family, and never thought his financial success would turn his daughter into what he called a "disrespectful phoney who lived off hard-earned money only to criticize the earner." Natalie heard his message and she could not ignore it.

She did not want to turn her back on her father, but she wanted the right to question things from her own perspective.

"Because I grew up in the 1950s and because I never completely threw over my father's values, I live a life similar to my parents," she says, with a touch of pride, a wry suspicion that she is perceived as an anachronism. "My husband is a doctor, my father was a grocer, and I hold closely to traditional values. I never found a real cause and I never rebelled against anything that took me across burning bridges. As a social worker, I get satisfaction from helping people, to help them get medical attention or food for the table, but I know I'm not going to change the world."

Natalie's daughter is eleven and she has watched *Rebel Without a Cause* several times on television, usually with her father. They both like James Dean. When the young girl is asked if she has a crush on the fifties movie idol, she looks surprised. She likes his movies, but when it comes to having a crush, "I love David Bowie."

Her father looks stricken. "Why, he often dresses up in women's clothes," he says.

"I know, Daddy. He's simply not hung up on heterosexuality."

Did this little girl understand what she was saying? In part, perhaps. No doubt she also wanted to needle her father, and she knew that she could do it by choosing to make a hero of a popular young singer who is sighed over by many teeny-boppers in spite of — or because of — his declared bisexuality. David Bowie, like other rock artists, offers instant shock value — and he may also offer young girls a terrifying glimpse of their own sexual fragility.

Freudians believe that there is a high degree of bisexuality in a young girl's crush, that she can love a female teacher as a heroine with the same ardent passion as she might feel for a male as a hero, because neither arouses strong sexual stirrings. Even so, these stirrings have usually been reined by parental rules. Paternal authority was still at work in the culture when Ed Sullivan introduced Elvis Presley to his first television audience in 1956, and the camera never looked below Elvis's belt buckle. Sometime after puberty, however, a different kind of crush stirs a girl's deeper erotic nature. A young girl still idealizes movie stars, rock musicians, even politicians, but she looks around for a boy who can share her eroticized interests. This crush allows her to safely pursue values outside her family with others her own age who are likely to live under similar constraints.

However, in the two decades following the first television performance of Elvis, constraints were loosened, and the power of paternal influence was severely curtailed in the home and throughout the larger culture. Television redefined attitudes. The commercials for designer jeans, disco records, and even hamburgers lead a young girl's eyes inexorably to the genitals and the soap-opera sexuality of television encouraged Daddy's Little Girl to be sexually precocious, if not promiscuous, and a good deal more verbally sophisticated than her mother was in the 1950s.

Later Developments

Often a daughter identifies the changes she has gone through before her father becomes aware of them, though a girl's verbal sophistication can mislead. She may not know what she is talking about. One father told me how astonished he was when, on hugging his fourteen-year-old daughter, she protested: "Be careful, Daddy. The only thing between you and me are my Calvin Kleins."

The sexual repartee between a father and a daughter in her early adolescence seems to dart out of nowhere. One moment she is a little girl sitting on his lap, and the next, such a scene looks like a parody from the pages of *Playboy*.

"I came home from work one evening and swept my twelve-year-old daughter in my arms with an exuberant greeting," says Henry, thirty-seven, a lawyer in Mobile, Alabama. "She looked up at me, her big brown eyes twinkling with innocence and mock adulthood, and said, 'Please, Daddy, not tonight, I have a headache.' She had only a remote inkling of what she was referring to, but she knew the humor in it, and I knew it was time to put the brakes on some of our robust affection."

If the father doesn't put the brakes on physical affection, the daughter probably will. Alfred, forty-two, recalls the moment at Los Angeles International Airport when his relationship with his eleven-year-old daughter changed. "Lucy greeted me at the gate when I came home from a business trip, and I wrapped her in my arms, holding her close as I had done since she was a babe in arms. 'Daddy, you can't do that anymore.' 'Why not?' I asked. 'Because I'm old enough to wear a bra now, and your hugs are sexier than they used to be.'"

All those vitamins and all that orange juice have changed a lot of things. Improved nutrition and better health care have accelerated sexual development in both boys and girls; maturity arrives earlier. "We have medical evidence that the age of sexual maturation has been [dropping] rapidly for boys as well as girls over the past 150 years," says Dr. Claude Migeon, a pediatric endocrinologist at Johns Hopkins University. "'Premature' sexual maturity today is a diagnosis confined to girls under eight. Today more girls are [physiologically] able to bear children in their early teens." [6] Many do, and most of them aren't married.

Today about 1.3 million children live with teenage mothers, about half of whom are unmarried. One of the reasons, according to Captain Carol Bryant, who runs the Salvation Army's home for unwed mothers in Chicago, is that thirteen and fourteen-year-old girls try to act older, "just like Brooke Shields," but they don't "connect sexual intercourse with pregnancy in any meaningful way." [7] A third of the babies born to white teenagers and eighty-three percent born to black teens are illegitimate.

Early development causes special problems in the family for fathers and daughters, especially in a culture that celebrates sexual liberation. A protective and concerned father wants his daughter to grow up slowly.

The first battle in the family is usually over the young daughter's changing body, and how she decorates it. The little girl who used to dress up in her mother's clothes knew she was playing a game, rehearsing to be an adult. When teenagers wear Mom's clothes, it signals Daddy that there is another woman in the house. He is often surprised, not only by what he sees, but what he experiences himself. Often he wants his daughter to hide what can't be hidden, even when she is shy and innocent.

"Lily was a sheltered child because we live in a quiet suburb," says Tom, forty-seven, an accountant in Oklahoma City. "She was a Girl Scout who sang in the choir at church, just the kind of girl you used to see in Norman Rockwell's covers for *The Saturday Evening Post*. I flew into a perfect rage one evening when she borrowed her mother's blouse to wear on a hayride. Lily was thirteen. I remembered what I had tried to do with the girls on hayrides and when I saw her in my wife's grown-up blouse I exploded. I told her to take herself back upstairs to put on something suitable for a thirteen-year-old."

In retrospect Tom realizes that there was nothing wrong with the blouse his daughter picked out of her mother's closet. What made him lose control was his recognition that his daughter had a figure that looked good in women's clothes. Although he had noticed that she had begun to wear a bra, the image he related to was a little girl, a woman in miniature. She was instead becoming a woman in fact. The next day he apologized to his daughter, explaining that he missed his little girl, but he was pleased with what a fine-looking young woman she had become.

Though not prepared for the changes in his daughter, he fortunately adapted to Lily's new phase. A father who is overly sensitive (or insensitive) to his daughter's body image can "infantilize" his daughter, elevating himself at her expense. A teenage girl is particularly vulnerable to his responses among family and friends where she is trying to establish a more grown-up identity. In an analysis of more than 160,000 teenagers, Jane Norman and psychologist Myron Harris illustrate the damage that can be caused by an unthinking father. Barbara, seventeen, tells this story: "My father always called me 'little dummy' or 'shrimp.' I was the baby in the family and I'm sure he was only teasing, but when I was little I really believed him. In fact, I believed it for a long time. It wasn't until I met my boyfriend and he told me how smart he thought I was and that he didn't think I was too short, that I began to feel I was OK. Unless you're very secure and sure of who you are, you believe you are what people say." [8]

Adolescents are constantly redefining themselves to adjust their emotional changes to their body changes. They are particularly vulnerable to younger images of themselves that portray them in unflattering or embarrassing poses. Home movies and photographs, such as those of a naked baby splashing in a bath or lying on her bear rug, should be put out of sight if a daughter is sensitive to them. She will look at them again when she is older or when she wants to make comparisons with a baby of her own.

A father must take care to show his respect for a daughter's newly acquired self-consciousness about her looks, dropping affectionate pet names from childhood that have less flattering significance in adolescence, ending playful teasing that is no longer appropriate.

In spite of what seems to be a super-sophistication portrayed by young girls on the contemporary scene, the teenage girl today is more, not less, sensitive about her looks than her mother was twenty years earlier. In surveys of 1,400 teenagers in the early 1960s and again in the late 1970s, researchers found those in the more recent group to be less secure. They described themselves as more easily hurt and more worried about their bodies than teenagers of two decades ago. In both surveys girls felt worse about their bodies than boys did.[9]

One of the ways a father can take the heat off the body image of his daughter is to begin to relate to her in a mature way. His tone of voice, the subjects he initiates for discussion, the way he includes her in his conversations, tell a young girl that he accepts her as a developing woman with thoughts of her own.

Adolescence is the time when a girl yearns desperately to be taken seriously. Expanding her outside interests, she continually challenges her father, until now the ultimate authority and arbiter in her life. Though this is all new to him, too, a father must learn to deal with her in a straightforward way, to listen carefully lest he miss what his eyes may not let him see.

An attentive mother holds certain advantages in perceiving how her daughter develops. Because she has been there herself, a girl's mother can anticipate changes as well as participate in them — she is often there when the daughter buys her first pair of

high heels, her first bra, her first tampons. She sees these rites of
puberty from the perspective of a wise woman, who can offer advice based on the good sense born of her own experience.

A girl's father is, after all, an outsider. He gets an occasional
glimpse or whisper of these female rites, but they are no less ar-
cane for being fascinating. The most sophisticated man is uncomfortable in a lingerie shop, or shopping for what are euphemisti-
cally called "feminine-hygiene products." Brash, usually crude,
male humor about menstruation is often nothing more than an attempt to compensate for ignorance of female mystique. Even in
the media-made culture, where everyone seems to know everything by the age of five, the most well-intentioned men remain ig-
norant of and insensitive to a woman's psychological changes as
she grows up. Fathers often hide bewilderment behind bull-like
bravado.

Phyllis, thirty-three, a housewife in Louisville, Kentucky, continues to feel physically awkward around her father because
he never accepted her adolescent yearning for a woman's grace
and femininity. Her story is dramatically painful, but similar in
theme to those told to me by many women whose fathers revealed
an inability to accept their daughter's budding womanhood:
"When I was fifteen Dad made a movie of my dancing. At
the time, I thought I was something special as a dancer, but
when we got the film back and Dad put it on the projector even
I thought I looked pretty silly. Occasionally Dad put the reel
on and everyone laughed, including me. 'She looks like a
chicken,' Dad would say, and everyone would laugh again. I felt
a *little* embarrassed, but I was with my family and no great
damage was done."

Phyllis could accept at fifteen what humiliated her after that.
Her father remained blind, unable to perceive the distinctions that
were all-important to her. "When I was nineteen Dad decided to
put the reel on at a family reunion, where we were surrounded by
fifty people who were more or less strangers, even if they were
distant cousins and uncles.

"As soon as I saw what he was doing, I begged him: 'Dad,
please don't show that one.' He grinned at me and continued to

thread the film through the sprockets of the projector. 'Please, Dad, I'm begging you.' He could hear the tears in my voice. But he paid no attention and there I was on the wall, looking every bit as awful as I remembered it. Everyone roared, and when Dad came up with his line, 'She looks just like a chicken,' everyone roared again. I sat there in the dark with tears of humiliation rolling down my cheeks. When the lights came on nobody even noticed. I can cry today when I think about it."

Phyllis's father refused to accept the changes in his daughter, refused to look beyond his projector to the young girl who was trying hard to be a woman. By playing to the crowd, and repeating the film and his joke about it, he was acting as if time had stood still. He hid from the psychological reality of his daughter, pretending it was of no importance. But it was extremely important for his daughter and for him.

Matters of Weight

Psychologists talk about adolescence as a mourning phase, when the young girl must experience the sadness of giving up her parents. This mourning process is essential to turning loose her parents, and in turning loose, the daughter learns to recognize her father's fallibility and disappointing qualities, and learns to live with them.

Parents mourn, too. They must learn to live with the loss of their little girl, and to accept the maturing adult. It is not uncommon for the first stage of mourning to be rage — a daughter rages against a father's insensitivity, and a father rages over his loss of control. A daughter's body often symbolizes his complete loss of control. A vain father, particularly, will expect a daughter's body to reflect his paternal authority. Armed only with a temper and a watchful eye, however, a father fights a losing battle as his daughter's figure succumbs to the ravages of calories. Literally hundreds of women told me how their fathers obnoxiously interfered with their diets, immediately criticized an extra pound, and in general acted as though they were raising Miss Americas, movie stars, and models instead of "plain ol' me."

Jeanne's father, for example, wanted her to have a Twiggy figure, model-thin, all firm skin and fine bones. It would be his way of keeping his little girl little, although he didn't know that. He established the most elaborate arguments about why his daughter should lose weight. Once, when she was fourteen, he threw her ice cream cone across the backyard just to let her know how important it was to him that she diet. In response to his tyrannical weight watching Jeanne learned to cheat. "Because he wouldn't leave me alone," she says, "I ate like crazy, but always behind his back." She got fat as if to spite her father.

A father who takes on his daughter's struggle with weight often is making a last attempt to maintin his paternal control over her, and usually this struggle helps him hide the other, more threatening, emotions he feels about her developing body, and other males who admire it.

Norma, a svelte saleswoman in a dress department of a Fort Worth, Texas, department store, says her father's attacks on her weight coincided with her growing popularity with boys. "I will *never, underline never,* forget the time some high-school friends and I were sitting on our front porch late of a summer afternoon, laughing, telling jokes, and sipping our iced tea, when my father popped his head out of the upstairs window. 'C'mon in, Fatty," he yelled at me, 'it's time for dinner.' I was mortified. At dinner I screamed at him and asked him how he could call me Fatty, especially in front of my friends. I wasn't fat, only plump. He played dumb, and in more ways than one he was. 'I was just being affectionate,' he said. 'I meant no harm.' "

Psychoanalysts have traditionally linked eating disorders with the "oral" stage of infant development, examining issues of love and security, and lack of them, that accompany our first associations with food. More recently, anorexia nervosa, a disease of young girls who on occasion even starve themselves to death through excessive dieting, and bulimia, a food-gorging illness, have come to be perceived as part of a pathological family structure. Therapists who work with these girls usually try to redefine intimate family relationships.

Anorectic patients frequently speak of being split into two people, one of whom is "the little man who objects when I eat," says Dr. Hilde Bruch, professor of psychiatry at Baylor University College of Medicine in Houston, who is a specialist in the diagnosis and treatment of the disease. Because the development of the disease is closely related to abnormal family patterns, she says, successful treatment must always involve resolution of the underlying family problems.[10] A family therapist often tries to engage an anorectic's father in a closer relationship with his daughter, one that may have nothing to do with food, but which helps reorder family alliances. Since the way a young girl looks is intricately related to her sense of self-esteem, the way a father relates to his daughter's demeanor as well as her body naturally influences her eating habits and her style.

Elaine, twenty-four, an interior decorator in a small town in New Hampshire, describes the effect her father's obsessive weight watching had on her: "When I was nineteen, I was overweight for about nine months (I weighed as much as my father!). Dad harped on me constantly about the way I looked, but always added that it was not because *he* really cared, but because he thought I was unhappy with my fat. He just wanted me to be happy and he was doing it for my own good. He constantly watched what I ate, supervised me on total fasts, monitored my weight, and he had me running and doing calisthenics. I developed a problem of going on binges, but I didn't tell him until I was thin. I was disgusted with myself as a fat person, yet I resented him as a diet-pusher. Our relationship affected the rest of the family, too, because they had to sit by and watch our constant tug of war. Once, in a restaurant, a family dinner was ruined when I sulked because he would not let me have a Salad Niçoise. I had already had a hard-boiled egg that day."

The experiences of Jeanne, Norma, and Elaine may be extreme, but they are repeated in many different versions in other households. A father's incessant criticism of his daughter's body is the emotional equivalent of bullying. Thoughtful compliments, on the other hand, can overcome thoughtlessness and unconstructive criticism. Surely a little common sense can tell a father that it's never too late to say something nice to his daughter. Even in a bad relationship the crumbs offer nourishment. The fathers who deprive their daughters of food often deprive them of love. A father's earnest concern for his daughter's weight must be tempered with admiration for her appearance and other virtues.

Beauty, we all know, has its own rewards, and good-looking women are often judged by others as more intelligent, well-adjusted, and easier to get along with than their plain sisters. But beauty is more than skin deep and is reflected often in how a person feels about herself. "If you tell a young girl that she's beautiful, even when she's not, she's likely to become a very attractive young woman," says Dr. Willard Gaylin, the psychoanalyst. "If you tell her that she's ugly, even the prettiest girl will believe it and act accordingly. So your [response] may determine whether it was true or not." [11]

How important it is then for a father to respond positively to his growing daughter's attractiveness. It is a rare woman whose father plagued her about her weight or figure when she was young who is not later self-conscious about those same issues.

Sharon, twenty-eight, a dental technician who lives in Wilmington, Delaware, suffers doubts and uncertainties about herself that grow out of her looks, but her father managed to get more than one "image message" across to her. "Even though my father criticized me often, and told me repeatedly that I had big thighs (which I do), he didn't ridicule me about my appearance. I always felt he was proud to be with me. When we'd go someplace together he would often tell me that I was the prettiest girl there. Although I didn't really believe I was, I believed he thought I was and that was enough. When I was in a blue funk, feeling fat and ugly, he told me not to be so vain, not to worry so about my physical appearance; I was a nice person and that my inner virtues radiated for all to see. That simple comment made me feel ten feet tall, and it was a message that saved me from total insecurity."

Visible Difference

Although a father often expresses exaggerated concern about his daughter's weight, he can be even more irrational about her developing breasts. The budding breast is the first physical sign of a young girl's sexual maturation and it is fraught with fears enough for all. For most girls, breasts or the lack of them complicate adolescence and the process of becoming a woman more than anything else. Breasts are visible, even when artfully hidden; or worse, when there's nothing to artfully hide.

The beginning of a daughter's menstruation, though a profound rite of passage, is only rarely a topic a father wishes to engage. That's mother business. Lillian Hellman, the writer and playwright, recalls how her father reacted when she tells him of her first period. He seeks to refer the subject to higher authority immediately:

"Papa, I'll tell you a secret. I've had very bad cramps and I am beginning to bleed. I'm changing life."

". . . Well, it's not the way it's usually described, but it's accurate, I guess. Let's go home now to your mother." [12]

Fear usually accompanies a father's knowledge of his daughter's menstruation: his baby can now give birth to a baby of her own. The swelling paternal pride can accompany the budding of a daughter's breasts because this is a less threatening recognition of sexuality. A father must take care how he shows his admiration, nevertheless. His daughter is likely to be extremely sensitive on the subject.

The cruelest teasing a girl endures is over her breasts. The year I went out for tumbling we ran in packs, like little rats, and the packs were comprised of those who wore bras and those who didn't. Gymnasts didn't. We were tormented by the "Boob Brigade" with epithets like "sweater girl," and "Hubba-hubba, ding, ding, Baby, you've got no-thing!" By the beginning of the eighth grade it was past, when the fortunate among us had no reason to be embarrassed anymore, and the rest of us were finally old enough not be to embarrassed by boorish behavior.

If a flat chest is a heavy burden for Daddy's daughter, Daddy sometimes acts as though his daughter's flat chest is a personal affront to his own masculinity. "My father embarrassed me mercilessly," says Madeleine, a middle-aged housewife in Des Moines, who now prefers the braless fashion. "Daddy used to look straight at my chest after I got my first bra and say, 'Aren't you rushing things a bit, Maddy?' I hated him for that one. Once, in front of his friends, he announced that I couldn't wait to be a sweater girl. I blushed and ran out of the room, but not before I heard him say that it was too bad I didn't take after my curvaceous mother."

Because breasts are the first sign of a daughter's sexuality, some fathers become irascible and self-conscious when confronted with their daughters' physical development. He simply doesn't know what to do or say.

In his novel *Something Happened,* Joseph Heller depicts a father struggling with thoughts over a young daughter's latest developments:

> I turn irritable whenever my daughter comes out of her room to chat with us wearing only a nightgown or a robe that she doesn't always keep fully closed on top or bottom. (I don't know where to look.) I either walk right out without explanation (seething with anger but saying nothing) or command her in a brusque, irascible voice to put a robe on or put her legs together, or keep the robe she does have on closed around the neck and down below her knees if she wants to stay. She is always astounded by my outburst; her eyes open wide. (She does not seem to understand why I am behaving that way. I cannot explain to her; I can't even explain it to my wife. I find it hard to believe my daughter is really that naive. But what other interpretation is there?) Afterwards, I am displeased with myself for reacting so violently. (But there is little I can say to apologize. Where am I supposed to look when my tall and budding buxom daughter comes in to talk to me wearing almost nothing, sprawls down negligently with her legs apart, her robe open? How am I supposed to feel? Nobody ever told me.)

The novelist's perplexed hero is not alone in not knowing what to do. Fathers of all kinds have spoken to me of their confusion at facing their daughter's adolescence. Their feelings are rarely discussed. Such topics are not for barroom banter.

One man told family therapist Frank Savard that he was disconcerted by his daughter, who was soon to be fourteen. "She has a habit of running up to me and hugging from the back, with her arms around my waist," he said. "I can feel the pressure of her bosom against my back, and I feel awkward. I don't want her to be self-conscious with me, but I can't help but feel that it's time to put an end to this kind of physical contact."

Young teenagers do not know the extent of their sexual power, and fathers often do not know how to confront it. A physician who remembers sitting on her father's lap until she was twelve says that all physical affection was limited between her and her father after puberty. "He made me feel that there was something nasty about becoming a woman. Recently I told him how I resented his abrupt withdrawal from closeness.

" 'You put me off your lap forever when I was twelve.'

" 'I know,' he said, 'but what would you have me do?'

" 'I would have let *me* know that you can have some physical affection without the threat of sexuality.'

" 'I didn't know how.' "

Father and daughter were reflecting attitudes commonly found in adult couples. Woman are more able than men to "separate the wish to be held as an end in itself from the wish to be held as a prelude to sex," says Marc H. Hollender, chairman of the department of psychiatry at Vanderbilt University School of Medicine in Nashville. Dr. Hollender, who for many years has studied the meanings of hugging between adult men and women, says that for men "being held and holding is much more likely to lead to sexual arousal." [13] Married couples who don't understand this frequently give each other confusing signals, signals that often grow out of the father-daughter relationship.

Adolescence is one of the two major periods when most rules have to be modified. The first period is when a child starts to walk. A teenager is more vocal than a "terrible two," but both age groups demand increased mobility, and care must be taken to help them expand their freedom while trying to teach them their limits, too.

Many fathers overreact. Dolores, twenty-eight, a restaurant cashier in Sacramento, California, still blames her father for her terrible feelings about her breasts. "I know my friends envy me my large bosom, but that envy doesn't erase the message my father gave me." When she started to develop, her father teased her all the time. "Be careful about looking too much like a woman," he'd say. "You'll get yourself in trouble." Or he raised the threat of danger. "You don't want to get raped, do you? Wear looser shirts and quit showing them off like a hussy on the street."

Without meaning to, Dolores's father made her feel as though she was deformed. "I still walk with a stoop as though I've got something to hide up front," she says. "I know a lot of women wish they had what I have, but whenever I see a man's eyes drop to my chest, I have an irrational terror that he wants to rape me."

Dolores's father is not greatly different from Joseph Heller's fictional father who thinks up retaliatory remarks when he sees his daughter's bra, left lying about instead of around her bosom. "No wonder they say dirty things to you when you walk past," he imagines himself saying. "You're asking for it. If you get raped you deserve it."

Unfortunately, such fathers do not know how to offer words of caution without being cruel, though what they are reacting to are their own fears for their daughter. A father wants to protect his daughter, but her world is now much bigger than her own backyard. He knows that after puberty a new set of dangers is lurking beyond that backyard, and that adolescence quickly separates the girls from the boys.

Neither Separate nor Equal

Freedoms of thirteen-year-old girls are curtailed differently than the freedoms of thirteen-year-old boys. All children when small, young, and weak are protected equally, but as they grow out of the extreme vulnerability of their early youth the girls become uniquely vulnerable by the very virtue of their sex. Independence for adolescent boys grows in ever-larger leaps, but a girl's freedom is carefully monitored within certain fences and hemmed by specific fears, defined along certain routes and ordered by specific routines. Young girls naturally chafe under these restrictions, so arbitrarily imposed. But are they unnecessary?

"What else can we do in the face of the reality of their greater risk?" asks Ellen Goodman, essayist and columnist. "There is one statistical fact that slams down like an iron door against their freedom of movement. The fact of assault. Last week there was hardly a neighborhood in which a woman was not raped. That is the painful truth that divides the lives of growing boys and girls." [14]

A concerned parent inevitably choses excessive safety precautions over excessive risk; far better to be safe, even at the price of a noisy domestic scene, than sorry. Fathers traditionally are the major agents of this protection. Linda, twenty-eight, a legal secretary in Albuquerque, New Mexico, always thought that her life was doubly proscribed because her father was a cop.

"He saw a lot of seedy people in his work, and he would be quick to comment when I had on too much makeup or when my hair was ratted too high on my head. He also made sure that I wore a girdle when girdles were still just in fashion. I almost always complied. But when miniskirts were in style, I rebelled, and began wearing those. My father would tell me, 'One of these days someone is going to grab your ass and you're not going to like it,' and one of those days someone did, and I didn't. That was the last time I ever wore a short skirt. I learned many things the hard way."

Because of his criticism, Linda is well-groomed and fashionable today. She takes special pride in the way she looks, and likes hearing a man admire her perfume, her dress, and stylish hair fashion. She also prefers men in their forties or fifties (her father is fifty-one) because they have an old-fashioned sense of what it means to be a man. "I feel more protected."

As much as he might like to do it, even a sheriff cannot play the policeman with his daughter for long, unless he devotes his entire life to it. A teenager, like the rest of us, must learn some things from experience. Perhaps the greatest distress the father of an adolescent girl feels is his inability to protect her from emotional growing pains.

Joan, twenty-nine, who lives in St. Joseph, Missouri, recalls her father's discomfort when her date for the senior prom didn't arrive on time. "He spoke to me about how it was important to be myself and not waste time on boys who didn't appreciate me because they were too stupid to know better. When he finished his little speech he went upstairs and got dressed in his tuxedo, determined to take me to the prom himself. Horrors! Fortunately, I was literally saved by the bell, my date was at the door and Daddy pretended that he and my mother were going out to a dinner-dance at his lodge. My date thought it a little odd that my father was in formal clothes and my mother was in a housedress." She loves her father for the sentiment, she says with a smile, now that she is old enough to appreciate a parent's emotions.

In those first piercing experiences of adolescence, a father who realizes that he can no longer assuage hurt pride may instead look for ways to blame himself for his daughter's unhappiness. She takes a major step toward independence when she finally sees her father as having a certain measure of complexity, with the feelings and prejudices of a man as well as the anger and anxiety of a father.

"My strongest memory of my father is of the time I was in the sixth grade, when I was already well into adolescent problems," says Melissa, twenty-two, whose father is a jeweler in a small town in Montana. "I came home from school crying because the other kids had made fun of me, for a reason I can't even remember. I collapsed on my bed in tears. Dad came into my room (which was unusual) and closed the door behind him. He came over beside me and put his arms around me and asked what was wrong. I told him that the other children had made fun of me. I noticed the sad and strained look in his face and he hugged me harder. 'It's because of my ear isn't it?' he said, involuntarily putting a hand to his cauliflower ear. I think that was the first time he had displayed feelings of sensitivity in such a way that I could recognize them. He took on a whole new character in my sight. Of course I was saddened by his thinking that he was the cause of my mockery and I began to cry even more. He cried also! That was a very special moment for me and I will *never* forget it."

Melissa's father, like most men, finds talking about a daughter's childhood pain difficult. That past, like many of the topics that divide father and daughter, is confronted reluctantly when it is confronted at all. The most difficult experiences, Melissa's father says, "were those times when my daughter's feelings were hurt somehow by other people, and I had no power to prevent the hurt and no power to make her feel better." This is a miserable feeling of powerlessness that all parents know, and fathers, upon whose male strength ancient tradition decrees the security of the family ultimately rests, feel this powerlessness most of all. Such injury to the vulnerable female child who sprang from his loins is ultimately a challenge to his very manhood. For daughter, as for father, adolescence is the most treacherous passage, the Cape Horn of her childhood.

CHAPTER EIGHT

Sex and the Single Daughter

I was standing next to my father at the registration desk at the Eden Roc, trying not to show how impressed I was by the fake marble all about, the pseudo-crystal chandeliers above our heads.

My parents had taken me along on a midwinter vacation in Miami Beach. The other guests were Biggie, the richest of the gamblers from my father's old crowd, and Lorna, his latest "best and closest friend." When the room clerk pushed the register toward Biggie, handing him the pen to sign in, Daddy leaned close to whisper into Biggie's ear. I heard the admonition, too: "Biggie, you have to get separate rooms, because my daughter is with us. She's just a teenager. Connecting rooms are okay."

Biggie nodded, smiling. He wasn't at all embarrassed. He agreed entirely with Daddy's reasoning. I was mortified. Didn't Daddy know that I knew that the door connecting hotel rooms was designed to be easily unlocked during the night? Didn't he know that I knew that a man and woman did not necessarily have to be married to make love?

Biggie and Lorna got their connecting rooms, and nothing was ever said about their sleeping arrangements. Daddy did not care who slept with whom, so long as his little girl didn't have to know. But what Daddy didn't know was that nothing he could have said or done would have enhanced the sexiness, the attractiveness, of illicit love-in-a-hotel-room quite like his whispered request to his pal. It was the kind of irresistible love-in-the-shadows that died with the movie fadeout into a crackling fireplace, blushing brides, and steamed-up Studebaker windows on Lovers Lane.

Sex in the 1950s was not, as popular mythology holds, altogether dead. It was everywhere — but where *I* was. In those days adolescence was closer to childhood than to maturity.

I learned what sex was, more or less, when I was nine and my friend Ginger took me prowling through her attic. "These are some things my sister's boyfriend sent her from the South Pacific," said Ginger. "He's a marine. They're *very* private and my sister doesn't want *anybody* to see them."

So I helped Ginger slip the rubber bands from around the shoebox. The first thing we pulled out was a cartoon torn from *Stars & Stripes:* a man with the body of an electric plug chasing a woman, whose body was shaped like an electric socket. Beneath them was the caption: WHEN THE LIGHTS GO ON AGAIN ALL OVER THE WORLD.

That was the light bulb, so to speak, that went off over my head. For years afterward, whenever Ginger or I got a crush on someone we spoke of feeling "bright lights," but a metaphor was all it was. By the standards of my children's generation, our lives were one great blackout.

I gave up my crushes on sports heroes at the age of fifteen and looked for boys closer to home. I discovered Rudy Dawson, the super-sexy senior of Calvin Coolidge High, when I was a sophomore. When I tell my children about Rudy, I tell them he strongly resembled Fonzie, the prototypal Mr. Cool of the TV series *Happy Days.* Rudy had a pompadour, which he slicked down with Fitch's Rose Hair Oil and combed — and combed, and combed. Rudy never passed a store window or brightly polished Chevy without bringing out his comb. He wore a soft leather jacket, which made him look a lot tougher than he was or needed to be.

Rudy worked at Rock Creek Pharmacy on Grubb Road, where I started hanging out every afternoon after school. To have an excuse to talk to him, I soon had an enormous inventory of Ipana, Lavoris, and roll-on deodorant. Rudy would have thought I had the worst halitosis and B.O. at Calvin Coolidge High, except that fifties girls were ethereal creatures who did not perspire, tire, or have physical needs and appetites.

I first saw Rudy in the corridor between Biology and Spanish, as I ran to get to class on time. I was wearing new loafers, the ones with a little slot on the instep to hold a penny, and slick leather soles that made me slide into a group of seniors around Rudy's locker. My notebook and all its contents flew out at Rudy's feet. He helped me up, observing that my new pennies seemed to be not very lucky. This was such wry maturity. When he helped me pick up my papers he touched my hand. Stan Musial had never given me such a tingle with a bases-loaded single, nor Sammy Baugh with a last-minute touchdown pass to beat the hated New York Giants.

I saw Rudy often after "the fall," and he always gave me a big smile that became the lodestar of my universe. I finagled his entire classroom schedule from my friend Tissa, who worked in the attendance office, so that I could change my own route to all my classes.

By running down the hallway past the boys' gym after leaving American History, doubling back past the auditorium, and racing up the back stairs, I could get a glimpse of Rudy running in the opposite direction and slip into my desk on the front row just as the tardy bell rang. We were reading *Romeo and Juliet* and Rudy was more than enough reason to memorize Juliet's soliloquy perfectly. I knew Juliet well; I was in love with love, too: "Rudy, Rudy, a rose by any other name . . ."

I would have spent the rest of the semester racing that bell to English lit, chasing Rudy's elusive smile, had it not been for Al Capp's comic strip *Li'l Abner*. My sorority, Sigma Pi Sigma, had the same idea that every other high-school sorority had. We held a Sadie Hawkins Day, where for one wonderfully awful day the girls had to pursue the boys. The day was climaxed (and this is definitely not the operative word) by a Sadie Hawkins Ball.

Dare I ask Rudy? I hung about the pharmacy for days. I bought nearly a case of Ipana and enough Lavoris and Listerine to sanitize the entire 4077th M.A.S.H., just trying to make up my mind (I never knew what my mother thought when she finally found that inventory in a little-used closet off the basement game room). Finally, one Thursday afternoon when I couldn't put it off any longer, I popped the question: "Would you, uh, like to, ummmm, you know, ah, takemetotheSadieHawkinsBallthreeweeksfromSaturdaynight?"

I knew he didn't have a girlfriend; I also knew that nobody, unless he was going steady or had pinned someone, made plans three weeks in advance. Rudy tried to be a gentleman. "Let me check my calendar," he said. "I'll let you know the next time you come in for toothpaste."

But I knew. I *knew*. The next day I happened to be in the neighborhood, and suddenly found myself on Grubb Road, and since I was there anyway I sort of waved, nonchalantly, like Merle Oberon or Olivia de Havilland would have done had she found herself on Grubb Road, needing toothpaste.

Rudy waved back and called me over. He had looked at his calendar. He was awfully sorry, but . . . It was my first rejection. I was afraid I *would* live, and the humiliation was so great that I did not want to. Daddy, my mother, my best friend Ginger tried to console me: Daddy stressing the value of self-worth, my mother reminding me that I was still the smartest girl in my class. Only Ginger made sense: Rudy was a turd.

I went back to my original route to class. Giving up that race to English lit was a relief, and soon I was able to feel chagrin not for the humiliation of rejection, but chagrin over having had so little taste in men. Sometimes, when I am brushing my teeth I smile at my innocence, and at the intensity of adolescence and naive schoolgirl earnestness. I appreciate again the eagerness of Daddy, my mother, and my friend Ginger to ease my pain. Then I think: Ginger was right. Rudy Dawson, wherever he may be, *is* a turd.

Mind over Body

Self-esteem during adolescence derives more from opposite-sex friends than from those of the same sex. A prerequisite to falling in love is the adolescent's need to feel independent, to psychologically relinquish the security of the family.[1]

In the month following Rudy's rejection of me, my father and I had several heart-to-heart talks. If the talks didn't assuage the pain, at least they gave me a degree of secure male admiration in the family I was not yet ready to leave behind. I had tested the waters of my romantic feelings and had failed to walk on them.

After Rudy, my high-school years exemplified innocence reinforced by the conventional culture: dates where boys came to the door of my home to fetch me and stayed to chitchat with my parents, with my father about the three-hitter Bobby Shantz had thrown at the Washington Senators, to my mother about the movie we were going to see, or about her chocolate-chip cookies in the earnest hope that she would offer a few to go. All the boys took me out with respect for my one o'clock curfew, and the grunting and groping and heavy breathing on a living room sofa was occasionally punctuated with a parental voice echoing down a long hallway, suggesting that it was "getting late."

In class, I stared truly in awe at the long-legged Lilah Rafferty, who was reputed to have done "it." At my twenty-fifth high-school class reunion, she confirmed all our suspicions as she accepted the award for being the first grandmother in the class, telling us: "I never expected to get an award for getting knocked up in high school."

Lilah had done what most of us only fantasized in our fevered dreams. We read the prescribed "hygiene" texts and learned all about chickens and eggs, but true sex education was gleaned from novels like *I, the Jury; Tobacco Road;* and *What Makes Sammy Run.* The boys giggled over pornographic comic books, called either "Little Books" or "Hot Books," which usually featured crudely drawn illustrations of Popeye eating more than spinach or Dick Tracy catching more than crooks. Condoms were something furtively glimpsed in a father's bureau drawer, hidden beneath the underwear and handkerchiefs, or in an older brother's wallet, where they were carried for showing off. The boys carried them in a way to be seen when they reached for the money to buy the tickets at the movie, but the condoms disintegrated unused from the rigors of perspiration and age. Some of the boys pretended to be passionate followers of the fortunes of the University of Southern California when they were around girls, and there was much coy discussion of the Trojans, accompanied by the winks, pokes in the ribs, and slapping of backs. Birth-control pills were gleams only in the eyes of biochemists, and abortions were illegal. When Ingrid Bergman gave birth to the son of Italian director Roberto Rossellini without benefit of either divorce court or clergy, she gave us a topic for endless cryptic chatter in the lunchroom, but I do not recall a single person speculating upon whether she had considered an abortion. Teenagers were chaste, whether they liked it or not. "Going all the way" was the most powerfully enforced sexual taboo. For many of the girls of this generation, filial chastity was defended by their fathers with the zeal of a medieval knight.

In the 1950s, the father as head of the family determined the family-centered values, and protection of the family image meant that girls should remain chaste. The sexual revolution that ushered in the era of self-fulfillment in the sixties knocked Papa off his pedestal and gave the adolescent rebel more power than she had ever before had. But the issue of a daughter's sexuality remains a problem for her father.

Taboo or Not Taboo

Adolescence is the age that most consciously calls up the unconscious rebellious stirrings against the incest taboo: observe any group of fathers at the beach or pool, where their adolescent daughters are splashing about or parading past male eyes, attired only in bikinis or seductively styled one-piece suits. The men are appreciative, often struck with feelings closely akin to awe, and are most likely to make admiring jokes about the *other* girls parading with their daughters.

The plot thickens, as the hide-and-seek game becomes an ever-more-dangerous exercise. The French movie director Claude Berri deals with this in his film *One Wild Moment.* In it a forty-four-year-old man beds the daughter of his friend; the girl, who is eighteen, is the friend and confidante of his own daughter. The outcome is inevitable: the seduced girl's father is enraged, not so much for his daughter having an affair as he is enraged by his friend in the role of seducer. If society forbids a man to be his daughter's lover, how dare a man his own age fall heir to such fabulous fortune? And the seducer's own daughter is pleased, in a way, but she is enraged, too. The fact that her own best friend becomes her surrogate is almost more than she can bear.

Fiction also takes up this theme, cutting beneath the surface of propriety. We are again privy to the prurient speculations of the father in Joseph Heller's *Something Happened:*

> My daughter doesn't really like her friends very much . . . and neither do I, with the exception of one classmate a year older who is slim and pretty and secretive and who, I am just about convinced, is flirting with me, leading me on. (I encourage her.) She is not, my daughter tells me, a virgin anymore. She has a knowing, searching air about her that sets her apart from the others. She keeps her look on me when I am near, and I keep mine on her. I'm not sure which one of us started it. . . . Sixteen would be *too* young, even for me. (Or would it?) *Someone* is going to be laying that provocative, pretty, hot-pantsed little girl soon, if someone isn't doing it already, and why shouldn't it be me, instead of some callow, arrogant, wise guy of eighteen or twenty-one, who would not relish her as much as I would, regale and intoxicate her with the spell of flattery and small attentions I could weave, or savor the piquant degeneracy of it nearly as much as I would be certain to. (Although I'm not so sure I want to tell anyone about this one.) No, sixteen *is* too young (young enough to be my daughter, ha, ha . . .)

Heller perfectly captures the "new morality" that permeates the culture and how it affects the father-daughter relationship. "More and more of us don't really care what happens to our children," he writes in this book, ". . . as long as it doesn't happen *too soon.*"

In the past two decades the kind of childhood innocence venerated by Jean-Jacques Rousseau in the eighteenth century and propounded by the Romantic poets has changed radically.[2] Adolescent love once emphasized the unattainable, the perfect and chaste ideal. "We did everything *but,*" we often boasted on mornings after big nights before. Today's teenagers, impatient with the mannered and teasing rituals of courtship, are more likely to do *nothing* but. It is a new sexuality that poses difficulty for both father and daughter.

One father told me how shocked he was to discover a bill from his daughter's doctor, itemizing the costs for an examination and fitting of a diaphragm. "Don't you think she ought to pay for this herself?" he asked his wife. Probably, agreed his wife, but as a practical matter, how did he expect her to do so? The girl did not work, because she had too much homework. The father deducted it from her allowance at a dollar a week. "If she's old enough to have sex," he said, "she's old enough to pay for her contraception, and she ought to get in the habit of taking care of herself because men aren't going to do it for her." The daughter was happy to pay for it, she told her mother with more insight than she knew, but she thought her father was making "a thing" about the diaphragm simply because he was jealous.

About the Matter of Double Standards

In spite of the new morality, the double standard lingers. Women young enough to enjoy the sexual revolution may feel more free but their fathers rarely do. Lydia, twenty-four, a housewife in a small town in Florida, is representative of many woman who tell how the mixed messages on sex were received from the father.

"When my brother was sixteen my father found a rubber in his pants pocket, and he bragged that my brother was a man. When I was sixteen, he got stricter with me because it was clear that I could get pregnant if boys were not as careful as my brother was with his girl friends. My father seemed to hate the boys I went out with, but he winked when he talked about the girls my brother took out. When I talked back, he called me a slut. When my brother talked back he yelled at him, reminding him that he was not a man *yet,* but he didn't impugn his sexuality."

The teenage years are too long to be a point of passage, and as such they are a recent phenomenon. There was no adolescence in the Middle Ages, and adolescence today creates a limbo of double standards. Notes Carlos Sluzki, the psychiatrist: "A father says to his daughter: 'You must stay in this house and let me support you, but you must also let me tell you what you can do.' The child says, 'I want to do what I want to do, but I want you to give me the money to make it possible.' "

Children once attended school from age six to fourteen, and after that they were expected to earn money that went as a matter of course to their parents. In the years of the Great Depression, 1929 to 1941, there were few jobs, and high schools began to add eleventh and twelfth years so that children could be kept out of the work force. Even today it is difficult for children to work, yet they mature sexually earlier than before.

We treat them as dependent children beyond any logical reason, and when conflict occurs we should not be surprised. Once a daughter discovers sexual intercourse, she is not likely to give it up. A parent who does not help a daughter learn about birth control runs the risk of losing a daughter's confidence and trust.

In 1979, the Alan Guttmacher Institute reported that family-planning services like Planned Parenthood prevented 400,000 unwanted teenage pregnancies. In a recent study by the institute, researchers found that one-fourth of the teenagers who applied for contraceptives said they would no longer ask for them if their parents were notified, but only two percent said they were willing to refrain from sexual intercourse.[3] (Could some among this two percent have lied?)

Nearly fifty percent of girls between fifteen and nineteen have had premarital sexual relations, by some estimates, and this percentage is nearly double the estimates made in 1971.[4]

In the debate over whether groups like Planned Parenthood should notify parents when a child applies for contraceptives, even those who insist that this be done usually want to allow exceptions, such as for those children who might physically suffer if their parents find out. Nevertheless, the potential for harm is difficult to measure.

Women who answered my questionnaire frequently told me that when their birth-control pills or diaphragms were discovered, verbal abuse by their fathers followed. Whore, harlot, slut; such were the epithets. Why should there be such paternal vituperation for a beloved daughter? Typically, these daughters report, their fathers had not wanted to discuss the issue; they wanted only to roll back the clock and calendar, to make their daughters whole again. Failing that, they wanted their little girls to refrain from further sexual intercourse until they were safely and respectably married.

Most parents are concerned enough to want their daughters to learn about sexuality within a close, loving relationship, and are frightened by the prospect that someone will exploit a young girl's vulnerability and inexperience. This often includes the father who is driven to irrationality by the evidence that a man has known his little girl. But it is also possible that some of these fathers are terrified of the fantasies that haunt their own imaginations upon learning that a daughter is sexually active.

Suddenly, a father sees in his daughter a younger version of the woman he married, and he longs for her, and for his own youth. Or he realizes that he was powerful when his daughter was a child, and now her maturity reminds him all too well that his power is rapidly waning. As a father he is no longer providing for a little girl, but is supporting a woman who offers her most precious and intimate favors to other men. On a deeply primitive level, he feels his own manhood under attack. He becomes the fall guy in her sexual drama, supporting her for someone else to enjoy. This is truly tinder for conflict, if not for war.

Where Reason Fears to Tread

Few fathers could sit down to talk reasonably as a mature adult with a daughter to discuss the profound and complex implications of the sexual experience. Fewer daughters still would want their fathers to do that. Such mortification is surely available elsewhere. But conscientious fathers who want to draw a helpful distinction between love and infatuation could profitably cite this distinction from Ann Landers, drawn in a column that is often requested in reprint.

Infatuation, she writes, is instant desire, a set of glands called to action, marked by feelings of insecurity. Love, by contrast, is friendship first, quiet understanding and happiness, strength in patience and trust, an acceptance of another person's imperfections. Infatuation leads you to do things you'll regret later. Love makes you a better person than you were before.[5]

The way a father imparts such values, how he talks about the meaning of love between two people, can exert a powerful influence. If this influence is not seen immediately, it may be later. As a daughter acquires her own experience, she remembers the actions and attitudes of that first man in her life, and if he has been concerned and respectful to her she will expect to find another man to be that way, too. Bad experiences with father, on the other hand, usually beget bad experiences with other men.

"One of the most painful memories of my father," recalls Norma June, a woman in her midthirties in Savannah, Georgia, "was his anger when I came home late from a date with my first boyfriend. We had parked to watch the moon rise over the pines. I was fifteen and had just begun to learn how much fun kissing could be. When I got home my lipstick was a mess.

"My cousin, who was sleeping over, arrived home with me and she looked even worse than I did." Norma June's father hardly saw the cousin, but he took one look at his daughter and told her coldly: "I know what you've been doing, you little whore, and I won't have it." He slapped her across the face, not hard, but she still feels the pain. He was crushed, too, struck instantly with guilt and remorse. She thought he would cry.

"I had never heard him say a single mean thing to my mother or to my brother, and Lord knows he had never been anything but love and kindness to me. I understand now the anger that was surely more at himself than anger at me. We were never such close pals again."

Norma June has married twice, the first time to a cold and insensitive man and the second to a man who thought beds were something to collapse in after a big meal. In both marriages sexual disappointment was ordained. "Most of the fault is mine," says Norma June. "I dearly love men, but when the time comes to go to bed I just can't, no matter how much I want to. Some people are terrified of airplanes and some people are terrified of those glass elevators that run up the outside walls of skyscrapers. That's the way I feel about a big bed with a randy man in it."

No one has come up with a comprehensive explanation for sexual problems, though many have tried, but an unavoidable conclusion drawn from my interviews is that a father's response to a young girl's blossoming sexuality is crucial. He sets the terms for a young girl's perception of herself and of the men who are attracted to her.

A father who is not comfortable with his own sexuality signals his daughter to beware of others like himself. Irma, who is in her late twenties and the mother of a young son, describes her lingering sexual inhibitions and dissatisfactions. Like many other women who talked to me, she believes her sexual inadequacies are a direct result of her father's attitude: "When I was a teenager, Dad more than my mother took an overly active interest in my personal appearance. If I looked anything other than a tomboy he was upset. He banned makeup, sophisticated hairstyles, short skirts, low necklines, pants or slacks in school, and nylons. His fear of my developing sexuality has made me sexually unsure and afraid today. He called me a 'hussy.' I felt guilty if I looked too sexy or too pretty. I still can't think of myself as attractive or sexy, despite admiration I receive from others. When men admire me as a woman I unconsciously think, 'you *animal!*' " That was the very word her father used to describe all men. If her father could not accept her sexuality, then she was sure it was vulgar to develop it or to flaunt it, and men were dirty-minded to like it.

As a result of her father's attitude, Irma left home when she was eighteen, and did not speak to her father for four years. Just before she left, however, she performed in a minstrel show with her father. In one of the rehearsals he was singing "Daddy's Little Girl." After getting through two lines of it he suddenly stopped, broke down, and cried like a baby.

The demons that beset Irma's father are easy to identify. Many men cannot outgrow the madonna-whore image of women. His desperate need to control his daughter, to keep her a virgin, was the only way he could manage not to lust for her himself. His problems were not his alone, however.

Two Steps Forward, One Step Back

An adolescent is bewildered herself by the many changes taking place in her body and mind. The girl child and the woman inhabit the same space inside her body. The battle raging between them has not yet found an internalized referee. She is often at the mercy of an uncontrollable conflict of past and future selves.

Young adolescent girls particularly affect enormous swings of moods, often within minutes, from belligerent defiance to child-like surrender. A teenage girl typically reverts to mock baby talk after a loud and violent argument with her father, making an innocent attempt to put things back the way they were. Such a female is perfectly capable of manipulating a man, of course, but usually this mixture of babylike coquettishness is born of desperation: she wants to preserve tender feelings between herself and her father and she is not sure how to do it.

If it is true that girls mature more rapidly than boys, it is no less true that the culture makes the transition from girlhood to womanhood easier than the passage from boy to man. A young girl will take from home to college a favorite stuffed animal, a calico cat from a favorite uncle, or a gingham bunny, to be the necessary sentimental tie to home, a security blanket to make a dorm room seem not so far from the familiar room she has left behind.

But unless he is the eccentric Sebastian Flyte of *Brideshead Revisited,* a boy who shows up with a teddy bear will be thought bizarre, odd, or worse. Boys don't do things like that. A boy cannot cuddle up to his mother or father after puberty; he cannot leap upon their bed after an evening out to tell them of his romantic quests and triumphs. A girl, on the other hand, can camouflage her leap into femininity with little retreats into childhood, seeking affection with the little-girl wiles she will eventually leave behind.

This makes adolescence all the more treacherous for her father, who must respond to her overtures for affection without seeming to pander to her babyishness, without exploiting her vulnerable budding sexuality. Occasionally a father fails. A father and a daughter who continually fight during the daughter's teenage years, trapped in a hidden terror of incest, are pushed about by emotions they don't know how to control. Often only an outsider can show them how these unconscious destructive forces work.

Mary's father began to beat her when she became a teenager. Her mother had died when she was quite young and he had assumed the responsibility for raising her alone. They got on well until Mary became an adolescent. After the beatings started, father and daughter became family-therapy patients of Carlos Sluzki.

"Together we were able to identify a pattern of the beatings," says Dr. Sluzki. "They formed a circular cycle that had to do with closeness. Whenever Mary and her father found themselves getting too close they began to fight. The beatings became a regulating mechanism. Both father and daughter were afraid of becoming too intimate with each other; the intimacy forced them into a fight that put distance between them."

A beating was their thermostat. It functioned as well as a lovers' quarrel; they unconsciously began to anticipate the bliss of making up. The rules of the father-daughter relationship precluded that kind of bliss, so the quarrel helped them to experience the safety and security of distance. They oscillated between titillation and separation. Therapy became a quest for the right distance. Once they could recognize a fight coming on they were able to change the punctuation and talk about what they needed from each other. They no longer felt a need to hide behind their strong emotions.

With neither wife nor mother to absorb the turbulent crosscurrents of emotion, Mary and her father found it difficult to neutralize their unconscious sexual feelings, and fighting protected them. Some fathers and daughters find effective protection only in the courts.

Breaking the Barrier

In a Baltimore courtroom, Clarence, thirty-seven, pleaded guilty to sexually abusing Bonnie, his sixteen-year-old stepdaughter. "I don't want to blame anybody for my wrongdoing," he says, "but Bonnie would stand in front of the picture window in her thin sheer nightie. I'd say, 'Get away from that window,' and she'd go on standing there, teasing me like she wasn't my daughter but some woman I didn't even know."

Clarence is an electronics technician, working the early shift. His wife is an operator for the telephone company, working the late shift. They did not see a great deal of each other, and Clarence was the parent who was home in the afternoons when Bonnie arrived from school.

"One thing led to another, but the one thing that didn't change was the way Bonnie stood in front of that window, wearing that nightie that made it absolutely clear that she wasn't wearing anything underneath it."

Bonnie is a stepdaughter, but Clarence has known her since she was eighteen months old. It was then that he moved in with Bonnie's mother. He often bathed her and fed her when she was an infant. "I'm no pervert, and I know that incest is wrong. I never touched her anywhere until she was fifteen. I touched her breasts one day when I was drunk and she wouldn't let me forget it — and she had already had two abortions.

"So I got mad. 'Okay,' I said, 'you want to play for real, you take off your clothes.'

" 'Not today. But tomorrow.' "

The next day Clarence was at home, as usual, when Bonnie arrived.

" 'Okay. Now.' "

He describes what happened next: "She started taking off her sweater, slipping it over her head, real slow like, stretching her arms and pulling her breasts up tight, and then her bra. She really teased me with the way she unbuckled her bra and took it off, grinning at me. She unzipped her jeans and slid them down her thighs and she stepped out, first one leg and then the other. She stood there for a minute with her hands on her hips and then she hooked her thumbs inside her panties and worked them down her thighs. When she got them to her knees she stopped and wiggled her little bottom. She stepped out of her panties and kicked them away and stood there grinning at me, licking her lips, standing there just as naked as you please."

Bonnie kicked off her panties for her stepfather again, and then again. When their trysts were discovered Clarence pleaded guilty and was told he had two choices: he could agree to participate in a therapy group run by the Baltimore County family-services administration, or he could do nothing and the district attorney would seek to have him sentenced to prison. Like most men caught molesting their children, Clarence chose therapy.

In therapy sessions the men seek to learn why they did what they did. Not all go so far as to actually penetrate their daughters; some draw their daughters into oral sodomy or mutual masturbation.

Under the law in many jurisdictions, incest is both civil offense and statutory crime. If a parent is prosecuted under the criminal statute, the child, as the only witness, must be called to testify.

This is a disagreeable prospect for anyone and is often a shattering trauma for a child. To avoid this, many prosecutors file civil charges of child or sexual abuse. The proceedings are referred to a social-services agency and the child need not be called as a witness. The agency provides protective care for the family while the father is referred to appropriate therapy. Second offenses are rare.

Typically, the incest victim is not yet an adolescent, but usually a young girl of eight or nine who at first enjoys the special attention of her father without knowing where that attention will lead. The father does not know how to be close or affectionate outside of a sexual relationship. His insecurity is stressed by the outside world and he uses his daughter as an emotional buffer against that world.

Contributing to the increase in incest, nearly everyone agrees, is the growing isolation of the American family as a technological age advances upon old values. Rita and Blair Justice, in *The Broken Taboo*, cite the restless movement of America. More than 50 million Americans move each year, going from job to job, house to house, state to state. As a result, the family that historically served as a refuge for the bruised and the battered has become itself beset and buffeted by unfamiliar winds of change. "Instead of acting as a shock-absorber, the home for many has become a pressure-cooker," say the Justices, who studied this problem in more than a hundred families.

They identify seven different personalities of incestuous fathers: the tyrant, the introvert, the rationalizer, the teacher, the protector, the elitist, and the sexually free spirit. The *tyrant* thinks of his child as his personal possession; he is enraged if his daughter shows even a flicker of interest in boys of her own age. The *introvert* has no friends, seeks shelter from the cruel outside world in the security of his home, believes that indulging in sexual acts outside his marriage is a sin, and that his daughter, because she is within the family circle, is a legitimate alternative to his wife. The *rationalizer* argues that it is better that he introduce his daughter to physical love than to throw her to the hot hands and mercy of the evil-minded little boys she hangs out with. The *teacher* considers it his duty to teach his daughter the right way so she won't get hurt later. The *protector* wants to keep sexual expression in his family free of the corruption of dirty old men. The *elitist* is determined to keep his family's royal blood and purple genes unsullied. The *sexually free spirit* is proud of his open-mindedness, pious in his permissiveness, and devises games the whole family can play.[6]

"They always have lots of reasons, but the cases read like Xerox copies," says Dana Levitz, assistant district attorney for Baltimore County, who prosecutes incestuous fathers. "Daddy begins by giving the child something special, extra attention and affection. Touching, fondling, feeling, nothing bad. But he gets more demanding as the girl gets older. She begins to feel guilty. It feels nice, but it *has* to be wrong. Her girl friends are getting interested in boys and her father sees boys only as his sexual competition. She has come a long way from jumping into his lap, but who can she tell? She can't tell her mother that she has stolen her husband. How can she say, '*I'm* the other woman!' "

Although the daughter feels wretched over the sexual activity, she usually blows the whistle in the course of protesting something trivial by comparison, such as her father's imposing a curfew on the night of the senior prom, or his refusing to let her take the family car for a night out with her friends. One daughter in Baltimore told a school counselor about her affair with her father only after they argued over which television channel to watch.

Some young girls have no one to tell, or are afraid to go public with the news. They know the effect the scandal will have on their families and on themselves. Often the mother, who is initially outraged when she hears that her husband and daughter have engaged in sexual activities, will scapegoat the daughter later when the "bills" start to fall due. Who will support the family? Certainly not the daughter. Even a pervert who is earning a paycheck is usually thought to be preferable to a father in prison. Mothers who think this way often sacrifice their daughters to foster care or institutions.

Sybil, twenty-five, a social worker in a small town in upstate Wisconsin, weighed her options about her "father problem" and decided not to press her charges against him because of the damage that *she* would inflict on the family. She speaks of her trauma with lingering sadness, frustration, pain, and bewilderment.

"I have blotted out most of that period of my life but I do make a conscious effort to deal with it now. I think it started when I was eight. There would always be times at home and on trips when Daddy and I would be alone together for a few minutes. He started by having me touch him through his slacks. Later he exposed himself to me, and touched me with his hands. He always wanted me to kiss his penis but I never would.

"I developed early and fast. By eleven I had large breasts and lots of pubic hair, and I was already getting my period. He fondled my breasts and compared them to Mom's. He tried several times to masturbate me and I wouldn't allow myself to feel anything."

Sybil wondered whether all fathers acted with their daughters as hers did with her. She was not even sure it was wrong until she was thirteen, and she did not know what to do. "I couldn't tell my mother or my brothers, but I didn't want to deal with my father anymore, either."

One afternoon when she was fifteen, her father tried to have intercourse with her. By tensing her body, she discovered, she could prevent his entering her. But she was determined to do something to prevent his even trying again. She went to a counselor at a private agency, who worked with her until she was nineteen.

"I first learned that I could go to the juvenile court and they would put me in foster care and arrest my father. It was horrible just trying to decide. If I went to court, my family would be destroyed. My brothers would never understand. How would we live? In the end I couldn't risk breaking up my family." Instead, she started running away from home, taking drugs, getting high, even joining a "religious" cult. Her parents couldn't control her and she couldn't control herself or the rage and hurt she felt. "All I wanted was to be loved, to belong."

With the support and help of the male counselor and a man she met through a telephone crisis line, she made it. The men who helped her became surrogate fathers; the man from the crisis line is still a close friend. After living away from her hometown for several years she moved back, carefully choosing a neighborhood far from her parents. For more than a year she declined to give her parents an extra key to her place. "My father never approached me again, but the damage was done."

She has had to "unlearn" her defense tactics, and it has not been easy. "Only in recent years have I learned enough to allow a man to penetrate me. I never have an orgasm and this frustrates my lover. He doesn't know about my father and I'll probably never tell him."

Sybil does not yet understand why she became an incest victim. Her mother acts as though she knows nothing about it. But how could she not? Sybil turns this question over in her mind often. "If he was coming to me, he must not have been going to her," she says. Those who make a study of incest differ in their views of the wife's role in the matter. Most experts think Sybil's reasoning that a mother knows, one way or the other, is generally correct. (However, the fact that her father was indulging in sex with the daughter is not necessarily evidence that he was abstaining from sex with the mother; one appetite might very well have sharpened the other.)

Black-Widow Mother

Typically the wife and the incestuous father have a sour marital relationship, however, and rarely achieve true sexual communication. Often the wife's attitude, expressed directly or by implication, is one of resignation if not relief: better that the "other woman" be their daughter than a twenty-five dollar whore, or someone else from outside the family.

"What's often forgotten with incest is that a mother, like the black-widow spider, frequently sets up the whole thing," Diane

Everstein, a psychologist at the Mental Health Research Institute in Palo Alto, California, told me in an interview. She works with children of violence. "For the mother, incest is a way out sexually. If she wasn't involved in it, wouldn't the child run to the mother and enlist her help? Wouldn't you have run to your mother if you had needed her help?"

But mothers are not the only persons unwilling to help a little girl in distress. "I was about eight when 'it' first happened," says Marina, thirty, who is now the mother of young children of her own. "I remember it clearly because it happened just before my first Holy Communion. It was my first confession." This is how that confession went:

"Father, I did an impure thing."

"What was that?"

"I let a man touch me."

"Who is this man?"

Marina swallowed deeply, took a new breath, and replied: "My father."

"I'm sure it was nothing. He was just expressing affection."

By dismissing her confession, the priest dismissed Marina. "Do you know he never again asked me 'who?' although I confessed again and again? He knew very well who I was. He was the pastor of our church."

Finally another priest heard her confession, and he would not grant absolution unless Marina promised to tell her mother what she had told him. "But how could I tell my mother?" Nevertheless, Marina had to find a way because the new priest was adamant. She went to the cafeteria where her mother worked, pulled her aside, and told her: "The priest said I had to tell you: Daddy has been kissing my bottom."

"Mom was furious — with me."

Her mother talked with her father, who denied everything. Then he told Marina never to say anything to anyone again, and continued to pursue her. "I prayed for certain birthdays to come, thinking that I would then be old enough to insist that he stop. I reasoned that since Jesus reached the age of reason at twelve, that would be my magic birthday, too. This, too, would end, and I wouldn't have to resist any longer.

"When I started menstruating, Daddy finally left me alone. We had never had actual intercourse, but we did everything but."

Marina was still wracked with guilt, and when she was seventeen she went to still another priest, a young and inexperienced padre, who told her that she was right to feel culpable, that most of it probably had been her fault. "You got pleasure from all this," he told her. "You turned your father on."

He was not altogether wrong, Marina believes now. "I was not doing it for pleasure, but there was some pleasure in it even though I tried not to take pleasure. I felt powerful, that I was Number One in the family. Daddy did not single me out for presents, but when he was in a good mood he brought gifts for everybody and I felt that those good moods depended on me."

Marina was shocked when she learned that her father went to her younger sister when he let up on Marina. She worries now about her own daughter, who is three. "I don't want to deprive my daughter of a grandfather, but I will not allow her to sit on his lap."

Although the incest taboo is universal — no known culture allows unrestrained sexual relations among close relatives — scholars in various disciplines offer different explanations for it.[7] Biologists justify the taboo in terms of inbreeding. Close-kin mating often immortalizes undesirable genes. Hence the celebrated hemophiliacs of the Hapsburg family, the ruling house of Austria for six hundred years. Sociologists say the taboo is necessary to assure the proper environment to raise children; erotic attachments between parent and child blur generational boundaries and retard the sexual passage from the family to society, from immediate sexual gratification to the more restrictive social morality. Psychoanalysts, taking their cues from Freud, stress the need for peace in the family. The incest taboo, according to this theory, inhibits sexual rivalries, expecially those between father and son. Anthropologists see the incest taboo as a founding principle of social organization, what Levi-Strauss calls the "rule of the gift," allowing families and tribes to exchange women through the institution of marriage, insuring trust and stable mutual relationships, the ultimate guarantee of security.

Modern feminists argue that the taboo also acts to reinforce the male-dominant culture with rigid sexual division of roles. "Women are encouraged to commit [a surrogate form of] incest as a way of life," says Phyllis Chesler, a feminist psychologist. "As opposed to marrying our fathers, we marry men like our fathers . . . men who are older than us, have more money than us, more power than us, are taller than us . . . our fathers." [8] Feminists like Miss Chesler blur issues, too. By seeing incest as a patriarchal plot, they put the burden on society rather than on the individual father.

The taboo must be rigidly enforced precisely because the incestuous attraction, like certain deadly poisons, can be effective medicine in the proper dosage. "Incestuous attraction between a parent and a child is the thread by which a parent pulls a child through the tumultuous developmental stages," says Diane Everstein, the psychologist. "It can be a very positive thing if used appropriately. It can help the child want to be like the parent, help the child want to grow up."

This thread, and how it is loomed and braided, is the thread that will later draw the developing child toward a suitable person of the opposite sex; the incestuous attraction, properly channeled, is a powerful force shaping the woman who grows out of the child. As with all powerful forces, it can devastate if it is allowed to run amok in a girl's life. A girl's father must come out of hiding, but he must emerge with great and thoughtful care.

CHAPTER NINE

Messages and Models: Sugar Daddies, Sweet and Sour

"Here we go, Suzanne." My father reached for my hand and propelled me into the doorway of a tiny boutique.

We were back in New York City for a weekend, back at the Waldorf, back on Park Avenue. This time there was no sudden illness, no tears, no terror. Daddy and I had been out for a walk, shopping the windows, watching the traffic, indulging the senses as is possible only in Manhattan on a balmy afternoon in spring.

I was looking forward to an early supper and then a cab ride uptown to Yankee Stadium. The Cleveland Indians and Lou Boudreau were in town for the first game of a three-game weekend series.

Daddy steered me to a counter.

"This is the one I saw in the window last night," he said, tapping at the counter top with a manicured finger. I wasn't sure he was speaking to me or to the woman behind the counter. She brought out a blouse, in red jersey with tiny pink-and-white flowers tracing a route around a modestly plunging neckline. "Can she try it on?"

I had never seen the blouse before, and it was beautiful. I looked quickly to the tag attached to the label, and I knew it was a blouse I would never dare buy for myself. As I followed the saleswoman to the dressing room, I imagined I detected the smallest smile flickering at her mouth, but I was not embarrassed. She was surely accustomed to men bringing their mistresses into her store to be fitted in expensive red-jersey blouses.

The blouse fit perfectly. "It's very nice on you."

"Well, if he likes it I'm sure it's just right," I said, affecting the nonchalance of a sixteen-year-old who was positive that she seemed at least twenty-four. "Whatever he wants. He has exquisite taste."

The saleswoman draped my jacket carefully over her arm. "Oh, yes," she said. "He certainly does. He picked out a gorgeous white-wool suit for your mother just this morning."

I felt my cheeks turning as red as the blouse. The blush was for my own comeuppance. I had never felt authentic jealousy of my mother; she was first with Daddy, and I was pleased that my parents were the envy of many of my girlfriends, who never saw their own parents touch, hug, and kiss the way my parents did when my father was particularly pleased with my mother.

Daddy was seductive; if the saleswoman had thought he was my sugar daddy I would have been pleased, but the truth was that my father never fostered competition between the two women in his house, not that I noticed. My parents had very different purposes in my life: my mother was to see that I always looked nice, my father was to see what she had accomplished and to admire us both for it. When a horse-player who owned a flower shop couldn't pay off a big tab, Daddy took it in roses and peonies. Every Sunday for years my mother got a large bouquet that she placed on the piano, and I got a minibouquet for my dressing table. Daddy never admired me or played to me *instead* of his wife, nor did he ever blur those generational boundaries. For that I would be grateful: when a father blurs those boundaries, he courts trouble.

In a healthy family, where a strong relationship bonds husband and wife and a strong relationship between father and daughter becomes possible, there can be a safe, close, and even eroticized tie between father and daughter. But if the daughter is expected to provide emotional gratification for her father, problems are inevitable.

When this happens, a man once again hides the loving father figure his daughter needs and is entitled to, destroying it with selfish demands of his own. Well short of molestation and incest, a father can be *too* seductive with his daughter for her own good as well as for his own.

Too Close for Comfort

For her book *Father-Daughter Incest,* Judith Herman interviewed twenty women whose fathers had been overtly seductive, though not overtly incestuous.[1] These fathers talked about sex with their daughters, often confiding intimate details of their love affairs, and constantly asked the girls questions about their own intimate affairs. Pornographic materials were left around the house, daughters were spied on when they were naked, and fathers looked for opportunities to be "caught" undressed. Some fathers courted their daughters like jealous lovers, bringing presents of flowers, expensive jewelry, even sexy underwear. "Although all these behaviors stopped short of genital contact," says Dr. Herman, "they clearly betrayed the fathers' intrusive sexual interest in their daughters, which was a form of covert incest." "Many women spoke of themselves as leading 'double lives,' and some in fact developed a secret life. One woman . . . alternated between a job in a massage parlor, which was concealed from her family and friends, and an unpaid job in her father's business. The implication was that she felt prostituted in both situations. Another developed highly dissociated 'good' and 'bad' personalities, each having a different name, different clothes, habits, and friends. The 'good' girl was subdued, compliant, and eager to please; she liked to stay home and cook for her husband. The 'bad' girl liked to go to dating bars, get drunk, and pick up men. She was vivacious, aggressive, and tough. This woman experienced her two selves as constantly at war and felt unable to control which personality would dominate at any given moment."

Daughters of seductive fathers have a problem that is usually compounded by their mothers' failure. Ruth Moulton, a psychoanalyst, describes three patients, whose fathers were seductive and whose mothers had no sense of their value as women. As a result, the daughters have an ambivalent identification with their mothers. Because they see them as rejected by their husbands, they anticipate a similar rejection from men when they become adults. "The fathers of these patients, although often seductive with their daughters, had such negative relations with their wives, for whom they had both resentment and contempt, that their warmth and support of their daughters were given inconsistently and mixed with hostility, thus reinforcing the girls' fears of men and male rejection." [2]

It naturally follows that daughters of seductive fathers are often locked in a complex rivalry with their mothers, and some of these women exhibit qualities of excessive femininity, always taking great pains to get a man.

Karen Horney, the psychoanalyst, four decades ago described "a common present-day feminine type," that fits these women today. They share a similar obsession with having to have a man. They have been so titillated by their father's seductiveness, a titillation that grows out of a father's stimulation and a daughter's seeming triumph over mother, that they crave the feelings engendered in sexual competition with women for men.[3] These women suffer an underlying anger toward their mothers, and until they overcome that bitterness, they can't respect other women, or themselves. Their mothers are usually ineffectual, an insignificant presence on the family landscape.

Just as the daughter of this seductive father is angry at the mother, so is the father angry at his wife. However, he takes his bitterness out on the daughter without knowing she is a victim of it. A dangerously seductive father has many reasons for exploiting his daughter's sexuality, growing out of his own feelings of inadequacy with his wife or other women. Especially vulnerable is a father who as a result of divorce has been forced to leave his wife and his children, and needs to compensate for his banished image; often he will play Don Juan, both behind the scene and in front of his family, and when he does, he usually overdoes it. Seductiveness between a father and an adolescent daughter may emerge when their conversations no longer obey the conscience of paternal authority.

Leonora, who grew up in Yuma, Arizona, remembers a sultry and electric experience with her father when she was nineteen, and with him on one vacation. He told Leonora about his difficulties with his lady friend, a middle-aged woman who lived with her identical twin. "Daddy had fallen in love with both of them and he told me how he was fascinated with this fact. I made some offhand comment like, 'Why don't you try some trisexuality?' He said he had mentioned it and they were not interested. I was lying next to him on the bed. We were both in our underwear. We often walked around half dressed in front of each other and it was no big deal. But now I could feel the heat of his body next to mine. We had been talking about his 'lover' and about sexual matters, and I could feel sexual tension in the air. I was suddenly apprehensive that he might 'try something' so I got up, found a sleeping bag, and lay down on the floor near the bed. He didn't do anything or say anything. I rolled over to go to sleep, but for a long time I lay awake, aware that he was lying awake, too, smoking. I watched the tip of his cigarette fade and glow, but I said nothing, just listened to both of us breathe, until I finally dropped off to sleep."

This encounter stimulated the youthful, impressionable Leonora's sexual imagination, making her uncomfortable. From her recollection of it, the encounter made her father uncomfortable, too. Few daughters, of whatever age, want to know about their father's sexual encounters and adventures; imagining and knowing are two very different things. Sometimes a girl's imagination is sexually stimulated by her father because *he* requires imaginative stimulation.

The Medium Is the Message

Yolande, forty-eight, an art therapist in Newark, New Jersey, tries to laugh off the stories she tells about her "seductive" father, but the pain is palpable. Her father was a typical traveling salesman, who loved to tell dirty jokes, show smoker films, and collect nudist magazines. When she was thirteen, she "borrowed" one of his dirty films and showed it at a friend's house. "We alternated it with animated cartoons someone else had brought, but the real animation came from the stag film," she says. "I still remember one plot where a magician pulled a rabbit out of a naked woman's pubic hair." Her father never touched her, but he was seductive in the things he left around for her to find and the way he talked to her. "He was always telling me that nice girls were virgins when they got married, and yet he seemed interested only in what bad women did. I have always felt a conflict between being a virgin and a whore. I like to look 'loose,' seducing Dad and my boyfriends with my well-made-up face and sexy body, but when my husband and I make love I'm incapable of having an orgasm. My husband is a supportive, loving man, in ways my father was not, but I'm afraid my husband won't be there if I really need him so I back away, afraid to need him."

Many fathers are like Yolande's, men who are at ease in a male world of work and virile camaraderie but who cannot adjust their interests when they move closer to home. Such a father may tyrannize his family with the smoke and stench of his cigar; he may litter the house with his beer cans and expect others to clean up after him; he may bring home the sensibility of the saloon and locker room without perceiving his effect on his family.

A father whose manliness becomes such a caricature that he feels ill at ease in the domestic scene is often unaware of the impact he may be making on his young daughter. He may be so concerned about proving himself a man who can stand up to the pressures in a man's world that he is oblivious to his failing to savor the gentling sensibilities in the woman's world of his wife and daughter.

Women often spoke to me of the indirect sexual messages they got from their fathers that confused them in many ways. If Daddy left *Playboy* magazine around when they were little, they got the idea that he liked the way bunnies looked. One girl went so far as to make herself a bunny costume on Halloween, and her father wouldn't let her leave the house for "trick or treat." The irony of that phrase was lost on the daughter, but not on the father.

"But you think *Playboy* bunnies are pretty, don't you?" she asked as a pubescent thirteen-year-old.

"I certainly don't want my daughter to be one," he yelled. When this young girl finally changed clothes to go out that night, she dressed as a gypsy: a full blouse, long skirt, lots of beads. "Now that's a costume you look good in," says her father. *Playboy* was never seen in that house again.

Children are much more literal than their parents often suppose, proof of the wisdom of the proverb: "What you do speaks so loud I cannot hear what you say." When a father wolfishly admires a big-breasted woman, referring to her as "a broad," he will invariably get the message across to his daughter that she would be perceived as "a broad," too. What should that tell her about her father in relation to herself? At best, his message would be ambiguous.

The most important people in adolescent lives are their parents, on whom they depend for self-esteem and the source of enduring fundamental values. Nothing so rocks the young, healthy adolescent girl than the conflicting sexual messages she receives from her family. The father, no matter how well-intentioned, may too easily offer conflicting values when he has no idea that is what he is doing. A father talks as an adult but his messages are interpreted through the innocent perceptions of a child.

Becky, twenty-nine, an airline stewardess, managed to channel her father's sense of adventure into her own career, but she had to learn how to do it with her own best interests in mind. "When I was growing up I heard a funny kind of mixed message from my dad," she says. "It sounded to me like, 'Be hedonistic.' He'd regale me with stories of *his* youth — riding a Harley, gambling with dice, watching and betting on cockfights, spending money on wild wardrobes and women. I didn't have a brother and I thought he was saying it was okay for me to be wild, too, because that was what he admired."

Becky didn't know how to sort out what he really meant, that what was great for Daddy was not necessarily what he thought was good for his daughter. She "slept around" on the sly all through high school, and when she hinted to him of her sexual exploits, he screamed at her. "It was as though he didn't know himself whether to treat me as a boy or a girl," she says.

He didn't know how to draw admiration from her without setting the wrong kind of example. If a father is going to talk about all the fun he had sowing his oats, he should be prepared for a daughter to want to sow oats, too. Did Becky's father pay any price for his "wild" life? It might have helped if he had drawn some complexity in his stories for an impressionable young girl.

A child requires more than a superficial message when it comes to issues of growing up, especially around sex. She needs clearly stated values. *Vivienne,* the true story of an adolescent suicide, told by Harvard psychiatrist John E. Mack and writer Holly Hickler, illustrates the adolescent yearning for direct statements and precise messages concerning sex. They tell how Vivienne and her sister, Laurel, were confused both by peer pressure calling for sexual experimentation and by their family's "open" attitude toward sex. Both parents walked around the house without clothes, stressing "naturalness" when what the girls needed were firm moral values. The teenage world did not offer such openness or naturalness, and the girls were ill-equipped to cope with the world outside their house. Vivienne sought reasons *not* to have sexual relations; Laurel became promiscuous. When both girls yearned for sexual guidance from a strong father and mother with solid values worth imparting, they got only "body rhetoric." [4]

Sex education begins the moment a child is born, though not in his seeing his parents walking through the house naked together or showering together, but in observing how they live together, how they touch, talk, enjoy each other's company, and show respect for each other.

Parents are needed to provide some reasonable balance and limits to teenage quests and tests that drive them into mature experiences before they are ready for them. Sexual stimulation leads girls into a pseudo-sophistication quickly, but this knowledge is hardly wisdom. Emotional maturity comes later. A sixteen-year-old confides that her friends think she's crazy for wanting to remain a virgin, though she doesn't yet even have a boyfriend. "I'm still trying to follow my father's judgment," she said. "He told me that sex follows commitment and I have a feeling he knows what he's talking about."

The daughters who had the happiest memories from adolescence were those whose fathers talked to them of their dates, asked about the boys' families, interests in school, and who engaged the boys when they visited the house. He was the father who provided "a firm masculine presence in my living room," one woman told me, who was typical of the daughters who *liked* their father during adolescence. "He let them know in a genial but firm way that he was going to be home when they brought me home," she says, "and that he thought they were lucky to be able to share my company. There were times when I hated his solicitousness, especially when I wanted to stay out late and I knew he wouldn't let me. But as I look back, his standards were the ones that influenced me when I was on my own. I always pretended that my father was looking over my shoulder and I had to consider what he would say. I was not nearly so wild as I expected to be when I left my father's house. The values he set were so clear-headed that I felt sure he would like the man I eventually chose to marry, and he did."

Many fathers told me that they asked their daughters to bring their boyfriends home for dinner, or family picnics. They engaged the young men in conversations about politics and current events. Sometimes they played ball together. In this way a daughter got to see her friend in relation to her family's standards and interests. Such meetings also help the young men to see a daughter in the context of her traditions. Without talking about sex, the family shows both girl and boy that there is much more to a relationship than sex.

Behind a Mother's Back

A father who is unable to wield his authority may actually be jealous of his adolescent daughter's freedom and will become rebellious along with her. Together father and daughter fight the rigidities of an old-fashioned mother, school, or society. Such behavior looks to be increasing, but it's always been around. A father and daughter who hide their conspiracy behind the mother's back is typical of a family where a father's power has eroded, where his contempt for his wife has grown.

Such conspiring may begin innocently, seeming to harm no one. Bertha, who is in her early sixties, tells how her father loved to make fun of her mother's "old-fashioned" ways. Because her mother came from an orthodox Jewish family, she had insisted on keeping a kosher kitchen, which meant, among other things, no mixing of meat and dairy products. When her mother went to the synagogue on Saturday mornings, Bertha's father got out the milk, bologna, and eggs, and together they feasted on the forbidden. Occasionally, he ran out to the corner store to buy slices of ham, forbidden at all times. "It was wicked of him," says Bertha, almost fifty years later, "but I loved having 'our secret.' I guess it was Daddy's way of cheating on her. He hated her strict old-country ways. Why couldn't she be more modern? he always asked." Bertha never expected to sympathize with her mother, and she didn't until she had a daughter of her own. "I always wondered if my husband and Sarah made fun of me when I didn't know it," she says.

A father who hides with his daughter while making fun of her mother is acting out childish aggression. He still wants to be a child, casting his wife into the role of his mother. It is his last-ditch effort not to grow up, not to take on paternal responsibility. When such behavior continues into his daughter's adolescence, he is hiding from himself.

Midlife Papas

A daughter's adolescence often arrives with a father's midlife crisis, his sense of powerlessness, that time in his life when despair begins to crowd him, and the taste of panic first comes to his tongue as he anticipates the failures in his future. "Unconsciously, this parent may be jealous of the adolescent's youthfulness, and may react either by attempting to find vicarious enjoyment through excessive involvement in the child's life, or by attempting to restrict the child's activities in order to avoid feeling envious," says Laurence Steinberg, a psychologist who studies psychological stages of human development.[5]

One way such a father restricts a daughter's activity is by criticizing her boyfriends. They are never up to *his* standards. In reality, his criticism says more about himself than about the boys. Cheryl's father is one such example. "The teenage boys I went out with were never 'good enough,' " says Cheryl, who is now thirty-one, and whose father was a midlevel executive in an Ohio shoe company when she was growing up. "He'll never amount to anything," he would always say. Her father was cordial enough to the boys when they picked her up, talking about the Buckeyes and the Rose Bowl or the pennant prospects of the Cincinnati Reds, and her dates usually liked his affable, easygoing manner. But he was obsessed with his daughter's finding someone who would be a doctor or a lawyer, who, in his words, "would be somebody."

Cheryl was determined to comply. She met a young law student at the state university in Columbus, and eagerly brought him home to meet her father. She was shocked when her father put him down, too. "He'll never amount to anything coming from a 'cow college,' " he said.

It wasn't until years later that Cheryl found out that her father hated his own job, that he felt he was a failure for never rising above middle management. She realized that he didn't really want his daughter to marry a lawyer or a doctor. *He* wanted to be that lawyer or doctor.

While most fathers want the best for their daughters, jealousy comes in many forms, and those fathers who are dissatisfied with themselves are not going to be happy for their daughters, no matter whom they bring home to marry. A father's jealousy of his daughter usually develops over those two little words Freud thought so important, *work* and *love*.

It has often been remarked that adolescent love frightens us with its intensity, and makes us envious of what we have left irretrievably behind. Such feelings may cause a father to hide from his daughter's boyfriends because he cannot bear to be reminded of himself as a young man. Worst of all, his daughter's sexual flowering coincides with his fears of waning sexual potency.

Louise, forty-one, a realtor from Sioux City, Iowa, was the apple of her daddy's eye until she started to date. After that he would only enjoy her company when they were alone, and then only as long as she didn't talk about any of the boys she was seeing. When a date came to pick her up, her father always disappeared. For one who loved his pipe in the comfortable chair on the front porch, he was conspicuously absent when Louise was going out.

The night of her junior prom, she had a new dress, a William Cahill original, a beautiful blue organdy that matched her eyes, and which she couldn't wait to show off to her father. But when she got dressed, he had already disappeared into his workshop in the basement and had no intention of coming upstairs to see her. So she lifted the hem of her organdy, trying to keep it from dragging in the dust on the stairs, and went down into the cellar to show off. He grunted. There wasn't a glimmer of appreciation. The doorbell rang and Louise left, feeling terribly let down.

"I was much too naive then to perceive that my father was jealous of my boyfrends," she says. "My parents had a terrible relationship, but I didn't understand then that that had anything to do with me. I understand now."

Louise's father is an example of a desperate man who cannot face life's maturing processes. He needed to hide in the basement rather than confront the young men in his daughter's life, reminding him of his lost dreams. Instead of extending Louise a hand toward the future, he preferred to close his eyes and irrationally hope that what he didn't see wasn't really there.

A man in his late thirties and forties is acutely concerned about his accomplishments, and lack of them, as well as his changing physical appearance and sexual power. His daughter's expanding options in work and love throw into relief a father's narrowing set of possiblities in both categories. While he needs to deepen his understanding of many things and develop the interests he has chosen, his daughter is able to choose from a smorgasbord of opportunities with lovers and careers.

Crisis of Competition

The "natural" antagonism between a father and a son has been long understood; the younger man replaces his father in society, and the impatience and resentment this breeds seem obvious enough. But when women find more worldly possibilities increasingly open to them, a father's sense of his own failure may increase antagonism to his daughter, too.

Colette Dowling, writing in *The Cinderella Complex,* says that a father often competes with a daughter as strenuously as he might compete with a son, and that he is jealous of her success.[6] However, a father's pleasure in a daughter's success, as in a son's, depends on his own self-esteem. Daddy's Little Girl makes Daddy feel like a Big Man, but when Little Girl moves away from that role, he is often left with no pride in his own achievements, and he may try to keep her from surpassing those meager accomplishments.

"When I was little and got good report cards, my father loved to brag about me, but once I got into high school, and was an honor-roll student, my father started to undercut what I did whenever he could," says Estelle, twenty-seven, a computer technician, whose father is a clerk in a paint store in Indianapolis. "Teachers were encouraging me to take college prep courses, and my father wanted me to go the vocational route. I think I scared him by my love of academic work. I don't think he was holding me back simply because I was a woman. I believe he would have done the same thing if I had been a son. Being a girl just made things worse. Pop never finished high school, and I think I embarrassed him in front of his friends when it looked as though I might be smarter than he was. He always hated working for someone else — and it was too bad he had to be grudging with me, too."

Estelle's father found it impossible to take pride in her computer studies or any of her adult achievements. She worked her way through college without any help from her father's paycheck. Because she's not married, it doesn't matter that she makes five times his salary in a respected career, she says. "He needs to believe I'm a failure."

While Estelle's father was unnecessarily cruel in denying his daughter's abilities, a father can be caught off guard when his daughter moves into realms mysterious to him. When a child goes off to college and has experiences foreign to him, the father may feel confused by her changes. He has no touchstone for her new information and social world. Long gone are the days when the daughter moves down the street and drops in from time to time. If she moves far away from the local landscape, she may return as if from another world. Communication is difficult on both sides, often unwittingly so.

Jenny, twenty-seven, speaks poignantly of her first trip home after a year of college in New York. She was visiting her father in Shreveport, Louisiana, when a woman friend called her to go out for a drink. That was something no women did in her father's generation. "Dad tried to be nonchalant about it, but I know he imagined my life to be much wilder than it actually was," she says. "He asked me where I was going, and I said that our plans were still fairly ambiguous. I'd let him know when we decided."

She still remembers the expression on his face when she said the word *ambiguous*. "Don't use that big college word with me," he yelled. "I just want to know where you're going."

Jenny was shocked, and fortunately her father could see that. He saw that she hadn't meant to be smart with him, and he apologized. The "big college word," plus his sense of her as a single woman in a big city school, frightened him. He had always wanted to go to college and now she was having an opportunity denied to him, and he felt doubly hurt by being left behind.

Jenny's father was quick to realize what had happened, and father and daughter were able to laugh at it later. He went to the dictionary and looked up *ambiguous* and they started playing a game about words the other might not know. There were plenty of things he could teach Jenny, too, and they mended what might have turned into a major tear in a close father-daughter relationship.

Recently, communication researchers have identified patterns of speech that intensify conflict, and this is particularly observable between a parent and adolescent. Dr. Vernon E. Cronen, studying "why people get trapped in patterns of conversation that are sources of frustrations," offers a typical example between a conservative father and a son, who attends a liberal college, but this conversation could just as easily have been between a father and a daughter.

FATHER: "Well, what did those radical professors teach you this week?"

SON: "If you weren't such a close-minded conservative, you would understand that what they are saying makes sense."

FATHER: "What I believe in is what this country was founded on."

SON: "What you believe in no longer exists." [7]

What is obvious about the exchange is how it is determined by the opening question. Each person is fixed in a response that he thinks he has to make, although it can only perpetuate antagonism. Such exchanges can be modified if each person keeps an openness. If a father asks his daughter what she is studying in history, he can also express pride that she has the opportunity to take such a course, particularly if he was deprived of that chance. He can acknowledge that her political interests afford her different kinds of interpretations.

Like Daughter, Like Daddy

Sometimes a father takes control by being overzealous on his daughter's behalf. We've all known the father who protests to the teacher his daughter's math grade, or objects to the drama coach that she did not get the lead in *Madame Butterfly*. It's as if he thinks that had he taken the test, auditioned for the part, he could have done it for her. Once in a while he tries to do even that.

In Japan, where patriarchy has traditionally been absolute, an adolescent girl from a middle-class family became seriously depressed a few years ago as she prepared for her difficult and competitive college-entrance examination. Her father believed that he could do it for her if he only had the opportunity. He dressed up in women's clothing, put on a wig, painted his face elaborately with rouge and mascara, and sat down at his daughter's desk. A professor, thinking the father looked a little too old, uncovered his identity. When the story became a sensation in Japanese newspapers, one of the most frequently telling comments was: "Such a thing could *never* have been done by a father before the War!" [8]

The Japanese father, for all of his misplaced ambitions, was at least concerned with *her* getting ahead. In the last twenty years, many fathers in this country, watching their daughters enjoying a taste of a world not available to them, have tried to find a way to play what might be described as a better-late-than-never game. This father dresses up for *his* lost time.

The long-haired, mellowed-out, middle-aged man has been satirized mercilessly in books and movies, but a daughter who has such a father is not only embarrassed. She feels deprived. Daughters speak with contempt in their voice when they recall how some of their fathers wanted to smoke pot with them. One summed it up this way: "I'd be needing advice about college or a boyfriend and my father thought he was an Indian. 'Let's pass the peace pipe and talk about it,' he'd say. I gave up smoking pot before he did since I realized that no one was going to take care of me, but me. I felt like the parent to my father."

Adolescents, we know, have difficulty in deferring instant gratification, and it may be a sign of the times that certain fathers do, too. In the 1960s, things changed. During this decade many parents supported their children's habits of sexual abandon, drink, and drugs; the parents sanctioned their children's rebellion. Fathers became rule-breakers rather than rule-givers, when what their daughters usually wanted were more thoughtful moral guidelines, offered with protection and love — even if the guidelines were to be the limits the rebellion sought to breach.

Yet, it is easy for a father to hide behind the generalizations of his daughter's generation, blaming the culture for his shortcomings and failures. One father I spoke to said he blamed "the hippies and long-haired losers, pot heads and punks" for his daughter's undisciplined, uncontrollable adolescence, until he realized that he must have played some part in it.

"She was a child of the sixties and I was a parent of the sixties," he said. "I blamed Vietnam, the new black 'awareness,' the breakthrough in civil rights, liberal soft-headedness and wimpishness. Today I'm certain that my own conduct contributed to her being very poorly equipped to deal with the decade of the eighties."

For the first thirteen years of his daughter's life, this father was a reporter on a morning paper, and that meant working nights. His wife was with his daughter, and he saw her very little. The paper and his friends took priority. Looking back, he sees that he was an absent father whose rules were uninformed with sensitivity and directly expressed affection, who discovered late that there is more to a father's rule than his right to rule.

"If I had it to do over again," he says, "I'd spend more time with her and try to listen to what she way saying and try to learn to accept her for what she is and not for what I am, and above all to tell her every day that I love her."

A teenager, like a toddler, craves loving authority. A four-year-old daughter, watching a horror movie on television, runs to her father and begs him to tell her not to watch. A teenager similarly pushes a father to the limits of his endurance, forcing him to make rules for her in a sexual relationship.

In *Endless Love,* novelist Scott Spencer dramatizes some of the confusing issues in contemporary father-daughter morality. In a passionate story of teenage love, a father in his frustration banishes his daughter's lover from the house for at least one month. The trouble, the girl's mother argues, is actually that the father had robbed his daughter of her childhood, that she had craved a strictness that her father had been incapable of offering. Daddy wanted to be hip and cool; they dropped acid together. He learned to his sorrow and anger that the family that can trip together does not necessarily stick together. Father had offered daughter a pop when what she really wanted was an old-fashioned Pop.

No matter how he tries, a father cannot reach a daughter as a peer. It is his responsibility to offer her some measure of wisdom he has acquired, at least, by virtue of being older. A fortunate daughter has a warm, attentive, and loving father who is patient, reasonable, and *firm* in the face of his daughter's rebellion.

The father-daughter relationship during her adolescence is more than ever a two-way street, and a daughter often exploits conflicts with her father in order to seek more freedom from him. The pattern is not so easily altered later when she wants to alter it. One father spoke to me of the battle scars earned during his daughter's adolescence. The fights were awesome: she slammed doors in his face, ran from the house against his instructions, and used language that he had learned only as a man. Then, suddenly, the arguments were over. An ugly duckling became a swan, graceful, serene, and composed. Nevertheless, the wounds had been inflicted, and they festered long after the vile language died, the vulgarly sophomoric posters had come down from her bedroom walls, the clangorous music had been shut down.

Adolescence is perhaps the most unsettling stage for the father of a daughter, as he first adjusts to having another adult woman in his house, and then as he helps her to plan for her future away from him. It is the stage in which a daughter crystallizes her sense of identity and moves toward new opportunities as she is thrust forward into adult life. What Gail Sheehy calls the "Seeker Self" will propel the late adolescent into a world beyond her father's house and protection. How a father encourages her in her choices, and how she makes those choices, testify to his fulfillment or his failure as father.

P A R T   F I V E

Marriage and Maturity

Mrs. Bennett rang the bell, and Miss Elizabeth was summoned to the library.

"Come here, child," cried her father, as she appeared. "I have sent for you on an affair of importance. I understand that Mr. Collins has made you an offer of marriage. Is it true?" Elizabeth replied that it was. "Very well — and this offer of marriage you have refused?"

"I have, sir."

"Very well. We now come to the point. Your mother insists upon your accepting it. Is it not so, Mrs. Bennett?"

"Yes, or I will never see her again."

"An unhappy alternative is before you, Elizabeth. From this day you must be a stranger to one of your parents. Your mother will never see you again if you do *not* marry Mr. Collins, and I will never see you again if you *do.*"

— Jane Austen
Pride and Prejudice

CHAPTER TEN

My Husband and Me

The mercury in the thermometer on the front porch had already climbed close to a hundred. The Bregman Wildcats, drenched with perspiration, trooped into the house after the usual Sunday-morning game, grateful to get out of the July sun.

I saw Daddy pull my brother Stanley aside. "Who is that skinny drink of water who played shortstop?" he asked.

Stanley pushed a hank of wet hair out of his eyes and took a cold long-neck bottle of Senate beer from my mother. "Oh, him. His name is Teddy Fields. I think Suzie probably knows him. He goes to Calvin Coolidge, too."

"Well," said Daddy, "he's a fine athlete. *Natural* ability. He ought to go places."

Stanley was wrong; though we both would be seniors at Calvin Coolidge High, we hadn't met. And for once, Daddy was wrong, too. Teddy Fields wouldn't "go places" on the baseball field, though his natural grace and athletic ability would stand him in good stead in other ways. What neither my father nor I knew then was that one of the places Teddy would go would be under a *chu-pah* in our living room to repeat the marriage vow.

Teddy and I had lockers almost side by side, but we might never have exchanged two words if Marlene Dodek hadn't come down with senior itch. Teddy and Marlene were An Item for weeks into our senior year, a constant source of lunchroom gossip, and I happened to be in the right place on the afternoon that Marlene told Teddy that she hoped they would Always Be Friends.

The corridor was dim and deserted, and I thought Teddy and I were surely the only kids left in the building, when Marlene came tripping down the corridor, earnest, determined, and breathy, as if she were trying to imitate Vivien Leigh as Scarlett O'Hara. She stopped when she got to us, standing between us as if I were not there. I stuck my face into my locker, making as much noise as I could with books and papers, trying to make myself look as disinterested as possible. When Marlene opened her mouth, I made myself as quiet as a mouse.

"I've got to tell you something," Marlene said, coyly, with the voice of a woman determined to get something over with so she could get on with something suddenly more important. "I've got to break our date on Saturday night. I think it's best for both of us, more for you than for me, really, and besides, Randy Jordan has been calling me a lot lately and I think frankly he likes me more than you do and even though you're really a sweet and wonderful guy we're really not right for each other and I've thought about this a lot and I'm sure you'll agree with me when you think about it."

By this time I was beginning to understand why Marlene always sounded so breathless, but she wasn't finished. Poor Teddy. He looked as if she had told him she was leaving for the moon. "We'll always be friends, won't we?" she asked, caressing his cheek with her hand. But before he could think of something to say, she was gone, and suddenly I began to wonder if there was something I could say.

I wasn't surprised; Marlene was the *femme fatale* who had gone through the senior boys like Stonewall Jackson through the Shenandoah Valley. Randy Jordan had three letter sweaters, in baseball, football, *and* basketball, and Marlene intended to get all three of them. Teddy Fields had only two, basketball and golf, and golf hardly counted with girls. Marlene was the girl all the senior girls loved to hate, and I was no exception. She was lavishly endowed, beautiful and blonde, always on the make, and worst of all she was a sophomore. She made us all feel so old. It wasn't that the senior girls wanted the senior boys for ourselves, it was just that we hated to see empty-headed younger girls (the "airheads" of my daughters' generation) make fools of them. We were very jealous of Marlene Dodek doing what we had wanted to do when we were sophomores.

Senior girls thought of senior boys as brothers rather than boyfriends. It was *declassé* for senior girls to date a *boy* in high school; all the popular senior girls went with "men" from Georgetown, George Washington U., American, even from the nearby University of Maryland. *Really* popular senior girls made their reputations with the occasional boys home for the weekend from Yale, Princeton, Columbia, NYU, or the Big Ten schools. Girls like Marlene Dodek brought out the best of our sisterly instincts.

I put on my most sympathetic sisterly smile when Teddy watched Marlene Dodek walk away. Teddy shrugged his shoulders, which were suddenly broader than I remembered, and looked more wistful than wounded. "You really are too nice for her, you know." My voice sounded like it came out of a balloon above the head of a girl in Love Comics.

"Well, I never understood her," he said, with a sigh. "I asked her out once and right away she acted as though we were going steady. I didn't have the money to take her to the movies every weekend and she'd get mad. I should feel bad, but I don't, except that I don't have a date for Saturday night."

"I'm sure you can get another."

"You wouldn't want to go with me, would you?"

The rest would be history.

I did not fall quickly "in love" with Teddy Fields, and in the beginning our intimacy was the intimacy of good friends, of brother and sister. There was none of the "love at first slight" that I had for Rudy Dawson. Since Teddy was "a man on the rebound" there were no illusions of deathless passion or a love for the ages; consequently we both could be open and free with our innermost thoughts and feelings. We did in fact become very good friends.

Our first conversations naturally focused on how awful the other woman was. I listened to Teddy's tales of woe, feeling very superior as I analyzed the transparent wiles of younger women. Teddy was only six months older than I was, but I took on the air of female maturity that separates teenage girls from teenage boys. It was real enough; the female of the species does mature faster. Together, we were close to the archetypal pattern of teenage "love": I was more open, sensitive, better able to speak out on issues of vulnerability; Teddy loved hearing how he was vulnerable, sensitive, misunderstood, a misbegotten exile from a Greek tragedy.

Because we were both seniors, with many friends in common, we found many occasions to hang out together, from pasting up pages in the Coolidge Corral, the yearbook, to auditions for the Coolidge Colt senior variety show. When I ran for senior-class secretary, he sang the inevitable campaign song off-key in my campaign quartet: "If you knew Suzie. . . ." When I won, he threw the victory party. Between senior parties and celebrations we talked about our future, our fears of leaving home and the anticipation of going to college.

We came of age in the Eisenhower years, "those fabulous fifties," and though we lived in the nation's capital, the political world held little significance for us. We lived in a Calvin Coolidge cocoon. I have friends who grew up in Maine and Oregon who remember more fifties political folklore. Our innocence is astonishing, compared to the generations of seniors in the following decades. I was introduced to Freud only when I went off to the University of Wisconsin that following year. I pronounced his name as if it rhymed with *prude*.

In a city where everyone is from Texarkana, Cambridge, or Sacramento, everyone is astonished to meet someone who actually grew up in Washington. So new friends are amazed when they learn that my husband was the boy who took me to the senior prom. Because we met when we were still children, we played out together the thrust-and-parry that most of us have with a procession of different people before we marry. We went together through the stages of mating that marked young love in the 1950s, moving up the hierarchy of going together, going steady, getting pinned, getting engaged, and, four years after graduating together at Calvin Coolidge High, getting married one warm June afternoon in my home on Yorktown Road. There was nothing but sunshine on the reception in the garden, which was ablaze with the geraniums, gladiolas, and the Paul Scarlet roses that make Washington such a glorious city in the late spring. During those four years before marriage we argued, dated others, even went off to different colleges in widely separated states, but we always ran back to each other, eager and anxious for the familiar and the comfortable.

My father liked Teddy, who took the trouble to charm my mother. For them he was a step up from the beer-drinking boys at the nearby universities. My father talked sports with him, getting him to play with the Wildcats on Sundays, giving him pointers on how to handle a fast ball and a subtle word to go slow with his daughter. My mother warmed to his boyishness and limitless appetite. No one appreciated her cooking more than Teddy.

But I don't believe either of them expected us to marry. Teddy was too much the boy next door, whom the girl leaves behind when she finds the real thing.

Great Expectations

But even in those first days, when a date with a senior boy lacked glamour, I had a tiny glimmer that Teddy would take care of me as my father had, that he had what it took to be a man, like Daddy. At sixteen, when we met, he had none of the makings of a Big Daddy, nor would he ever. But he had an easy sense of self, of his own masculinity, of enjoying the company of the boys almost as much as the company of the girls, and I had an inkling that he would learn to master worldly situations soon enough. But it did not happen overnight.

My mother, contrary to the usual script, was less thrilled than my father when we set the wedding date. I think my father knew Teddy better, calling on insights from his coaching days, watching him handle a ball with a tough hop, a 3-2 pitch when he was up at bat, with the winning run on base. I think he knew Teddy could stand stress. My mother, I always thought, dreamed of her daughter marrying a Yale-trained surgeon, a physician from Penn, or at least a Harvard lawyer, and Teddy was studying to be a dentist at NYU. But she never spoke against him. My father saw dentistry as a prosperous profession, no doubt remembering the protection of that upstairs dentist in those hectic bookmaking days. My mother saw us as very young with so much to learn, even though at twenty-one I was three years older than she was when she married my father.

They were both somewhat relieved, too. After all, I was moving from the safety of their house to a respectable married position, without having to taste the crueler, more adventurous world of work — and the temptations of sin — as a single woman.

In the year of our engagement, my mother threw herself into the preparations for our wedding and my father faded into the background, becoming the passive father who paid the bills of caterers and couturiers. I have no memory of my father during that year, not until a half-hour before musicians from the National Symphony played Beethoven's Third String Trio, disappointing the guests, who are still waiting for the familiar "Here Comes the Bride." He walked into my dressing room to admire me in my wedding gown, uncorking a magnum of Mumm's. The cork hit the ceiling, the bubbles in the glass made me high before I took the first sip, and my father told me not to be nervous. "Time will take care of everything," he said. He, too, was scared sober.

There was plenty to be nervous about. His daughter had moved the male center of her universe to another man, from a worldly man in his late forties to a twenty-one-year-old innocent novice. Having earned the right to wear white, and facing the delicious ordeal of learning what Lilah Rafferty, the first girl in our class to do "it," was believed to have learned in the backseat of her boyfriend's 1937 Ford, I was terrified.

The champagne helped. But for the photographs, presented later in the white-leather bindings my mother ordered, I wouldn't remember much of my wedding. I walked on my father's arm through an aisle to a circle of four friends who held the *chupah* over our heads, and this time when the groom stepped hard on the ritual glass, it splintered noisily. A kiss, and more champagne, followed by more kisses and champagne, until Ted (no longer "Teddy" to me) and I got into a blue-and-white Chevrolet convertible, a gift from my father. We drove off for a two-month trip across the country and into Mexico, but two blocks away and around the corner we stopped to cut the strings of shoes and tin cans streaming from behind the car, and several miles farther Ted found a car wash to clean off the boasts and admonitions his friends had scrawled across the car with soap and shaving cream: HOT SPRINGS TONIGHT! and WATCH WASHINGTON CROW! Ours was a wedding of its times.

The honeymoon was a succession of small shocks. I was shocked when I saw how tentative and unsure of himself Ted was when we registered for our first night at the Williamsburg Lodge. He didn't do it the way my father would have done it. Daddy would have walked in with commanding authority, and a fistful of bills at the ready, and we would have moved into our room with the assurance that we were doing things the way they ought to be done.

The next shock was that "going all the way" didn't seem nearly as wonderful as doing everything *but*. The earth stood dead still, it didn't turn; where were those whistles, bells, and golden horns? I couldn't hear even a squeak, not for a week of clumsy nights. And then *it* happened. The lights went on all over the world. I never wanted to live through blackouts again.

By the time we got to Mexico City we felt we had lost the newlywed look and thrilled at the abandon of being on our own, climbing the ancient Aztec pyramids outside Mexico City, laughing at the dismal tourist attraction called the floating gardens of Xochimilco, which we called the floating *salesman* of Xochimilco. Ted bought me a beautiful silver and copper bracelet at Tasco, and we glowed with anticipation for everything to come. Life stretched endlessly in front of us, one constant turn-on.

We roamed south to the Yucatan, over the Mayan site of Chi-chen Itza, where the Mayans threw young virgins into a sacrificial pool, and I laughed, enormously pleased with myself, when my new husband teased me about my lost eligibility for the rite.

The U.S. immigration officers laughed when they found a few grains of rice in the car when we crossed the border at Nogales, Arizona. "You shouldn't be carrying plant life around in your car," they said winking at each other. "But we'll let you go, you look like an old married couple." I felt pleased with myself again; my respect for Ted had grown enormously, too.

Las Vegas was to be the spree of the trip. Biggie, my father's friend from the old days, had arranged things. We were installed in a large bridal suite at the Desert Inn, where champagne was cooling in a silver bucket, glistening with beads of frost, next to a bouquet of long-stemmed American Beauty roses. The man at the desk handed over envelopes with assignments to ringside tables for Frank Sinatra, Sid Caesar, and Dean Martin and Jerry Lewis (who were a comedy couple themselves, then). Everything was on the house. Each night a clerk handed us an envelope stuffed with bills from Biggie, who wanted us to have fun in the casino, too.

All great fun, but it wasn't our world. Having become, in our eyes, experienced travelers, the real fun was searching out cheap motels, bargain-priced roadside restaurants, and inexpensive amusements along the way. The other was the extravagant world of my father's; the bargains were the world of my twenty-one-year-old husband, and it was his world that I was embracing with growing enthusiasm.

We drove east, toward New York City, where we would be living for the next three years while Ted finished his dental studies at NYU. I became a feature-story writer for *World Week* magazine, the current-events reader that many of us had used in junior high school. Our first task was to find an apartment, which wasn't easy, even then. We had some wedding-present money, but no bank account. No landlord would give us a lease; it was Daddy to the rescue. He flew to New York, signed the lease for a one bedroom on Gramercy Park, and paid the rent for three years. This was his wedding present, Daddy said; but I knew that it was also his way of making sure that his little girl could still live in the manner he thought she ought. Ted accepted the present, graciously and gratefully, and I didn't complain.

When the Husband Pays a High Price

In those first few years I alternately loved and hated my husband for not being like my father, and often loved and hated at the same time. I loved him for his easy openness, boyish innocence, spontaneity, his ability to laugh things away, as well as a reasonable respect for money. But I hated the square uprightness of his life, his naive trust in others, an inability to be extravagant without pain. I am mortified when I think of it now, but I hated our anonymity. I craved my father's flashy life, his connections with the sporting big time, the easy insiders, kibitzing with headwaiters and gamblers, his rendezvous with danger. I missed the bigger-than-life *scene* that always surrounded us when I went somewhere with my father. I still wanted a Big Daddy, but what I had was a husband drawn to true-to-life scale. Ted and I had still to forge a life together, and I still wanted a glamorous life handed to me.

In painful retrospect, I see myself trying to make Ted into my father by playing the helpless Little Girl to a Big Man image of my own construction. If I thought Ted seemed unsure of himself, unlike my father ever was, I tried to double my own insecurity, to feel more dependent than ever. If I thought Ted said something stupid, something my father would *never* have said, I said something dumber still, which was not difficult. Ted chose the restaurants, Ted got the theater tickers, deciding alone which price seats we wanted. I wouldn't even order from a menu without deferring to him.

"What do you want?"

"What do *you* want?"

Without meaning to, Daddy, who had not hidden himself from me, had hidden instead the harsh edges of real life away from my innocent girlish gaze. I was suddenly thrust into this real world, a world where most people aren't flashy and flamboyant, and a world where helpless little girls are neither cute nor successful.

Many women and men have spoken to me of the difficulty a father creates for his daughter, once she is married. As the husband struggles to exhibit manhood, she sees that he suffers by comparison to the more accomplished older man. A father maintains control of his daughter in fantasy and sometimes in fact. The most well-meaning father can intrude on his "helpless" daughter's new life with money and gifts. Bubba, a forty-seven-year-old man in New Orleans, told me his story of the unusual beginning of a marriage:

"I married the girl I had been obsessed with all through college. She came to me after an absence of a year with the story of a broken heart. Her boyfriend had run away when she told him she was pregnant, and married someone else as quickly as he could. That was a cad's way out in those days.

"Abortion was illegal and against all our beliefs, even if she and her family had thought about it, and when she poured out her story of pain and humiliation my heart broke. I gulped twice and asked her for the hundredth time to marry me. She said yes immediately. It turned out, she said, that she had always loved me. I didn't really care. My sisters were aghast. My mother was crushed. My father thought I was a fool, though I think he did grudgingly admire my clumsy attempt to make everyone think the baby was mine. I was finally going to wed my true love, and she was only a little bit pregnant."

Everything in this Southern Gothic tale might have turned out all right but for the girl's father, and in the beginning the father professed to be eternally grateful to Bubba. Once he was convinced that the baby was not Bubba's, he no longer wanted to hang him from the live-oak tree in his backyard. But he didn't want to relinquish his daughter, either, and the daughter didn't want him to. After the baby, a girl, was born, the wife's father took the new "father" aside and told him that he would pick up the bill for all the medical expenses. By this time the young husband realized that the situation he was in was fairly bizarre, and the only way he could hold on to his self-respect was to take *all* the responsibility for the marriage, the baby, and the bills. He borrowed two hundred dollars from his bank to get his wife and the baby out of the hospital. The father was furious and so was his daughter.

"When in the end I paid," says Bubba, "the father's bitterness over his daughter's sexual indiscretion was turned on me. The marriage was probably doomed, anyway, but there was no hope after she took her father's side in this dispute. The father wanted to hold on to his little girl, and she wanted to remain that little girl. She filed for divorce three months later."

Turning down gifts that make life comfortable is never easy, but if a father seeks to maintain his daughter's dependency on him through these gifts, the daughter will find it exceedingly difficult to make an independent life of her own. After a daughter marries, a father's role in her life is ambiguous and he must tread carefully not to intrude. Even without meddling, a father can become more fantasy than reality in a young bride's mind as the Big Daddy of her memory looms larger than the young husband with whom she has tied the knot for her future.

Life without Father

Colette Dowling identifies this cultivated helplessness as the Cinderella Complex. Her thesis is that "personal, psychological dependency — the deep wish to be taken care of by others — is the chief force holding women down today." [1] She examines the influences of parents and teachers, and academic, cultural, and political attitudes and interpretations that contribute to the feminine fear of independence. The only way to break through these inhibiting obstacles, she contends, is to emancipate the self from within.

Many women look at themselves and find a vaguely defined cultural conspiracy to explain why they cannot assert themselves. A fear of independence surely inhibited my behavior with Ted, and no doubt the larger culture contributed a malign influence. But a narrower lens with a sharper focus gives a more accurate picture

of the way we were. It was essential that Ted be smarter, more sophisticated, surer about everything than I was, because if he
wasn't I had surely married the wrong man: I had gambled and
lost Big Daddy.

I spoiled many evenings out, complaining about the table, the
wine, the tacky ambience. If our theater tickets weren't sixth or
seventh row on the aisle in the orchestra, as my father would have
ordered from one of his friends in the business, the evening was a
bust.

I never consciously compared Ted to my father. I never actually said, "Daddy wouldn't do things like that." I didn't even
think that. I simply thought that there was a better way of doing
those things and my husband didn't know how to manage them.
At the root of all my criticism, however, were those unconscious
comparisons to Daddy. Anger and irritation never intruded when
Ted and I went to art galleries, museums, concerts, and the opera,
the kinds of things that would have been alien to my father. Only
when I relived childish memories of life with father did I feel Ted
measuring short. But the short measure was contagious. Without
Big Daddy's reflected glory, *I* was a flop.

These patterns developed almost imperceptibly during the
years we lived in New York City, and they became pervasive when
Ted graduated and was ordered to military service as a captain in
the air force, assigned to command a dental clinic at an air force
base at Greenham Common in England's West Country. We got
an apartment without heat or charm in the little town of Newbury.
Because wives of American servicemen were not allowed to work,
I set out to read the books I had never had time for, and started
writing short stories of my own. Away from family and friends,
without those supports that help to keep a troubled couple together, our marriage began to fray at the edges.

When Ted's two years were almost finished, we began to talk
about our future together. Ted didn't think we had one. I was
dumbfounded. He wanted to travel in Europe for a while, alone.

"Without *me*?"

"Yes."

"Are you coming down with the five-year itch?"

"No, I'm finally facing up to reality after five years. I'm tired of your trying to make me into something I'm not and don't want to be. We've been married five years, and if anybody asked you who you were it wouldn't occur to you to say that you're Suzanne Fields or even Ted Fields's wife. In your eyes you're still Bo Bregman's daughter."

My mouth went suddenly dry and I couldn't have said anything even if there had been anything to say. But my husband wasn't finished.

"You want the flash and tinsel of a life that you think is glamorous and exciting and I can't offer you anything but an ordinary living in the ordinary world where you live, like it or not, Bo's life wasn't glamorous to him. Just ask him. Why do you think he left it?"

I sat still and silent, not believing.

"You're not Daddy's little kitten any longer, and you're not the professor's little pet, wiggling your cute little ass on the front row with the correct answer to the question. You're a grown woman in a world a lot bigger than the one you grew up in and if you don't want to take advantage of it, that's your misfortune. But it's not going to be mine."

I was stung and scared, but then reassured: Daddy could straighten this out. He would talk to Ted. He could make him understand why he couldn't leave. We didn't talk much for several days. Ted was busy with his airline reservations and his travel folders from the Greek tourist bureau.

I had never felt so alone, such a sense of abandonment. Having at last enough sense not to call my father, I retreated into private thoughts. Echoes of Emily Dickinson played faintly in my consciousness:

> I'm nobody! Who are you?
> Are you nobody, too?
> Then there's a pair of us — don't tell!
> They'd banish us, you know.

I felt banished. Where could I go? Not back to my parents, nor could I turn to a career. I had none. Maybe I should have a baby, quickly. That might be disastrous, but surely not impossible, I thought smugly. It was the beginning of a new searching of soul. For two years I had been writing short stories, putting each one away in the bottom of a drawer in a living-room desk. I began to keep a diary, confiding to it my every thought, seeking to find why I clung so tenaciously to the illusion that it was someone else who was to determine who I was, how I felt.

I went to Harley Street in London to talk to a therapist. He told me that I had entered into an unconscious contract with my husband, not unlike the unconscious pact I had made years before with my father. The contract went something like this: if Ted would provide the kicks, be the Big Man, I would pay any price to help him maintain his image. Ted wasn't keeping his bargain because the contract was only in my head. He didn't sign on. I was playing out the role of the little girl but I didn't have anyone to "play to." I was paying premium price for second-rate goods. Since I knew they weren't worth it, I complained, a lot. I tried to change not myself, but Ted. I wanted to sink comfortably again into the role of daughter, not wife; a dependent child, not independent woman.

I cried a lot, too. This time I had no father to toss me into the air like a beanbag, to help me forget what tears were about. I began to contemplate a life outside of marriage.

I knew I could survive. I had worked in New York, and I could work somewhere else to support myself again. Work was not the issue, and it didn't sound exciting or even engaging without having Ted to meet at home at day's end. The reasons I had for getting married were the reasons to stay married. Ted was the man I wanted to spend my life with, the man I wanted to father my children.

I could not reorder life's timetables, nor tell Ted to come back when I was older. Either we worked it out now, or never.

Shedding the Daughter Dependency

I knew that what I liked about Ted had nothing to do with the superficial comparisons to my father. At the root of the attraction were the substantial qualities he and my father held in common: an ethical core of judgment, a fair-minded willingness to suspend judgment until all the facts were available, a willingness to talk about whatever was bothering us, a desire to judge the self against the self, not against the superficial fashions of society, and most importantly, a sense of what it means to be a man, the courage to face without whining, rough-and-tumble responsibility in the masculine world. He, like my father, was not a complainer nor the wimp who became so fashionable in the years when we were young. He didn't want to talk endlessly about how awful the world was, but noted the defects, and rather than feel sorry for himself, looked around to find the best way to master the small part of it he lived in. I thought of a passage from Ring Lardner: "Life is real and life is tough, and three out of three people die. So shut up and ... drink, or deal." Ted was a man's man and a woman's man. When things were best between us I always felt the thrill of being a woman, protected by his commitment to me, safe in his love.

After five years of marriage, I still wanted to be a little girl. I had yet to understand that femininity was the natural expression of being an adult woman, too. I had not yet made the connection between feeling feminine and feeling competent. I remembered the thrill and the titillation of being Daddy's Little Girl, but I had forgotten the substance of our heart-to-heart talks, when he tried to show me the necessity of learning to look after myself because no other person could give me an identity. My relationship with my father had indeed changed from one of Big Daddy/Little Girl to Proud Father/Adult Woman, but when I married I had foolishly attempted to recreate a childlike past. I wanted love, but not responsibility.

When a love bond is *symbiotic* in the best sense of that word, when each person provides something the other wants and respects and does not have, it becomes the essence of a good male-female relationship, whether of father and daughter, or husband and wife. The nature of the symbiosis must differ in each relationship; had I confused the two?

Being meek, dependent, and extravagantly feminine, being a *wife,* surely entitled a woman to require that her man be more fa-

ther than husband. Little by little, I realized that I was "not enti-
tled," that my proper role was as adult companion, not as Daddy's
Little Girl. The Pauline admonition to the early Christians at
Corinth echoed in my Jewish consciousness:

> When I was a child, I spake as a child, I understood as a child,
> I thought as a child: but when I became a man, I put away childish
> things.
> For now we see through a glass, darkly; but then face to face: now I
> know in part; but then shall I know even as also I am known.
> And now abidith faith, hope, charity, these three; but the greatest of
> these is charity. (I Corinthians 13:11–13.) [2]

Time was at hand to put away my childish fantasies. This was
not easy, and it did not happen quickly. But I persuaded Ted to
play the odds that things could change between us, that if he could
summon the faith, there was hope that I could return the genuine
love of a real woman. We wandered through Europe together,
talked with growing confidence of the future, and returned at last
to America to settle once more, this time for good, in the town
where we grew up.

My father eagerly offered us one of his newly built houses in the
suburbs; this time we said no. We found the house we wanted, a
turn-of-the-century row house that had gone to seed as a flop-
house on a street of similar houses. The neighborhood was well
known to the rape and robbery details of the Metropolitan Police
Department, but Ted guessed (correctly) that the neighborhood
was on its way back.

Daddy didn't approve, but he had learned years before the wisdom of the proverbs: "If you can't beat 'em, join 'em." This time
we *borrowed* the money from Daddy to make our down payment,
and a few years later he took us out to dinner to celebrate our
making the final payment on the loan.

Ted ordered — and paid for — the champagne. Daddy was
right again: Ted *did* have "natural ability."

Father's Daughter/
Husband's Wife

I had learned, almost the hardest way, that marriage is a relationship that requires a mature dependency. Two people depend on each other for different things; each person carries a responsibility for the other, a responsibility that grows out of love, nurtured by concern. It is all so easy for a woman to cultivate an immature dependency on her husband, particularly if she marries when young, when she is still dependent on her father.

Dependency on my father was more a dependency of the mind than an actual reliance on my father. He did not interfere in our marriage. Even the rent payments were a present, generous and without strings. The strings were the strings to my emotions; they were not of my father's doing, but of mine.

Little-girl wives make the mistake of measuring their husbands, who are from twenty-five to forty years younger than their fathers, by the abilities, the personalities, and styles their fathers forged only through years of experience. At the root of this antagonism lies the fear that husbands will not take care of them as fathers had done. Little-girl wives have learned that they can trust their fathers; they have not yet learned this about the men they have married, nor have they learned to trust themselves. They have not allowed themselves to consider that a marriage is a combination of two people, but that what a man *does* cannot reflect what a woman *is*.

The half of the identity a girl-child inherits from her father is usually the half that engages the world outside the family. In the past, as in my family, it was the father's work that identified the family. The mother projected a strong identity *within* the house, but in the world beyond the front door, the father's actions reflected on all.

When I married I placed that burden on my husband when in fact we were starting with a new slate in a world that was very changed; husband-and-wife roles were not so clearly differentiated as once they were. Intellectually, I knew that; emotionally, I did not. Everything that Ted did, or said, or believed, reflected on me, or so I thought, and I criticized him (in the old days it was called nagging) to get him to change, to reflect a brighter glory. The mistake was one that many women share.

All know about the woman who "slaves" to put her husband through medical or law school, only to find that once he has his degree he wants a more educated, more intellectually rounded, and often younger wife. Such a compact works only where men and women build their marriage on clearly understood divisions of labor, responsibilities, and *commitments*. In the world in which we now live, where the implications of marriage have changed, radically, and divorce confers little if any stigma, the marriage contract, like William Butler Yeats's "centre," "cannot hold." A woman's responsibility in the home is secured by the man with increasing difficulty. Cultural assumptions as well as personal perceptions and economic foundations of the marriage contract have moved.

Often we are still trapped emotionally by old assumptions, even as we understand intellectually that things have changed. I saw changes around me, even espoused many of them long before I had experienced or understood them deep inside the heart, whence motivation springs. I was married in a time when a wife's responsibility was expanding in ways our grandmothers could never have dreamed of. Many of us suffered from an emotional "perception gap."

. In the years after we left London, Ted and I had to renegotiate our expectations. I went back to school and to work. He assumed the greater financial burden; I took on the greater responsibility for managing family matters. Because I taught at a nearby university and contributed to newspapers and magazines, I had the more flexible schedule. I spent more time with our three children. Nevertheless, he was a far greater presence in their day-to-day lives than my father was in mine. The expectations our children will carry into their marriages are impossible to foretell; marriage is, after all, a private institution recognized by public policy, and an institution that continues to move away from traditional moorings. Their marriages are likely to be as different from ours as ours was from that of our parents. Because marriage is both a personal relationship and a social contract, the statutory and natural laws that govern it are determined by the needs of two people *and* society.

Why do people marry? It's a question with many answers, the most obvious residing in the need to care for our young, the most helpless of all the species and for the longest period of time. But people marry before they decide to have children and often without intending to procreate. Having children is often the result of a successful marriage, not the cause.

Remembrances of Parents Past

Marriage is the "irreducible unit of social organization, rooted in biological reality," says Henry V. Dicks, the British psychiatrist who studies and works with married couples. Dr. Dicks and others who espouse the theories of the British object-relations school of psychology believe that two people come together not simply to raise the young or gratify the instinctual needs (Freud's explanation), but because they have a need to feel needed by another. How a partner satisfies this need, they believe, is determined by the influences of the former family life with a set of parents. "Our experience [at the Tavistock Clinic in London] based on the observation of guilt feelings in unhappy marriage partners, of their attempts to improve their relationships and to protect their children from witnessing angry scenes and . . . conflicts, leads one to think that deep down mankind is aware of the biological value of the stable, united family which also offers the spouses themselves one of the greatest and simplest foundations for a sense of personal worth and maturity." [1]

Marriage is also about feeling safe. In certain cultures and societies, such safety is physical, but in modern Western society, psychologists now observe, the safety is more psychological because it provides the expectancy that someone will be there with whom to face the vicissitudes of life. [2]

Because we are all concerned about security, both for ourselves and for our families, and because security dwells in our sense of self as well as in our physical safety, it should not surprise that most of us seek security in the familiar. If a father protected us, or we think he did, we seek a man who can at least do as well as he did. When we cannot find what we feel is familiar, we either weave illusions about our reality or we attempt to renovate the men we have, hoping to make them into reasonable facsimiles of what we think we want. Such enterprise is almost always doomed, but in the fortunate cases a crisis can help a couple reevaluate their marriage and establish a relationship more in tune with their changing perceptions of themselves.

Just as we go through many different stages of perception in life with father, so must we grow and change in relation to life with our husband. Ideally, we have some clarity about our relationship with our father before we chose the man we marry, and we are aware of the pitfalls that we must avoid. But like most of life's tougher lessons, most of us have to learn about our fathers, our husbands, and ourselves the hard way.

For example, women learn, usually the hard way, that it's a mistake to marry a man for what she thinks *he* will be in the world, because she actually has very little control over what he becomes. Martha, forty-four, a former wife of a former congressman, married her husband because she thought he had a genuine chance to be President of the United States. As she was to learn, her ambition was woefully misplaced.

Martha's father was the mayor of her town, a medium-sized city in the Middle West, when she was a child, and she loved the limelight. She often had her picture in the paper, eating an ice-cream sundae in a soda shop or modeling in a charity benefit. She wanted more. "In those days I didn't think of actively engaging in politics myself," she says. "Running for office and haggling with men I couldn't stand in smoke-filled hotel rooms were not things I wanted to do or places I wanted to be. But I was determined to do one thing: to get myself a fish bigger than Daddy, a real Kingfish. I got one, all right. By the time he was swimming in his little Washington fish pond he could have drowned for all I cared. The esteem was mutual."

Others wanted what Martha had. "There are groupies, of a sort, even for first-term congressmen, and by the end of his first term he had forgotten about me, about the people who elected him, and about why he had come to Washington in the first place. He wasn't reelected, but neither was I. There's always another woman in Washington, usually younger and with better connections. I wouldn't dream of marrying another politician."

Being the daughter of the mayor bore no resemblance to being the wife of a congressman. Looking for a shortcut to personal development, Martha found instead a short-circuit. By placing so little value on herself and too much on the man, she sacrificed a major piece of her identity for an illusion, learning too late that mature identity cannot be bestowed by another. Martha had to learn to distinguish the superficial from the significant. Martha the Mayor's Daughter made good copy; so could, on rare occasion, Martha the Congressman's Wife. But who was Martha? That's the question she had to ask herself, and she had no answer.

Daughters of politicians, stars of stage, screen, and tube, and sports celebrities frequently suffer from confused identity. They always know how they will be introduced to other people, how they will be seen, and can guess what people say when they leave; how tempting to seek another man like Daddy to perpetuate such an image.

Martha believes now that she was never in love with her husband, but in thrall to his prospects as she was in thrall earlier to her father's public image. Her husband's image, more than his love, was what she hoped to share. When they divorced she became invisible. She took back her maiden name and began to forge her own identity. When she realized that what she understood about politics was marketable, she found another mission on Capitol Hill, and helps to run another congressman's campaigns from behind the scenes. "I enjoy my invisibility," she says, "because I'm the one responsible for it."

In Pursuit of a Daddy-Fix

Because marriage provides us with obvious echoes of our parents' lives together and strong memories of our early lives in relation to theirs, early married life can be an intense psychological proving ground to show us who we are, separate from them. In it, we play out many different psychological levels of experience.

The way our mothers bind us with the uncut umbilical cord, tugging at us long after we have left home, has been much remarked. No metaphor so dramatically suggests our connection to our fathers. But the attachment is just as real, and fraught with a danger more deadly than an uncut cord: sexual addiction. A daughter says to herself: When I am with Daddy I feel so good; why can't other men make me feel so wonderful? The promise Daddy offers is love unconsummated, the stuff of poets, an omnipresent longing that goes unfulfilled. Appetite becomes craving. Like a junkie needing a fix, this daughter yearns constantly for a "Daddy-fix." When Daddy is no longer available to her, this daughter seeks a substitute elsewhere, searching for a high, a good feeling, blessed euphoria. Daddy becomes dangerous without knowing it.

The promiscuous heroine of William Styron's novel *Lie Down in Darkness* is such a woman. She cannot kick her Daddy-habit, and as though to punish herself for this weakness she moves from man to man, affair to affair, before her husband's eyes. She finally seeks the ultimate punishment in suicide, crying out: "Oh, my Lord, I am dying . . . and oh! my father, oh! my darling . . . I fly into your arms."

A parent, and particularly a father, must nurture capability and self-confidence through example no less than through guidance. A child, like a delicate new flower, needs both sun and shelter. The most painful truth a father must accept is that his daughter, for all her vulnerability to danger and her susceptibility to temptations, must be encouraged to *walk* to her independence or she will run to it prematurely, and she may run from man to man to man in search of her father, even as she thinks she is running away from him.

A woman who runs compulsively from her father's home to a husband's arms bypasses important stages of personality development, and is likely to get stuck in what psychologists describe as "the merger stage" of marriage.

The merger stage develops out of romantic love, echoed in the lyrics of the country song, "I can't see me without you." The merger stage of marriage tricks a couple into believing that two can act as one. Life teaches quickly enough that two cannot live as cheaply as one, and the statistics of divorce expose the absurdity of "psychological unity." The merger stage, nevertheless, is often a stage of marriage that must be muddled through.

The need to merge with the loved one has many explanations. It has its echoes "from the time when we were one with our mothers." [3] Psychologist Howard Halpern sees it as containing strong vestiges of "attachment hunger" for mother. [4] Nowhere is the merger marriage so clearly observed than in the formula melodrama with Daddy as Villain:

> "But you can't marry that man."
> "But I will marry that man."
> And she does marry that man.

The man is usually everything that Daddy is not: he is warm, loving, passionate, tender, *and* he saves her from a terrible, horrible no-good authoritarian father. In the movie, the fade-out leaves the daughter in the lover's embrace. Real-life endings are usually less romantic. Romance, in fact, wears off when there is no dragon left to slay; problems emerge as soon as the couple discovers the need for a little space between them. This recognition rarely occurs simultaneously in each partner, and the woman is likely to be the first one threatened. The fear, anxiety, anger, frustration, and ambivalence that she had felt toward her father is transferred to her husband, even as he is trying to achieve some separate existence.

So gradually does this occur that the wife cannot see or feel the change, not until a tiny voice deep within the recesses of her memory tells her: "I've heard this somewhere before." The knot in the pit of her belly is familiar, and the flash of memory merges with dawning recognition: she looks across the dinner table and the man opposite her suddenly looks, sounds, and feels like the man she grew up with.

What follows in this chapter are two life stories of women who ran from father to husband. In one a daughter thinks she is marrying her father's opposite; in the other, she thinks she is marrying someone like her father, only better. Coincidentally, both husbands were in the same profession as the woman's father. Not so coincidentally, both women were deceived by their expectations. In very different ways, their eyes were opened to distorted perceptions.

Each of these women finds out that without meaning to, she has shaped her marriage into a replication of her relationship with her father. Shana, the daughter of a judge, moves beyond the point of no return. For her there is no way out but divorce. Cathy, the daughter of a small-town Midwestern lawyer, uses her recognition to turn herself around. She chooses to stay married, but with a fresh understanding of who she is and who she will be to her husband. Both Shana and Cathy bring to their marriage their unique personal history, their special needs for security, *and* a powerful hidden desire to continue the game of hide-and-seek with Daddy.

Here Comes the Judge

First, Shana, thirty-eight, remembers how it was for her: "Joseph was more than I dreamed of. Tall, dark, and handsome, he looked like a young Gregory Peck. He was a judge, like my father, a fact that enormously pleased me. I didn't see any other similarities, not at first.

"Naturally, when my father met Joseph it was hate at first sight. He said Joseph was too old for me [the difference was twelve years], and was not likely to treat me kindly because he had 'cold eyes.' 'If it's a judge you want to take care of you,' he told me, 'you already have one.' I was sure my father was jealous."

The antagonism of her father only fanned Shana's passion. She was sure she and her Husband, the Judge, would live happily ever after because they did *not* have her father's blessings."

To Shana her father represented tough, masculine intellect; both Shana and her mother were put down constantly for showing too much feeling. Their arguments were usually dismissed as emotional and irrelevant. "My father always trivialized my contributions to the dinner table conversations," Shana said. "Only what he had to say was important. He was the sole arbiter of morality. I was belittled for 'thinking like a woman.' The awful part of it is that I believed he was right, I believed that he *was* more reasonable, more rational, more knowledgeable than I was. It made no difference that I was an all-A student, not to my father; I was supposed to purr like a pussycat."

Had Shana learned to challenge her father, when she was younger or over other issues, she might not have married someone like him, but the first serious opportunity to challenge him was the opportunity to marry Joseph against her father's will. Because she had fallen into a passive role, it was easy to continue in it with Joseph, who had "charisma."

"Now I realize that that charisma was his being a sexy version of my father. Where my father was a ruthless despot, Joseph was benevolent. My father was cruel, Joseph was unambiguously fair. My father was coldly intellectual, Joseph was heroically tough-minded."

Later, as passion between Joseph and Shana died, she began to see her husband as ruthless, cruel, and cold, too. She had come full circle, as well: "I acted the same way with both of them. When the temperature of our romance cooled, I had the same feelings of antagonism toward Joseph that I had toward my father."

In her other life — her career — Shana was a very capable lawyer, who won environmental cases against opponents with powerful, capable lawyers. The emotions her father held in contempt infused her intellect with power and eloquence. She became a mighty pleader. She did not defer easily to clients, still less easily to colleagues on issues of substance. But in her most private relationship she was her daddy's little girl. Why?

Childhood passions often erupt in adult intimacies. Sexual intercourse, the ultimate and most intimate human experience, engenders regression, Harold Kaufman, a Washington, D.C., psychiatrist, told me. "Passion puts people at the mercy of those whom they love. Losing oneself in ecstasy, surrendering to a powerful force, are very positive experiences in lovemaking. But the other side of sexual excitement can be anxiety, fear of loss, humiliation, fear of being dominated, renewed fears of dependency. For some women these fears overwhelm all else, and as passion for their husbands wanes, they feel doubly incapable of surmounting these supposed challenges to their vulnerabilities.

"Father-daughter patterns often do not emerge in a marriage until a lot of the 'modeling' has worn off," Dr. Kaufman says. "People act the way they think they are expected to act only for so long — an insecure daughter will willingly act as the submissive wife and the autocratic husband will play the part of the powerful protector. Other neurotic patterns of personality are hidden for a time by romantic expectations and passionate sexual exercises. Both partners try hard to please each other. But eventually married life becomes a daily routine instead of a romantic weekend.

An emotionally insecure woman will begin to look for slights, the sort of things she encouraged in the early stages of romance."

When their marriage exuded passion, when they were still emotionally inseparable, Shana agreed with almost everything her husband had to say. "He knew so much more than I. He was so intelligent. I thought I had married a man smarter than I was and I could relax in *his* intellect."

Shana is typical of a certain kind of high-powered career woman who desperately wishes her mate to be smarter, more well-informed, more powerful than she is, and she likes to advertise those very points about him to others. But if that is what she actually finds, or thinks she actually finds, she often finds him impossible to live with for long.

As the hypnotic effect of his presence wore off, Shana began to see errors in some of the things Joseph said. She took issue. Unaccustomed to her contradictory nature, Joseph grew angry, and retreated to an irritating judicial pedantry. To Shana, their arguments were echoes of angry years with an intimidating father. Instead of using her information like a lawyer, she reverted to an emotional defensiveness. She describes an argument that began with something read from a newspaper:

"That senator's voting record has not been bad on forest conservation," says Joseph, as he begins meticulously to recite the record.

"You know as well as I do that the senator is a prick, and you're just trying to bait me because I haven't memorized his voting record," says Shana.

"All I ask is that you consult the record," says he.

"Who cares about the stupid record?"

When Shana argued with her husband now she relied on feeling and scorned facts. She became a silly little girl with a pretty, empty head instead of the competent trained lawyer she was. In a courtroom she felt she was Shakespeare's Portia; at home, she was an earnest teenager who had just discovered that the world was stricken with injustice. Instead of talking to Joseph as she would to a man she had met in her life downtown, she talked to him as if he were her father the judge; she was intimidated and fearful of a man who might belittle her for arguing emotionally.

Shana was on a collision course with her husband. Either she risked entering the next stage, of putting emotional distance between the two of them, or their marriage would end. She was unable to find a way to do this short of physical separation. "He was too much like my father. He stirred up painful memories unwittingly." They parted. Her father handed down his verdict of guilty: "I told you so."

Shana continues to be a successful lawyer, but she still cannot relax in adult intimacy with a man. She becomes the little girl she cannot leave behind.

Premature Maturity

Some women are more successful than others in outgrowing childish patterns of behavior. How little any of us know when first we marry. We yearn for what one critic describes as "premature maturity," an irresponsible desire for the perks of responsibility, without the pain. He first understood the implications of his own premature maturity on the morning after his wedding night; when the glow of sated lust dimmed, he was left with the sour suspicion that he had made a terrible mistake. The trivial and familiar so often yield the first clue. When a new husband brought his bride's breakfast to their bed, she smiled, thanked him, and said: "You didn't cut off the crusts." He knew at once the marriage was doomed. [5]

Maturity is often thrust upon women who have not been prepared for it; as a concept, maturity has always been different for women. If she marries and does not work outside the home, a woman usually is not required to accept truly mature responsibilities until she has children, and child-rearing, crucial though it is to society, does little to equip a woman for the world beyond the home.

Gail Sheehy's memorable story of the ambitious but ill-prepared wife illustrates. Rehearsing for an important dinner party, when she would be seated next to her husband's boss, she devoured newspapers and newsmagazines for days, cramming as if for a final exam. On the big night she felt particularly pleased with herself, delighted to be free of her children's demands, sailing through a brilliant analysis of third-world politics with the aplomb of Barbara Walters, when she looked down at the table and discovered to her horror and to the astonishment of her dinner partner that she was also idly cutting up the meat on the boss's plate. [6]

If the only man a woman has dealt with before she marries is her father, she will carry habits learned from him into a marriage as surely as that mother who, by reflex, saw every dinner as the children's hour. We must become aware of bad habits learned before they can be put away, and even then it is difficult. Unconscious needs have a way of making anachronistic behavior seem necessary, even when it is self-defeating. Had Shana been able to look across the table and see even an opposing lawyer, and not her father, she might have developed a mature relationship with her husband. She might have been able to speak reasonably instead of always regressing to childish behavior.

To change debilitating patterns, Gestalt therapists sometimes lead patients through therapeutic rehearsals with imaginary people; the patients speak to the imaginary people as they might like to speak to a mother, father, or husband: they practice who they want to be and how they want to act.

Marriage counseling of husband and wife is actually between two "sides," with three persons to a "side": the spouse and the two parents each spouse carries inside. If the couple can free themselves from the others, they have a better chance to work things out. Certain women require long practice to free themselves from needing to find their fathers inside their husbands.

Marital Melodrama

Cathy, thirty-nine, comes from circumstances strikingly like Shana's. But her story is a different one:

"My father had to die before I could see that I needed a different kind of relationship with my husband. I had run away from my father to my husband with the same set of expectations, and I managed to maintain the status quo for ten years. My husband had rescued me, and I was willing to pay the female price for that rescue — submission."

Cathy, like Shana, is the star in a melodrama of her own making. However, the scenario for Cathy turns out to be different because of the way she learns in time to rewrite her script.

At eighteen, Cathy thought she was the luckiest person in the world. She was a small-town girl from Iowa who won a full scholarship to a Catholic college in New York. Although her father had been reluctant to let her go — he was extremely protective — he had been persuaded that the nuns and priests could properly guard the jewel of his family. How could he have known that there wasn't a priest clever nor a nun persistent enough to keep Daniel from stealing Cathy's heart?

Cathy was spoiled by her father's attention, and these attentions extracted a price, retarding her personality development. She was ripe for plucking by someone who could and would treat her as her father had done, and Daniel could, and would.

"You have to understand what it was like being my father's daughter to understand why I wanted to be Daniel's wife. Both were old-fashioned men who were willing to worship me if I did what they wanted. And doing what they wanted, at first, was like eating candy." She pulls out snapshots, to plead her case with exhibits.

Exhibit No. 1: *Cathy in front of a microphone, in a strapless gown, backed by a band of high-school musicians. Rhinestones sparkle in her hair, a Judy Garland smile illumines her face.* "I was fifteen years old. I look at least seventeen. I was quite tall for my age, and flat as an ironing board, but my mother stuffed my blouse with toilet paper. She curled my hair, made up my face with mascara, rouge, and eyeshadow.

"See the name on the bandstand — *Cathy and the Crooners.* The band was formed by my father and my brother. My father did all the arranging and my brother played the saxophone, the clarinet, and the bass. His buddies played everything else and I sang."

The band was so good that Cathy and the Crooners played college dances and fraternity balls all over Iowa. "Looks like fun?" she asks. "Well, it almost was, except that my father never let me out of his sight." If anyone asked her to dance, he'd run up to say, "She's my daughter and she's jail bait. Ha. Ha." When Cathy occasionally accepted a dance, her father would cut in and criticize her for disobeying him. "I was humiliated," she says, "but I couldn't quit the band, because I loved being onstage."

Exhibit No. 2: *Cathy holding a trophy and wearing a smile.* "I had just won the high-school debate tournament. That's Daddy next to me thanking the principal. Daddy was always there when I won my trophies. My father went everywhere with me." Between performances Cathy's father took her to all the football and basketball games, and he was usually a chaperone at the school dances when the band didn't play. Cathy was forbidden to date and she missed knowing boys her own age. She enjoyed being with her father most of the time. "All you had to do was look at his face to see how he adored me, and I adored him," she says. "He was handsome, the best-educated father in my circle of friends, the sons and daughters of plumbers, electricians, conductors on the Burlington Railroad. Daddy was a lawyer, which can mean being a big man in a little town. He gave the commencement address at my graduation."

Exhibit No. 3: *Cathy in high heels and a tailored suit, posing like a manikin.* "That's me as model. My father took that picture. One summer I got a job in a department store on the square, and there was a continuous fashion show in the front store window. My father came by every afternoon to watch, and then he would ask me to lunch. His friends dropped by our table to make cracks about his young girlfriend, knowing perfectly well who I was. Daddy loved it, and I didn't mind much either."

And then Cathy left for college. Cathy of Cathy and the Crooners seemed like Iowa corn in the Big Apple and she felt like Cinderella after midnight. The girls in her dorm were cool, laid back, but drab as church mice, and she was secretly terrified she was going to be just like them.

Enter Daniel, a lawyer seven years older than Cathy, a lawyer who was already beginning to make a little money. He was looking to be someone's Svengali, and Cathy was the ideal someone.

"Danny was the first Jew I had ever seen up close, exciting, exotic, and to tell you the truth he seemed a little dangerous. He wanted a *shiksa,* and though I was hardly the first *shiksa* Daniel had seen up close, I was his first Catholic *shiksa* from Iowa, and that made me fairly exotic in his circle."

He took Cathy everywhere, to places that she had seen in the movies, and introduced her to people with names she recognized. He wanted an undemanding woman, and what was there for Cathy to demand? Daniel was a man, not a boy, and he was a lawyer, like her father. Daniel seemed already more successful than her daddy. She loved him.

Six months into her freshman year, Cathy decided to get married. "I wrote to my parents, asking them to invite Daniel home to meet them during my spring break. My father practically had a stroke. He called the priests and they forbade me to leave the campus. Daniel invited me to move in with him, but I was a good Catholic girl — I could never have done that. I thought I could go home and work old magic on Daddy, and Danny, reluctantly, agreed to let me try."

From the moment she stepped off the plane in Des Moines, life was hell. The day after Palm Sunday she was locked up in a mental institution on a commitment order signed by her father. "Over the next two weeks," she says, "I saw enough Catholic doctors and priests to staff an Iowa Inquisition. But for a sympathetic Jewish doctor on the staff of the hospital, I might still be there. Together we developed a plan to get me out of the hospital and safely back to the man I loved."

The doctor gave her a warning, though: "Once you get out of this hospital, you must never come back home again, not as long as your father is alive. I have had long talks with him and I think you and your boyfriend would be in serious danger if he were to see you again."

Daniel telegraphed Cathy an airline ticket and she left with the clothes she was wearing and two half-slips tucked into her purse. When Des Moines disappeared beneath the clouds, she never expected to see those familiar green fields again.

The prognosis for Cathy's marriage over the long run was poor. She set out to please her husband as she had pleased her father, with a woman's sure knowledge of where the power was. She knew her husband was attracted to the same qualities her father loved: she could protect, preserve, and manipulate a male ego with a courtesan's grace and a childlike tenderness. She assumed the role of wife and mother with the passion that she had spent in singing songs and winning trophies for her father. She had chosen security, at any price.

Cathy had sought the physical and emotional safety of a husband who could secure her life away from her father, ignoring her own economic and psychological development, and replicating her original father-daughter relationship.

She did not understand this until her father died.

"An enormous weight was lifted. It was as though a prison term had ended and I could walk through unlocked doors to a world of infinite possibility. My role of wife had been totally determined by my role as daughter. But there was a catch: now that I was no longer my father's daughter, I couldn't find any reason to be my husband's wife. My children were in school, needing me less and less. A voice inside said, 'Your husband has served his purpose. Let him go.' It may sound screwy, but I was very confused and depressed."

A child buried deep within Cathy's psyche had awakened, and wanted out. That little girl who failed to grow, whose dress front her mother had stuffed with tissue paper to cozen and deceive, whose father kept her from meeting boys her own age, wanted to come out at last and test herself in the adult world. Cathy was having a delayed "identity crisis," a phenomenon which is common for women who learn late that total submission to a man in a marriage can camouflage an undeveloped personality. Some women do not find this out until after menopause, says Jean Baker Miller, the psychoanalyst who studies problems of women.

"Women who may have avoided the task of building a valid sense of identity in adolescence and early adulthood now face even worse anguish at a time when they have much less chance of finding a successful solution."[7]

Cathy was young enough to make major changes, but first she felt panic. She lost control through tears and temper tantrums. The props for the structure of her world could no longer support her. She felt the weight of a crisis that required a change.

Little Girl, Little Woman, Woman-Wife

As we all know, a crisis is not necessarily all bad; it can help us redefine what we want for ourselves. It can speak to us of possibility even when we can't quite see what the future holds. Before we can change, however, we usually look around for someone to blame for our problems. Cathy didn't have far to look. She blamed Daniel for keeping her a prisoner of his male chauvinism. He was as bad for her as her father had been, she thought.

It was a time when the sound of resurgent feminism was upon the land, encouraging women to break away from their restricted traditional roles. Cathy heard feminist Germaine Greer sound a warning that was aimed straight at her: "Women who fancy that they manipulate the world by Pussy Power and gentle cajolery are fools. It is slavery to have to adopt such tactics. [8] Miss Greer would herself soon drop out of the movement, moving to a small town to keep house for a new man, but Cathy felt that she had found a soulmate; like Nora in Henrik Ibsen's *The Doll House,* Cathy felt trapped in a comfortable world that wanted to keep her a child.

She wanted to break free of her silk and satin shackles, but she didn't know how. Education? Work? Divorce? She was like Nellie in Janet Hobhouse's novel *Nellie Without Hugo,* who becomes dissatisfied with her marriage when she realizes that only Hugo, her husband, "creates the space for me to be me. And I don't always want to get my space from him." Cathy needed space to be who she was, in space she created for herself, not only what Daniel created for her.

Newspapers, magazines, and TV screens were ablaze with stories of women leaving their children and husbands for adventure and ambition, but Cathy couldn't do that, nor was she equipped to hold a job. She thought she still loved her husband but she loathed the way she was totally dependent on his wishes, and if he was part of the problem, how could he be part of the solution? Could she change without leaving Daniel? She thought she would at least try.

She told him that she wanted to go back to college, to pick up where she left off ten years earlier. At first he balked; that was not part of their marriage contract. He worked enough for both of them. Her husband, like her father before him, was threatened by the notion that she would be out in the world meeting people beyond his control. But he saw that she was desperate. "We struck a child's bargain," she says. "He gave me the money to go back to college, and I promised to stop being so depressed. 'I'll give you a nice treat if you promise to be good.' Like a teenager, I had to ask for money. Nevertheless, it was my big step, my big chance."

Cathy did well in her classes, particularly in psychology and sociology, and began writing short stories for family magazines, vignettes alive and green with remembrance of small-town America of the fifties, drawn from her benign personal experiences. In the next few years she would feel like Alice in Wonderland, a child who tried on hats and shoes, gloves, ball gowns, and finery of many sizes.

Cathy flourished. Daniel turned out to be a flexible husband, learning even to enjoy the pleasures they could soon afford on a second income. The transition from Daddy's Little Girl to Husband's Little Woman and finally to Woman-Wife was not easy for either of them. Their marriage survived because both partners were willing to change. Cathy and Daniel were able to give each other the room they needed to develop a new kind of understanding based on a renewed respect for what the other had to offer. They felt changes in every aspect of their relationship.

The keys to a good marriage are flexibility and mutual toleration, in the formulation of Henry V. Dicks, the British psychiatrist, and these qualities apply to aggressive and sexual issues of self-esteem and security. This flexibility is another way of describing the ability to absorb, to endure, to temper; these are the abilities crucial to all human relationships, the ability to "contain hate in a framework of love."[9]

To absorb, to endure, to temper — these were the tasks of Cathy and Daniel, and to succeed they knew they had to work hard. They succeeded; the proof of it is that a quarter of a century later they are still succeeding.

Cathy's story differs from those of many other women only by degree. By requiring, by demanding, a Daddy figure to protect her in the first stages of adulthood, she limited her potential for growth, and before she could feel whole, she had to understand her past with greater clarity.

One way to discover the myths of childhood is to go back home as a grownup and seek out family members from a new perspective. Cathy did just that, visiting her mother. She discovered that her parents had had a miserably unhappy relationship, that she had been the sole consolation for her father's frustrations. She was forced to submit to her father's will when her mother would not.

"You know," her mother said, long after dinner when the conversation had grown intimate and honest with the clock's striking of the wee hours of the night, "you broke your father's heart."

"I know," Cathy could say, with regret but no guilt. "I know that, because he broke mine, too."

Cathy realized that her innocent mistake was one that many have made — men and women. She had tried to live her married life in the same way she had lived as a child. Such enterprise seldom succeeds.

Nobody will ever say it better than Thomas Wolfe: "You can't go home again." Because we can't go home again, to that special time and place where we were always children and our fathers were forever handsome and our mothers eternally beautiful and everyone was going to live happily always after, we are tempted to recreate that world in those most intimate relationships long after we have outgrown the home of that childhood.

Cathy and Daniel have now been married for twenty-five years. They have raised two children, who are in college. Cathy works full time at her writing career and she is successful, publishing in national magazines. She still exaggerates her femininity with high heels, an expensive hairstyle, and deep-red fingernails. Her happiness, she believes, developed out of a mix of marriage and career. She needed to test herself against others and she was unable to do that until she freed herself of the need to please only one man.

When forming a love relationship, it's helpful to have your sense of identity clear and firm, says Howard Halpern, the psychologist. "But if you must get some affirmation from the reflected appraisals of others, and most of us do, it is far better to get it from *many* people than to be dependent on it from one person. Any person may have a distorted view and an ax to grind, and, above all, it can make that one person too important to your sense of selfhood."[10]

Women who depend only on their father's appraisal for their self-esteem suffer a thwarted psychological development. It isn't a question of whether a woman chooses marriage, family, or work when she grows up. What's important is that she freely chooses who she wants to be.

Just as a young girl needs to separate from her mother's image of who she is, a daughter must eventually learn to discriminate between herself and her father's conception of her. She goes through stages to achieve autonomy. In the early years, stage one, her experiences with her father are likely to be echoes of his. A second stage is one of ambivalence toward his ideas; she accepts some, she discards some. In the last stage of a healthy development, a child evolves into an independent person — "individuation" in psychological jargon — with a recognition of a separate, independent self, capable of making choices. Cathy, like many women younger and older, was stuck at stage one for many years of adulthood.

None of us escapes the forces that forge the patterns in those early years. In the best of circumstances, we can with hard work learn to mold those patterns to suit our adult desires. Cathy's psychological development had been arrested at the point where she could merely repeat her father's expectations of her even though the form of those expectations excluded him. The independence she eventually developed, however, she worked out with her husband. It was not the kind of independence that Germaine Greer had told women to find. It required a give-and-take that had more in common with traditional values than radical feminism. Marriage and an ability to act authentically in her own voice, she found, were not mutually exclusive, after all.

"The courage to be oneself is never completely separated from the other pole, the courage to be . . . a part," writes Paul Tillich, the theologian.[11] Cathy's father, like many fathers, deprived her of learning that lesson when she was a girl growing up under his protection and tutelage. Like many women, Cathy learned the lesson late. But the most important fact is that she learned it.

CHAPTER TWELVE

Coming to Terms: The Long Voyage Home

When I became a teenager and my father left his bookmaking behind, he started calling himself a has-been. He was only half joking.

He discarded his identity as "Mr. Magic," the identity that had so enthralled me, and became "Mr. Straight," which pleased him.

Taking on this new identity was not always easy. Headwaiters continued to greet him warmly, and the good tables at the window, between senators and quarterbacks, continued to be available, as if by magic. Headwaiters liked Bo, the little guy with the big tip, and he could have been a bookie, a builder, or even a bishop for all they cared.

The people who began to show up in our living room on Quackenbos Street, and later in a new house on Yorktown Road in a tonier part of town, were somewhat less colorful than Beanie the Beanstalk, Tink, and Jew Boy, but the parties and dinners with family and friends continued to bubble with champagne well into the shank of an evening.

In less than a decade I was on my own: married, raising a family, working at a job. In the heat of my young adult years I was playing hard in the game of life and my parents seemed to me as part of the entourage that sat on the sidelines. My children fell heir to their legerdemain. Bo took them to the races, staking them to the Daily Double at Charlestown and the exacta at Laurel Raceway, and when they lost he saw to it that they got home with a few dollars more than their parimutuel stubs could possibly have been worth. My mother's world of baking expanded from pumpkins and hearts to elaborate shapes of Snoopy (with and without goggles), Charlie Brown and his nemesis Lucy, Big Bird, and an infinite assortment of Muppets — none of whom had been around in my childhood.

I realized how fortunate my children were to have vigorous and prosperous grandparents, and I knew how lucky I was, especially when I was approaching a work deadline, that one of them would offer to take a child or two or even all three to the doctor for a pre-camp checkup or to Roy Rogers (the hamburger emporium, not the old cowpoke himself) when they complained of having to eat so many of my peanut-butter-and-jelly sandwiches.

In those hectic years of young children and a career, life seemed to extend limitlessly, not so much because it was filled with anticipation, but because there simply wasn't time to think about what was going to happen next. The mix and flux required total concentration.

Work of an absorbing nature, philosophers are wont to point out, frees us from thoughts of our own mortality, our essential aloneness. (Courage, Hemingway noted, is much easier in the middle of the afternoon than at three o'clock in the morning). So long as we are busy it is not so difficult to be unafraid.

But somewhere in the middle years there whispers that ominous voice we had not heard since adolescence, asking, What does it all mean? Threats of war, nuclear weapons, the Russians, pollution — these all have the power to frighten young as well as old, but in the years of their youth most men and women feel competent to cope, to find answers and solutions, even to survive in the absence of solutions. "No young man," wrote the poet William Hazlitt, "believes he shall ever die."

But as we get older we take more time to think, and to contemplate a future that suddenly seems to be not so limitless, and it becomes fixed in a philosophical focus: How will I face the inevitable aging of those whom I love? Of myself? How will I face the death of those I love? How will I face my own death? Is the promise that the wind is tempered to the shorn lamb the very best we can hope for?

Such questions gather a mournful momentum of their own as the number of sheep available to count decreases, dropping one by one. An obituary of a high-school chum: Hector Bob, the Coolidge Colt quarterback with the two first names, dead of cancer at thirty-five. Didn't that forty-four-yard winning touchdown pass against Woodrow Wilson High, our most hated rival, guarantee him eternal youth? Surely the fact that he was the first boy who kissed me endeared him to me forever. Uncle Fatty, who was never fat, who was never sick, the brother who looked most like my father, fell face forward into his afternoon newspaper as he sat behind the counter of his little candy store, dead of a heart attack at sixty. We knew that he had died of a broken heart years before, so there was no need for this second death, and besides, he was too young. Worse, he was only a year older than my father.

The roll call lengthens with each year. For whom does the bell toll? We giggled at the sentimentality of that line in sophomore English, but I was not laughing now. Surely that bell is not tolling for me, nor for those I love, not now. Not yet.

The telephone rang in my hotel room in Los Angeles. My father had had a heart attack, his first. I braced myself against the wall, waiting to hear the worst.

"How bad?"

"Not major."

"I've just about finished my interviews here. I'll fly right home."

"No need."

"Are you sure?" But she had already said the magic words: No need. I was determined to make her say the words again. "I can come home now, really."

"There's really no need. Finish your work and then come

home. If I thought there was an urgency and you ought to hurry I'd tell you. Really."

I was finally persuaded by my mother that there was no need to rush home, that the worst was almost over, that Bo was doing well, that it was really something as trivial as the food poisoning on the long-ago weekend in New York. But slowly, in the middle of the night that followed, I began to wrestle with the idea that my father might die. I knew that a heart attack was never trivial.

Like the movie of our lives that we are said to watch in the instant before death, frame after frame of my life with my father sped through the projector of my mind. Dreams, nightmares, and night visions, powerful images of the past, haunted my consciousness.

I was three years old again, waiting for the ambulance to pick up my father. "No! No! Take Jakie! Don't take my daddy!" A maroon Cadillac slipped into the driveway of my hotel, and behind the wheel sat a grotesque man, calling my name. *"Because I could not stop for death — He kindly stopped for me."* My heart pumped, jumping about noisily; the heart-to-heart under attack. I climbed into the Cadillac and we sped away on the Santa Monica Freeway, careering wildly toward the vast ocean. I saw my father on the deserted beach, a stick figure in the sand, beckoning me. "C'mon, Suzie, one last swim for old time's sake." The water was sinister, the color of ink beneath a sky without stars. Should we tempt fate this way a second time? "One last swim, Suzie, just one." We ran into the roiling sea, hands clutching hands, jumping the waves, daring Neptune to pour it on, two mortal mites animated by terror on a burnt-out planet hurtling through an uncharted universe. Suddenly a wave separated us and I fell to the floor of the sea. Small jagged rocks cut into my thighs. But it was all right, he would find me again, soon his hands would be under me pulling and lifting me to safety just like the last time. But no hand reached for me, and the pull was from the undertow, sucking and tearing at me, taking me farther and farther from the shore; and then it loosened its grip for no earthly reason, and I bobbed to the surface suddenly riven with dread. I looked for the familiar laughing face even as I knew I would not find it. He was gone: gone, gone, and gone. Where was he? Daddy!

Daddy! Where are you? Oh, Daddy! How can I live without you, Daddy? Daddy, Oh! Daddy, Oh!

At last the images faded, and I fell into a merciful sleep. When I awoke, staring at the unfamiliar furniture, a moment passed before I remembered where I was, and why, and then the conversation with my mother. I stared at the telephone, filled with enormous gratitude that it had not rung during the night. Gingerly, I picked it up to call the front desk downstairs; were there any messages? No, none. Were they sure? Yes, they were quite sure; there were no messages. Never had I thanked a clerk with such heartfelt sincerity.

I called Washington. Everything was the same. Nevertheless, I raced through my work, compressing the tasks of three days into one, determined to be aboard the coast-to-coast "red-eye" and to be at my father's bedside just as soon as Boeing could get me there. My father might be "doing fine," but I was not.

I had never before envisioned the world without my father — and my mother — in it. I had written about middle-aged children confronting the problems of aging parents, but it had never occurred to me that any of this would ever apply to me. I had an intact and healthy family, a mother and a father still willing to run interference against the world that threatened loss.

As a young child I had experienced fears of abandonment, and those fears never disappeared, not quite. But what actual abandonment would mean I had never contemplated. In coming to terms with the mortality of ourselves and of those whom we love, our natures inevitably mellow and we become more expansive in expressing the way we feel to those who care about us, those to whom we denied the tangible assurances of affection in the years we were struggling toward independence. But soon enough we no longer have to work so hard to accept the parents we see in ourselves. More aware of our own complexity, we become more aware of theirs.

So my book becomes largely a quest for coming to terms with life, for examining memories in hopes they will inform perceptions in a search for understanding, if not wisdom. When I flew home from Los Angeles I raced from Dulles International Airport straight to George Washington University Hospital, on the campus where I had walked with my father in happy times. He looked well, well enough for me to marvel at his recovery and good spirits. He was pleased to see me, and reached into an ice bucket on his bedside table. He pulled out a split of Mumm's.

"You're still Mr. Magic, I see."

"Well," he said, with the grin I had grown so accustomed to, "I guess I'm not a *total* has-been. Not yet." The cork popped. I was safe at home, one last time.

For Everything Its Season

Fortunately for me and for my father, he was able to ripen with the grapes of his own season and to enter into old age with much of the same mellow flavor that enriched his younger years and the years of my own childhood. Many fathers and daughters are not so fortunate.

They have instead faced the sad reversing of roles, when the child must become the mother of the man. These middle-aged daughters often hear the voice of their mothers when they speak to their fathers, telling them what's right and what will work. Such a daughter helps a father direct his energies toward worthwhile things in his retirement, eventually taking him into her own house or placing him in a nursing home. Often such a daughter finds herself reminding him to "be nice" to her mother.

A daughter comes to the height of her powers as her father's power and strength wanes. Such is the specific cruelty of aging. As we achieve this height of creative power, warming to a sense of growing fulfillment in our own children and in our work, our parents move into the uncertainties and infirmities of old age. We inherit mixed opportunities. At best, we can learn to relate to Daddy in a new way, sharing thoughts and affection. At worst, we must face the frustration of never being able to come to terms with the painful, sad, and permanent "new reality."

Ideally, we come to recognize our father's aging to be as natural as the maturing of the tree he planted for us when we were children. One woman in New Jersey describes just such an experience: "When I was entering adolescence, my father built a new house in the country, and he took me with him to work at his side on weekends. He decided to plant seedlings there instead of trees, and as we walked together through his woods, he would bend down, urge me to come closer, and show me a tiny sprout from an acorn: 'Just think, one day this is going to be an oak tree.' His joy and awe of life have been passed on to me, and it makes his aging seem less frightening."

Her experience and the emotions she felt were described by Longfellow:

> For age is opportunity no less
> Than youth itself, though in another dress,
> And as the evening twilight fades away
> The sky is filled with stars, invisible by day.

The subtle rewards of old age that Longfellow saw, that the woman in New Jersey recognized as possible, would be reward indeed but for the solemn recognition of the fact that at the end of old age waits death. In the infirmity, the weakness, and the enfeebling that overtake our parents we see the prospect of things to come for ourselves. The prospect frightens, with anger the only defense, and the anger is often directed at the one man who had once seemed invincible.

Whatever we do, however, we are never quite able to let go of the child within us when we are with our fathers, and he can never quite see the adult we become.

Tema, thirty-six, tells how the hide-and-seek game perpetuates itself as the father grows old. In the best of situations, a ripening of paternal love opens up new possibilities even as the pattern is preserved. Each allows the other to see a little more of the private self. Says Tema: "We let each other see as much as we can bear to be seen."

Tema was preparing to visit her parents after a separation of five years and 2,500 miles. Her father, an Indiana farmer who had held fast to traditional values, was eighty-five, his health failing. This would be the first time she had been home as a married woman with a three-year-old son, his sixteenth grandchild. She was anxious to see how he would react to her new family and her new sense of herself.

When Tema had first introduced Bob, the man she would marry, she was in a very different position. So was Bob. He had long hair, affected a Buddhist life-style, and expressed pride in "living in sin" with Tema. Tema was a "radical feminist," active in the civil-rights movement, and working in a slum of a large Midwestern city. The couple had kept most of these details from Tema's father, who was a Christian fundamentalist, a man who believed that a woman's place was to serve her husband and her family, not society. The races should be equal, but separate — "it is God's will."

A college friend once told Tema that everything she did was an act of rebellion against her father and his God, but if that was true Tema was careful never to let her father know it. When she went home for a visit, she left her rebellion at the front door: "I was as straight as Gerald Ford."

Away from her father, Tema became a slavish follower of another fashion, a woman who considered wearing anything but the costume of her contemporaries a compromise too dear to bear. The faded old jeans and bib overalls that became the uniforms of radical chic and the laid-back seventies were all that Tema wore, clothing that could be easily misinterpreted by an Indiana farmer who was country before country was cool. By his lights, denim, like flour-sack dresses and leather brogans ordered out of the Montgomery Ward catalog, was a reminder of the hard times he had known only too well. His daughter deserved nothing less than a dress cut from real cloth.

Tema had read her history well: "When in Rome . . ." To do anything less was to invite banishment from her father's house, and almost nothing was worth risking that. During college years and after, she deliberately protected her father from the painful knowledge of her as a "new woman."

She wore modest clothes and suppressed her most unorthodox political opinions because she knew he would not like what she had become, even to the point of despising what she had become. She wanted his love, not his contempt. But on this new visit, she believed, things would be different. She was more secure in her attitudes, more understanding of his. She had not moved so far from him as she had once thought, at least not where it counted. Had he been born in 1950 instead of in 1896, she was sure he would have understood the need for the recognition and protection of the civil rights of black people, and for the opening of greater opportunity for women. He was a man of principle, after all. Besides, she felt herself becoming less strident, and possibly less radical. Bob, who was now an accountant and respected in his community, was still a political activist, but Tema felt herself becoming reserved and even conservative like her father, at least to the extent of wanting to preserve and protect certain values to pass down to her son.

Like so many young people who grow conservative when they are old enough to have accumulated beliefs and values and something to conserve, Tema no longer wants to persuade people by shocking them. She wants to perpetuate the best part of her past without ignoring the need for change, gradually. "Now that I, too, am a parent in a small town," she says, "I understand why my father didn't want to rock the boat too often. When my husband takes on the Republican congressman at town meetings and in letters to the editor of the local newspaper, I am both proud and frightened at the risk he incurs for our safe world.

"Above all, I guess, I miss my father's romantic, steady, solid appreciation of the world. My father used to read poems to me, Longfellow and Keats and John Greenleaf Whittier, and my husband reads only political tracts and selections from the Tibetan Book of the Dead. Now that we have a child I find it harder to adjust to my husband's view of life. He is not a father as my father was a father. Where I was sheltered too much, Bob does not shelter enough."

Such were Tema's thoughts as she planned her visit to her

hometown, a trip she expected to be her last to that place. Not until she sat down with my questionnaire, she told me, had she opened the windows on her memories, calling up perceptions and recollections of her life with her father. "I could finally plan my trip home with positive expectations."

The More Things Change, the More Things Stay the Same

Tema expected her arrival to be the kind of family event she remembered from her childhood. "One or two of my brothers would be there, with Mom looking out the kitchen window while fixing supper, Daddy out at the barn keeping an anxious and eager eye out for us. I called ahead to insure just such a reception.

"When we drove in, the place looked deserted. I told Big Bob and Little Bob to wait in the car while I went in the back way. Mom was in the kitchen, all right, dozing at the table. The air conditioner was running on high speed and she hadn't heard the car. Daddy was asleep on the living-room sofa. Everything was still and empty, and I suddenly recalled how my grandpa's house had scared me when I was a child, with the same empty-and-waiting feel to everything.

"When I looked at my father I could see that he had brushed close to death — that he was still very fragile. I didn't want to wake him, such was an aura around him. I'd seen the same thing around other older relatives, but never before understood. I felt that if I could have a few seconds I would grasp it . . . I'm sure it was the echo of his younger, larger body, his stronger active spirit. . . . My mother came in and shook him awake with a start and a grunt and then he looked at me, focusing his eyes with effort. He took my hand, shaking it, pulling himself up on it.

"We hugged and cried and kissed each other, and he insisted on helping us carry our stuff in. We went out to the car and he and Bob exchanged rather formal greetings. Mom and Little Bob bustled about, keeping the moment short. We spent several minutes unloading and talking about the trip. Dad pretended not to notice that we only let him carry the lightest stuff, and we pretended not to notice how weak he had become."

The visit was an occasion for compromise on values. They all tried to be themselves without giving offense. Bob earned his father-in-law's acceptance. The old man recognized the younger man as a responsible husband and father, and they took long walks in the woods. The older man drove Bob across the farm in his battered old pickup. "Few people dared drive with Daddy any longer," said Tema. "Bob was showing his respect and Daddy was warmed by it. Bob actually seemed to enjoy their talks." The three generations of males hung out together in a way that pleased and surprised Tema.

The young couple didn't go to the services at the little Methodist church with Tema's parents, but they participated in the Bible readings each evening after supper. The readings from the old family Bible, with its familiar verses of hope and reassurance, its straightforward wisdom, its pages for the family tree, brought back the happy memories that Tema yearned to live again.

Because she was the youngest in a family of six children, Tema had always been "the baby," and in the old days she had sat on his lap while he read. He sat in a fat red-brown fake leather chair, a lamp standing behind him as straight as a pole in a row of beans, and selected a book from a cabinet his brother had made for his Bible and volumes of poetry, biography, and history. In the daylight hours her father might have selected a volume of Wordsworth, a Victorian schoolbook, or a worn black-and-white speckled notebook of poems he had copied down himself. He laughed until tears streamed down his face when he came to a familiar passage about a mad dog that bit his master: "but 'twas the dog that died." In the evenings there would be more somber selections, from John Bunyan's *Pilgrim's Progress,* from the Apostle Paul's letters to the Corinthians, a Psalm, a selection from Proverbs.

"The sure way for me to show off was to be the best at Bible quizzes, and I always did my best," Tema recalls. When they talked about the Bible on this trip, Tema felt at home again. Later, there was a family discussion about Christian schools. Warmed and emboldened by the good feelings engendered by the Bible reading, Tema dared speaking directly on a subject she thought would alienate her father. "When I said I wouldn't send our son to a Christian school because such schools don't teach children to use their minds, which I think is the main purpose of education, my parents didn't respond." They did not want to fight, nor did they look at her as though she was a monster. She thought they simply didn't understand her point of view; perhaps they understood very well, and grieved in silence. In the event, she chose not to press her point.

The other rocky moment occurred when her father asked about his son-in-law's politics: was he Republican, a Democrat, or a Communist? "The truth was," said Tema, "he was none of the above, but rather than go into Bob's status I replied, 'Strictly Democrat.' " To her father, who thought William Jennings Bryan the last trustworthy Democrat, she might just as well have answered "Communist." But this moment passed without rancor, too.

Tema felt a compelling need to suppress her disagreements, keeping quiet that angry, rebellious person inside her, because she wanted to give her father only love. If she angered him he wouldn't understand, nor realize how much she cared about him. The entire trip was a present to her father and to herself, given out of a need to let him know how much she loved him and how much she yearned for him to accept her not just as his daughter but as "an adult and as a friend."

It helped when she saw the old man with her son, watching him with the little boy, patient and kind as he had been with the little girl she had been. He was as gentle and as trusting as she had remembered him to be. The two, man and boy, did farm chores together, and when he felt strong enough the old man took his grandson to the barn to play on the tractors and in the hay in the loft.

Simmering beneath the surface of everything they felt was her preparation for saying the final goodbye. He knew that, too. On the day they were to leave, the old man came in from the barn with Little Bob and spoke to Tema. "What a fine young man you have borne," he told her. He hoped Little Bob would not grow up to be like his grandfather. "I will die a disappointed man."

The remark rocked Tema to the depths of her understanding. Daughters are never ready to hear their fathers make this declaration, common though it is to all men who reflect upon the deeds, misdeeds, and missed deeds of their youth. At the end of his life Winston Churchill, who was haunted through life by "a black dog that sits upon the foot of my bed, grinning at me," lay mortally ill. He told his daughter his life amounted to nothing. She reminded him of the admiration bordering on reverence in which the English-speaking world held him. "Yes," replied the old World War II prime minister, "all of that, to amount to nothing very much at the end."

Tema hardly knew what to say, either. She thought she knew what he meant, but she had never expected to hear it from him. Perhaps she understood; perhaps she, like all of us, would know and understand only when she was in her father's place at the end of a life. Tema wanted to say that he had believed too easily, that he had expected too much of his simple life. She couldn't say that, so instead she said the words that fathers have told me they yearn most to hear a daughter say: "You are a great man to me."

Although Tema had gone home to visit her father because she knew he was failing, she was not prepared for the physical and psychological changes she found. When she saw him sleeping, she wanted to linger to look again, hoping to find the young man she once knew as her strong, stern, loving protector. Instead, she saw an old man. He was, however, a more accepting man, a man for whom quiet pleasures in life were the significant ones, a man who was willing to risk his vulnerable side by telling his daughter that he had been disappointed by life. He was a more passive man than she remembered.

Aging Angels and Devils

This passive man is often the person a man becomes after middle age. Middle age is a time when a man begins to show an interest in philosophy and art, ideas he never took the time to cultivate when he was younger. "A certain softness, even tenderness, may emerge," writes Pierre Mornell, the psychiatrist, of the elderly man. "By middle age, he may begin to relax."

Dr. Mornell looks at the changing roles of men and women and notes that, historically, men refuse to expose their vulnerability until the "emergency of parenthood" has passed. A young father's traditional role means that he has to spend those early years providing shelter and security for his family. Even in a technological age, the father's work (or lack of it) continues to determine his family's place in society.[1]

Some observers of the "new" phenomenon of older women bearing children see an advantage for a child in having an older father. The father usually is more financially and emotionally stable, with his work approaching peak earning capability. Says Dr. David Reuben, a psychiatrist, of mid-forties fathers: "From the father's point of view, a new baby means more responsibility. But at the same time, for so many men in their mid-forties the excitement of competition in the business world is beginning to fade. A new baby comes along at just the right moment to bring a new interest in their lives." He cites the remarks of one such father: "After twenty years at the same old job, there wasn't much that turned me on. But now I call home every day at noon to see what new tricks that baby of mine is up to, and I can hardly wait to get home at night."[2] The daughter of this man is likely to meet a father more open and less than stern when she enters her adolescence. He is likely to be less threatened by the emergency of parenthood because he is already secure in his work. She may benefit from some of the "grandfather" in the father.

David Gutmann, who studies crosscurrents in traditional male-female roles, points to the frequency of a role reversal after middle age: Grandma become more decisive, tough-minded, and intrusive. Grandpa becomes sweeter, more affable, but rather vague.[3] And so it was in Tema's family. Tema was shocked at her mother's aggressiveness toward a dying aunt, her father's favorite sister. It was favoritism that was often expressed at the expense of her mother. "When we visited my aunt's sickroom," says Tema, "my mom was as cruel as I have ever seen her, and it was the first time that I realized how bitter she was. She had never revealed that before."

Such role reversals, Dr. Mornell says, are obviously the point of an ancient Moroccan parable: "Each man is born surrounded by a hundred devils; each woman by a hundred angels. With each passing year a devil is exchanged for an angel. So, by one hundred years of age the man is surrounded entirely by angels. And the woman by devils." The parable obviously reflects a well-worn misogyny, but it nevertheless contains the notion that even in the most traditionally structured societies women develop an assertive personality after their child-bearing years are past. Men, freed of the responsibility of bringing home enough bacon for hungry mouths, become more vulnerable.

A father in the United States who liberates the vulnerable side of his nature late in life offers opportunities to a daughter that she never had when they both were younger, particularly if the source of the difficulty between them was rooted in his show of authority and her rebellion against it.

Stormy relationships during a daughter's adolescence threaten to break the bond between father and daughter, and often come close to sundering this relationship irrevocably. But as both father and daughter grow older, the abrasive edges of personality are softened by experience, and where this is a love bond they can usually learn to respect each other as independent adults. Many women have told me that their bond with their fathers has deepened with age in this way. Fathers have confided that in the hectic early adult years, when making a living seemed to be a twenty-four-hour job, they felt they had little time for family ties and almost none to cultivate the intimacy of close relationships. It's almost never too late, fortunately, to bring these dormant feelings to vibrant life.

Many young men, as we have seen, are afraid to show vulnerability; to do so brings back painful memories of being a child totally dependent on an all-powerful female. Having worked so hard to free themselves of their real mothers and the strictures of "petticoat discipline," they fear succumbing to a second "mother." Yet, when the vicissitudes of age and the inevitable illnesses of a deteriorating body break down their emotional barricades in the second half of life, a mother is exactly who most men want. This mother is often a daughter. The kind of vulnerability that enhances a daughter's new understanding can lead her father to become painfully dependent on her as he ages, often exacting a price few women willingly pay. The strong, powerful, protective father sometimes seems to have no reserves when, late in life, his wife falls seriously ill. Women who have been manipulated and intimidated by men, women who think frailty and tears can be male virtues, often change their minds. Devils of a different species haunt the timid.

"Twice a Child"

"When my mother went into the hospital with a kidney ailment," says Glenda, fifty-six, "my father fell apart. He couldn't take care of himself. I lived twenty-five miles away and he expected me to come and clean his house and fix his dinner. I did all of that for the first week, but then I told him he had to make other arrangements.

"I was shocked at his emotional deterioration, and I began to wonder if he had been the strong, silent man of my childhood, never buckling or bending, or whether it was my mother who had made him seem so tough, so like the Rock of Gibraltar.

"I hope both of them live a long life, but there's no doubt in my mind that if my mother dies first my father will follow her shortly. I don't think he can take care of himself without her. If I sound unsympathetic, it is because I am. My father still wants to think I am thirteen years old and refuses to accept me as a mature woman who had raised four grown-up children, lost a husband, is still a widow and with some life ahead of me."

Glenda's father would like to order her around as he did when she was a teenager. Ideally, he would want her to move next door to wait for him to call. But he has no further influence with her, because she has finally learned to cope with his anger and poor disposition. She understands that he grew up in poverty and that his life was rough, but she feels pity and not sympathy. "I have survived," she says, bitterly, "and so has he. Ha, ha. But at least *I'm* happy."

The way in which Glenda responded to her father may even have been good for him. Psychologists have discovered that old people who must control their lives have much greater potential for psychological well-being than those who give up control to others. Residents of nursing homes who are encouraged to make their own decisions about meals and recreation show a significant improvement in mental health and activity over those for whom decisions are routinely made by others.

Giving up can lead to physical illness and even death, and doing too much for a loved one, especially an elderly loved one, can make him imcompetent.[4] Glenda, of course, had little choice. She knew that her father was not likely to change, nor could she likely bend her behavior to his deteriorating will. The conflict for an adult in his middle years is between generativity, an expansion of mind and body, and stagnation.[5]

The Yiddish language has a word for the man who is generative, a *mensch,* a man eager to be generous with lively spirit and good heart. Opposite generativity is regression and personal impoverishment. The father who stagnates begins to act like a child; he becomes the person who must be taken care of by others. Glenda's father was trapped in stagnation of his own making. It makes no difference to him now that he has been a success in business, that he has fathered a daughter whom he could, if he but knew how, enjoy as an adult. But he wants only to be cared for. If his wife can't or won't do it his daughter must; so he earnestly believes. He suffers from what Erickson calls "excessive self-love," the inevitable result of a "too-strenuously self-made personality." He is a psychological invalid.

Glenda had few choices. Had she wanted to lead her own life, she would have had to abandon her father. This is a problem many daughters have with aging fathers. Such old men, as Shakespeare noted, are "twice a child."

Work Sweet Work

Karen, forty-four, was shocked when her father entered old age. He had always been a big man in a small town in the lower Mississippi valley, and she had always believed that he would remain that way until he died. With two large general stores, each dominating the square in adjoining towns, he was the center of attraction for everyone. If he didn't have the feed, seed, fertilizer, or dress pattern a customer asked for, the customer could be sure he would have it the next time. The slogan on the front door, "If we don't have it you don't need it," was not entirely a joke. His word and generosity were personal advertisements for quality goods and personal service, and in his corner of the world he was glamorous, famous, and a legend, a beneficent businessman to the farmers who loved him.

He lent money, not foolishly, but quite generously. When a new fertilizer or strain of seed was introduced on the market, he encouraged the farmers to experiment and he assumed the risk. "If it works, you can pay me for it, and if it doesn't, it's worth it to me not to order it again." When a new tool came to the store, he lent it out before he sold it, just to make sure it worked the way the designer said it would. He loved his work, and his devotion was repaid many times. He grew rich.

In short, he was Big Daddy to everyone but his four daughters. He seemed to love his work more than his family. He hurried home for dinner, sitting at the head of the table to preside over elaborate and delicious meals his wife prepared with the same kind of love and devotion that he lavished on his own work, and as soon as he drank the last of his coffee he was back at the store, working on bills or going over inventory. Nothing was said about the quality of the meal. Says Karen: "It was just a place to refuel, so he could do more work."

In the middle years, Karen's father, in the vernacular of the hills, "got religion." He turned back to his no-nonsense, straight-forward Scottish heritage, and instead of going down to the store to work on his books on Sunday mornings he drove instead to the little Presbyterian church. Soon he was practically running the church, like the store. He sat on the board of deacons, headed the building fund, became the superintendent of the Sunday school. He was the parishioner a pastor dares not hope for.

"As a Type-A aggressive and energetic man, he seemed never to tire of doing things for and with others," says Karen. "But suddenly he got old. Worn out, depressed, lethargic. And who do you think he wanted to take care of him? Not the farmers who loved him, nor the fortunate preacher nor the men on the church board who admired him. Who but his wife and daughters, the wife whose table he always left without a warm word right after a hot dinner?"

Karen's father was a model of success in every material way; even his church work was more materialistic in substance than spiritual in tone. Finally, at seventy, he decided that money hadn't brought him happiness, peace, or spiritual contentment; he had no intimate relationships with friends or family, and the de-pression that settled over him like a shroud was cold, clammy, constant, and complete.

Others have observed that it is not death that the aged fear so much as the prospect of their lives ending uncompleted. Karen's father despairs because he eschewed the value of intimacy with his family: his life was an incomplete life. He bought the easy praise of the marketplace with acts of generosity to those who in the end did not care for him for himself, but for what he could do for them. His family, willing to accept him as he was and eager to love him deeply in return for minimum gifts of himself, were left with the crumbs from the table. At the end of his life he is left with only despair for his missed opportunities, rather than with an eagerness to press on in the search for new ways to bring meaning to his life.

Missed Opportunities

"I think the reason my father is so moody now is that he doesn't want to die and he has no deep spiritual feeling to sustain him," says Karen. "He's terrified. His depression has taken him to three different hospitals and no one has ever found anything wrong with him. He has consulted psychiatrists, psychopharmacologists, and a variety of internists. Mother even got him to consult a marriage counselor, who, after hearing about his behavior to his family, turned to him and said: 'You are truly a terrible man.'"

Karen's father is not wholly responsible, however. His wife contributes, too. With all four daughters gone to homes of their own, she filled her empty nest with the biggest baby of all. She waited on him hand and foot, encouraging him to consume her entire life. When she asks help of her daughters, they rarely say no, but Karen thinks now that all erred in being too readily available to indulge him. This trap is easily fallen into.

Karen gave her father a child's ultimate gift for his seventieth birthday. She called him from her home in New York City to give him a half hour of her total attention, to let him talk about nothing but his symptoms and imagined illnesses. "I didn't cut him off, not once. I sympathized. I told him it must be terrible, and in fact it was terrible because that was all he had to talk about. I thought it was a wonderful present, but the sad part of it was that he didn't even know that I had given him anything."

A father like Karen's is totally vulnerable. His dignity hangs by a slender thread, and a daughter cannot bear to be the one who cuts it. So she condescends. She patronizes him in a way that makes her cringe with self-contempt, all the more agonizing because Karen identifies with him. She is a magazine writer-editor with major administrative responsibilities, driving herself to work long hours.

"I work as hard as he ever did," she says, "but I don't have a wife or family. Actually all I could afford in my life right now would be some kind of passive companion who wouldn't demand much. I wouldn't marry and have children if I knew I had to work as hard as I do, as hard as my father did." Is she afraid she will be like him as she grows older? "Let's hope not. I think I've spent my whole life consciously trying to imitate his working spirit, and now I'd like to change the pattern before it's too late."

Karen is typical of hardworking women who sacrifice intimacy for careers, seeking professional rewards in the place of the rewards of love and intimacy with another person. A job is real, and the challenges are at hand, and to cut back on her drive to succeed on the job to seek a relationship might in the end be a pursuit of gossamer. Meanwhile, someone at the office is always standing by to breathe down the neck of she who hesitates.

"My father told me a story about a man who came into his store during World War II, when everything was hard to get and building nails were impossible to get. But Daddy had a few, which he kept in the back for his best customers.

" 'I understand you have number-ten finishing nails.'

" 'I might have a few.'

" 'How much?' the man asked.

" 'Thirty-five cents.'

" 'Thirty-five cents? Ames Hardware only charges a quarter.'

" 'Then you ought to buy from Ames Hardware.'

" 'Well, Ames is out of nails right now.'

" 'Oh,' Daddy replied, 'if you're willing to take the nails I *don't* have I can let you have them for a dime.'

"I've never forgotten that story," says Karen, a wistful smile playing across her mouth. "Giving up something real and possible to go after something that isn't there, and may never be possible, has always scared me."

Karen's experience is not unusual. Fathers who completely

suppress their tenderness in their younger years often crave tenderness as they grow old, and the only way they knew how to seek it is to demand it. The angels of affability are alien creatures to them. Without the diversions of the marketplace, such fathers are thrust into the domestic world they had ignored, and they behave like the proverbial bull in the china shop, running over people instead of plates.

When a Father Wants a Mother

Like Glenda's father, who wanted his daughter to become a full-time mother, men like Karen's father cannot get enough care and attention. In their yearning to be nurtured, they often confuse daughters with their own mothers.

Lucille, fifty-four, an advertising account executive in Chicago, tells of the vigil at her father's bedside at his last hour.

"It's so good to have you here, Mother," he told her. "Let me make a little more room for you."

"I'm glad to be here, too, Daddy. But I'm Lucille. Lucille, your daughter."

"Oh, I'm so sorry, Lucille. I get so confused." He turned to look at the clock on the wall, and his voice took on the anxious vibrato of a child. "Is it time to take my pill, Mother?"

Would the fathers of Karen and Lucille have so regressed to embarrass themselves by seeking motherly nurturing from a son? Our society, particularly the society in which Karen's father came to manhood, requires at a minimum that a man face adversity "like a man" when in the company of other men, and most of all in the company of a son.

Karen does not think of herself as a nurturer. She inherited an unblinking Calvinist ethical code, a willingness to stare unpleasant facts in the face, and then to deal with them. She brings to her concern for her father the virtues that guided his dealings with his customers. If her father eventually requires nursing-home care, Karen can make the arrangements.

She is a woman who has developed an independence that heretofore has been largely the province of men like her father. She earned her autonomy through hard work, breaking with many traditional values that have kept families together. A half-century ago a daughter was a man's insurance policy for old age: a son was lost to the woman and the family he married, but a daughter was expected to be always dutiful. Infirm parents could move in with an adult daughter, or if there was more than one daughter, move from female child to female child.

Today, the nursing home has taken over much of the day-to-day responsibility that once rested upon a daughter's shoulders. Daughters, like sons, work outside the home and cannot give the solicitous attention of Florence Dombey in Charles Dickens's novel *Dombey and Son,* a woman who nurses her crabby and intolerant father in his old age despite painful remembrance of the cruelties he inflicted when she was younger.

Maxine Hong Kingston, the author, tells the story of her grandfather: Ah Goong has three sons and wishes for a daughter so that she can sing for him as he grows old. When his wife bears a fourth son, he puckers with envy for his neighbor's infant, a tiny and dainty girl whose parents dress her in rags. Determined to have this girl as his own, he persuades the parents to exhange her for his own son, whom he has dressed in fine silk. When his wife discovers the switch, she demands that he return to the neighbor's house to reclaim his son. He does so and, weeping, discreetly takes out his penis; he chastises it, asking it whether it is yet capable of producing the daughter of his dreams, one who could sing for him in his old age.[6]

Rare is the modern daughter who will sing for her father in his old age, and almost as rare is the daughter who cheerfully assumes the care of an ailing father. Such filial devotion is a virtue that disappeared with ruffled panties for piano legs. Mary Gordon's novel *Final Payments* describes a daughter's eleven years of selfless service to a suffering father. The devotion is all the more remarkable for the complexity, and Miss Gordon's contemporary father-daughter relationship sounds as though it was

planted and came to flower in the nineteenth century; a game of
sexual hide-and-seek played out on a plane of spirituality and suf-
fused with *agape,* the love uncomplicated by eroticism

The protagonist's father, a professor of literature in a Catholic
college, finds her in bed with his prize student. Three weeks later
he suffers a stroke. Why did Isabel engineer a sexual liaison that
was so obviously fraught with danger, and in her father's own
house where it was likely to be discovered? She had many reasons,
and not the least was the nature of her relationship with her father. She would make him see her as a daughter who was growing
up and capable of attracting other men, capable of being identified as someone other than her father's daughter. More important, it was a way to keep her father for herself. She analyzes the
scene where she is caught *in flagrante:*

> Was I trying to punish my father for something; for his lack of
> attention to my obvious adulthood, for his lack of jealousy at the intru-
> sion of so clear a rival? He didn't even tease me about David. Perhaps I
> was outraged at his lack of outrage at what could so obviously have sep-
> arated us. Would it be so easy for him to let me go?

Letting go of Daddy means letting go of the child in ourselves.
It means taking responsibility for our own sexuality, and this is the
most difficult of separations because it exposes us at last as abandoned in a universe with only ourselves as protection. Women
have only rarely been schooled in thinking that they can take care
of themselves, and having a daddy, of one kind or another, keeps
us forever the child.

When a Time to Live Becomes a Time to Die

Letting go of Daddy also means forgiving. Recognizing
his fallibility and his mortality helps us to recognize our own.
Priscilla and Claire are two women who spoke to me of the difficulty of giving up their fathers, but for very different reasons.
Priscilla had trouble forgiving her father for not being closer to
her. Claire hated her father for falling sick and requiring constant

care. Both women were able to come to terms with their fathers at
the deathbed, experiencing in different ways the profound liberation of expressing love. With their farewells, they reached a
greater awareness of who their fathers really were, and consequently reached a more profound understanding of themselves.

Priscilla, thirty-five, a public-health nurse in Alaska, remembers her thoughts at her father's deathbed. He was a doctor who
had instilled in all of his children the sense of duty to care for
others. Most of the children had, in fact, gone into different kinds
of medical service. One was a doctor and two were nurses. They
resented their father's close attention to his patients; to his children he seemed more interested in the needs of his patients than
in the just-as-real needs of his children. This particularly bothered
Priscilla.

"The love was there, but the bridge connecting the love was at
best a series of slippery stones in the water. I had to forgive him
for that, I knew, but it was difficult. I was both attracted to his life
as a physician and repelled by it, attracted by his generosity and
unstinting service to others and repelled by his lack of concern for
my scraped knee, my fevers, my childish tears that he hardly had
time to notice after a long day at the hospital. Yet I knew that I
had become a nurse so that I could carry on his work, that it was a
fulfillment of his faith in me. I feel my father's strength in my own
professional practice."

At his deathbed her love and forgiveness for any shortcomings
or failures had no qualifications. She wanted him to know that. He
had had a tracheotomy tube in his throat and could not speak, but
his eyes said everything. She could see that he was close to "being
with mother, his one great love." She could see how he loved her,
and her brothers and sister; she could see him struggling to live
and struggling not to live.

"I told him, 'Go ahead, Dad, it's OK. We are here doing good
work and we will carry on your values, each in our own way.' "

Priscilla returned to Alaska and was at her work in an Aleut
village when the call came. "I had told only one native person of
his death, but all day long the children brought me wild flowers,

saying nothing. Just before the little plane that was carrying me out of the bush took off, two men went to their fishnets and returned with a huge red salmon. It was the saddest and the happiest moment of my life."

Priscilla was able to forgive her father, and as a result she is able to give other men in her life "more room." It is easier for her to let them be the way they have to be. Says she: "I explore ways to move toward intimacy without expecting the impossible."

Death always teaches lessons for the living, and the death of a father usually offers us an opportunity to contemplate both his strengths and his weaknesses. Because her father was ill for ten years, Claire found it difficult to forgive him for becoming such a burden, for taking so long to die. This, she knows, was unfair, irrational, unreasonable; her anger almost kept her from going to her father before he died. She was at last able to reach out to him in his final days, however, and in doing so she spared herself the supreme regret of her life.

"After a series of strokes, my father became a total invalid, and my mother kept him at home, tending to him for years. Feeding him, dressing him, taking him to the bathroom, cleaning him — she did it all. He couldn't talk. He could make grunts that made no sense at all to me.

"I was married by then and could run away from it all, and I did. I just couldn't handle it. I was angry for his not trying to get better, and I resented the demands he made on my mother. At times I'd go to visit and my mother looked so drained and exhausted, having stayed up all night with him. I hated him. I lay awake to pray that he would die. He was killing my mother, and I wanted to get on with my own life."

He contracted pneumonia on a bleak February day and they took him to the hospital where he could have intensive care. Over a period of weeks his condition deteriorated steadily, and her mother cried tears of guilt and remorse: "I can't let him come home anymore," she said. "I'm sorry, but I just can't do it."

A week later Claire found within her the ability to put her arms around his emaciated body and say to him: "Daddy, I love you."

He tried to smile and he managed to get an arm around her and for just one instant she was at peace. "I was once again his little girl."

And then he was dead. "I felt as if someone had taken a long, wicked razor and sliced open my body," recalls Claire. "To this very day when I see an old and feeble man who reminds me of my father I am flooded with yearning to do for him what I refused to do for my father for so many years. I want to run over to the stranger and tell him I care. I want to protect him with my own body."

When a father dies, memory makes us heiress to many modest loves and stunted hates. Then one special love or hate asserts itself with a powerful force as though it lives within us, an emerging gene that we feel we can pass on to a child of our own.

How we say the final farewell determines how we live thereafter with the piece of our father we forever carry within ourselves. Priscilla knew she would continue her medical work, that she would cherish what her father left to her rather than act on the bitterness of all that he had deprived her of. Claire began to see old people for the first time, and she opened herself to sensitivities she had blocked by refusing to acknowledge her love for her dying father.

We don't get a second chance to say a final goodbye. With bitter voice, one woman told me how she cannot forgive herself her father's death. In the heat of the sixties' anger over the Vietnam war, she left her father's bedside, where he lay ill with a heart attack, to go into the streets to lead a demonstration. When she returned he was dead.

"Instead of protesting the war I should have been protesting his treatment at the hospital. In his last hours they fed him salt-free baby food and took away his cigarettes, and I believe that's what actually killed him. Who wants to live like that? I should have been there. They would never have missed me at the Pentagon, but I know he missed me at his bedside."

Before he dies, a man usually comes at last to accept his fate, and communicates nonverbally. At this time a daughter can let her father know of her love by her presence, without saying a word. Holding his hand, listening with him to the song of a bird outside his window, even sitting silently by his bedside with a book, allows her to accept his death, too.

Giving Up the Ghosts of Childhood

We do not have to wait until a father dies to come to terms with who he is, and thus who we are. Rachel, a sculptor, tells how she began to understand the influence of her father on the day she began to make a sculpture of his head. He went to visit her in San Francisco and she thought it might be their last visit together. He was eighty-four, she was fifty.

"I had always wanted to do his head, and this visit seemed to give the project urgency. He was to meet me at my studio at noon. I was there early, preparing the clay, trying to remember him in my mind, to recall all the things I loved and despised about him.

"He was a charmer, a man of promises, promises, promises. Because my mother died when I was a child, he had full care for me for years, and he met his responsibility only some of the time. He parceled me out, along with my sister, to relatives from time to time, saying he would see us in a day to two, but the days stretched to weeks, the weeks to months.

"When he would finally arrive he'd sweep us off our feet, taking us out to dinner, telling us how lovely we had become. He was extraordinarily seductive, so we could never be angry with him for long. But the stretches between visits seemed almost unendurable."

All those recollections came flooding back to Rachel as she worked long, slender fingers through her clay. She shaped the clay feeling as if she were Giacometti, preparing to make one of his skinny, almost invisible men, a man who wasn't there. She would give the head a fullness with large, brooding, seductive eyes, speaking of a love that he had never spoken aloud.

"I didn't notice time passing, I was so engrossed in memories that would inform my work. But soon the light was not as bright as it had been and I realized the hour was long past noon. By the time the clock struck two I began to cry, like a woman who was being stood up for a date she had eagerly anticipated.

"Annoyance became hysteria. The sculpture became therapy, not art. I raged at it, knocking the clay about in ways that I felt my father had knocked me about. I began to choke the slim neck, screaming at it: 'You bastard. You never gave me enough. You were never there for me except in your charm. You were never a father. You were a charmer, a charmer! I accepted that, too, but not again, not this time!' "

Rachel broke down, sobbing, hurt, broken, angry, not only by her father, but by all the lovers who had treated her the way her father had done. "I idealize charming men, and they stand me up, just like my father. The men I go for are just like my father. They charm my pants off, literally, and then they disappoint me. They make promises they don't keep, and then I seethe with hysterical anger because I feel just like I did when I was a little girl, disappointed by my father."

Eventually Rachel's father arrived, explaining with his usual insouciant charm that he had had to wait for the doctor; the examination took much longer than he had expected. She accepted his apology, and began to make a head, much more realistic than she thought she wanted to make. The crisis had opened the way for her to work through some of her need to idealize him. "I need to lower my expectations of him and of my lover," she said, upon long and sober reflection. "I need to forgive my father for the wounds of my childhood. Most of all, I must learn to stop blaming my lover for those childhood wounds, too."

The last time I saw Rachel she was busy with a head of her boyfriend. It, too, is realistic — much more so than she had ever dared expect.

At some point we all, like Priscilla, like Karen, like Claire, Rachel, and the others, must give up the ghosts of childhood, those familiar phantoms who prowl our psyches and who so often turn out to be only our fathers, like the men we remember moving about our bedrooms after we had put out the light to fall asleep. To us was given the need to search for order and meaning, to stop pushing and pulling at the disparate parts of ourselves. Though too late to change our personal histories, we can still, if we try, integrate the bits and pieces of our emotions to create a coherent inner voice.

Recognition is important even when we must recognize that a father is less than we hoped he would be or once thought he was. He is the only father we have and we must learn what it is that he means to us even if we learn that he doesn't mean very much at all.

When Erik Erikson talks about the eighth and final psychological stage of "ego integrity," he describes it this way: "It is the acceptance of one's one and only life cycle as something that had to be and that by necessity permitted no substitutions: it thus means a new, a different love of one's parents." [7]

Wrenching though it usually is, it is at this point that we must finally call quits to the game, to stop seeking the Superman we knew as Daddy — to be content with the reality of the flesh-and-blood mortal we have found in Superman's place. We have drawn Daddy out of his hiding place as best we can. For better or worse, he is a part of the woman we have finally become.

Driving into the Future

"Life must be lived forwards,
but it can only be understood backwards."

—Søren Kierkegaard

CHAPTER THIRTEEN

Goodbye, Big Daddy

The sun slipped below the roofline of Griffith Stadium
and suddenly the air was cold. I wanted to go home.
My older brother, Stanley, didn't.

"There's still a minute to play," he said.

"The Redskins are behind by ten points. You *know* how the
game will end."

Stanley shielded his eyes with a scorecard. The sun was gone
but Stanley liked the way he looked, with the rolled-up scorecard
pressed against his brow. "Never over 'til it's over," he said.

My mother agreed. "A fumble, an interception, and it's a new
game."

"I'm still cold."

Daddy stood up, buttoning his overcoat. "Come on, Suzie.
We'll walk on ahead and get in line for the streetcar. Stanley and
your mother can catch up with us at the car. If we're moving you
won't feel the cold."

We trooped down the ramp to the street with the outriders of
the crowd, eager to make the first trolley car up Georgia Avenue.

Taking the trolley up Georgia Avenue to our car, parked on a side street away from the crush of traffic at the stadium, was another of our little rituals of Sunday afternoon. When we stepped out of the stadium the full breath of a late-November cold front hit us squarely, and by the time we walked the two blocks to the car line I was shivering. I hadn't dressed for the falling temperature.

My father, standing next to me in the queue, hugged me closer to him, trying to still my shivering body and chattering teeth. Suddenly, he whipped off is overcoat and draped it over my shoulders. He guided my left arm into the left sleeve, and then ducked inside the coat himself, slipping his right arm into the right sleeve. He hugged me close and together we struggled with the buttons. We were buttoned up together when the streetcar arrived, and we hopped aboard the trolley like a pair of Siamese twins.

The conductor looked at us, perplexed and grinning. "I don't know whether I should charge one or two fares. I've never taken fares from Siamese twins before."

"I think two," said Daddy, handing over a handful of coins. "Two heads are better than one."

I still chuckle thinking about that afternoon, remembering the closeness of my father, the rugged masculine texture of his cheek against mine (not smooth like Mom's), the bittersweet fragrance of talc and Bay Rum. The moment stands out in my memory like a snapshot remembrance of something wonderful past. I never before nor have I since felt more safe, more secure, and more loved. But more than remembered charm, the incident foretold to a small girl an approaching understanding of male and female, masculine and feminine, of the bond between father and daughter. I luxuriated in the flirtatious seductiveness of the moment, and beheld a glimpse of the richness of attracting opposites. My mother and I could not have engaged each other so in a similar moment of playfulness.

Every child has memories of the special differences between mother and father. These are the differences that in that best of all childhood worlds provide a secure balance of influences. Certain patterns repeat themselves with the imprint of archetypes.

For example, I remember those many nights when I fell asleep in the car, driving home from my grandparents' house, with my head resting on my mother's lap, my body all but blending into the soft, downy contours of hers. Once home, it was my father who carried me upstairs, his angular strength supporting me. I felt weightless in his arms. He *was* the strongest man in the world. My mother was supple, my father was muscle. My mother was *always* there, *always* loving; my father always came through on those special times when he was needed. My mother nurtured us with milk and tender touch; my father kept the beasts of a child's imagination beaten back from the hearth with his strength and cunning.

This book has been about fathers and their influences upon their daughters, and about a particular father, my own, and how his unique influence shaped the kind of woman that I came to be. But it is a book that is no less about mothers, and the mother's ultimate gift to a daughter. A mother makes the father-daughter relationship possible and is herself the fragile bridge upon which father-daughter bonds are forged.

Though the occasions on which my father brought the big maroon car to collect me from school or a friend's house stand out in my memory because they were so rare, it was my mother who was the parent most *often* there, driving me to the dentist, dance lessons, the parties and social occasions that first open a child's eyes to the larger world outside the home.

It was my father who "papered the house" for my dance recitals, buying fistfuls of twenty-five-cent tickets and collaring his Runyonesque friends to make sure that Miss Adalaide Courtenay had a public to whom she could present her students of tap and toe. It was my mother who practiced the dance steps with me, who kept after me to practice, who instilled in me the confidence to perform. If my father gave me a dollar for every A on my report card, it was my mother who stayed up late helping me color the flags of the different nations for a project on the United Nations, who drilled me in my spelling vocabulary every morning before school.

Such were the parental distinctions in the late 1940s and

1950s, distinctions maligned in the years since, as sociologists argue whether biology shapes culture, or whether cultural prejudices distort and amplify biological differences that are otherwise inconsequential. Has nature programmed women to nurture the young in a profoundly different way than men, or is this a skill that can be learned? Could my father have practiced my dance steps with me, or colored my flags? Could my mother have learned how to run the book and the crap game just as well as my father? Nobody knows; this is an argument that will surely endure for as long as men and women endure. But it seems clear to me, from hundreds of interviews and questionnaires, that most women expect that fathers, whether their own or the fathers of their own children, being men, will always be something other than exactly what women think they want them to be. In the main, men are going to be what *they* want to be.

What Do Men Want? (What Do Women Want?)

Most men, like our fathers, will continue to hide; such is the nature of the beast. We learn their hiding places and flush them from these secret places, but only occasionally, and then only temporarily. The raising of female expectations along with the raising of the female consciousness has created a paradox for women: we want fathers to take more responsibility for the care of their children, and like it when they do. But most of us have also learned that for our own survival and for the best interests of our children we must be prepared to assume the bottom-line responsibilities ourselves. The world will be the world as it is until it becomes the world we want it to be, and in the meantime we have to live in it.

In attempting to change their own lives, seeking opportunities for themselves that have been denied them both at work and in the home, many women are tempted to extremes in seeking changes from men. A clamor for men to become coequal nurturers, for example, though well-intentioned, is surely wrong-headed because it assumes that men will cheerfully relinquish the qualities we don't like while continuing assiduously to cultivate the qualities we do like. Some men will, as we shall see in this chapter; when they do, we may not always like the result, as we shall also see.

Though few fathers today boast, like my father, that they never changed a diaper, some of the modern rhetoric to persuade fathers to become mothers is, at the least, naively unrealistic. One well-known feminist writer urges men to study the "details of feeling" from their wives, the better to transform their "useless 'manhood' " into a different kind of fatherhood. Manhood, in this odd view, is perceived as something that can be separated from the male gender.

Men who can afford it, financially, are told to cut off their day's work at six, refuse to volunteer for extra work, and look for opportunities to change jobs, to become poets, potters, or housc-husbands to relieve their wives and get to know their children.[1]

The clamor from many feminists is for a sameness of the sexes. Little boys should become less competitive; little girls more. Fathers should be more like traditional mothers; mothers, less like traditional mothers. Marriage contracts, setting out shared "parenting" and equal time for the same tasks, are goals of many of these feminists and the unspoken complementary behavior of my parents' generation is looked upon as "sexist."

Yet the question persists: how realistic is the quest for sexual sameness and how desirable is it in the long run for fathers and daughters, daughters and husbands?

Vive la Différence

A theme of this book is that men and women, fathers and daughters, are different. *Vive la différence.* It is this very difference that enhances a daughter's self-esteem when she has a good relationship with her father.

Fathers and daughters are heirs to an abundance of possibilities because they belong to different sexes, and when they enjoy a good relationship, a father becomes an important influence on a daughter's sense of her femininity and competency.

The ideal father, as we have seen, is the man who in the first years has a "love affair" with his daughter. He first responds to her femininity by admiring her hair, her smile, the way she walks, the way she talks. He shows his pleasure by holding her, kissing her, cuddling her, and playing baby games with her.

This father is an important audience for her first steps, words, recitations. Because he is not around as often as her mother in the early years, his admiration, approval, and encouragement validate each new success in a way very different from her mother's.

A mother's love *feels* unconditional, providing a generalized security which is a daughter's due. A father's love *is* dangerous, and thus is more qualified. As the first man in her life, he sets the pattern of her expectations of men later in life. He provides safe sexual titillation even as he marks her achievements.

Because her mother is most closely associated with a daughter's first months of dependency, a father is also a dashing knight who rescues a girl from a mother's occasionally smothering protection. He is her insurance against harmful dependence.

But just as her mother has to learn to let her baby go, a father gradually must loosen his authority as she grows older. Many fathers and daughters never adjust to change. They are stuck in a trap of psychological dependency, so that a mature young woman remains Daddy's Little Girl, or they become locked in a conflict so that they never get to know each other as adults.

Since a teenager, like a toddler, craves loving authority, challenges and restrictions should be extended judiciously. As we have learned, a father should replace his robust demonstrations of affection with unhurried conversations, showing above all that he respects, admires, and takes seriously the young girl who is becoming the woman. He expresses values by the way he lives, which say that he expects no less from her. His is the wisdom that is passed on from the older generation, an attentive, reasonable, and firm authority figure who guides his daughter to a satisfying social and intellectual life by helping her to appreciate her femininity and developing abilities. Through the turmoil and turbulence of her changes, he is her anchor of responsibility until that time when she must leave him for the larger world. She will then have the confidence to assume her own care and protection. For better and worse, he is the standard against whom she will measure the men she meets.

We often see our fathers, in the way we usually see our mothers, through the distorted lenses of our own childhood. None of us can truly know what a father was like when he was a child. But when we become adults we can understand more of who he might have been. We can finally appreciate the struggling and the yearning of his own youth, and thus better come to terms with our own struggles and yearnings. Those of us who were fortunate to have had a father when we were young can do certain things to assure a warm and close relationship with him as we both grow older.

We can first put aside the father of our youthful fantasy. By doing that, we can better appreciate the father we each carry within ourselves. We can at last realize that if father did not always know best, he nevertheless usually did the best he could. He was only a mortal; this may be the most painful realization of all.

Less fortunate among us, the women in my study showed me, are those who grow up without a father. Today, because about one in five American children live in fatherless homes, many girls are cheated out of a father-as-protector. They lack the strong male guardian to defend them against the real dangers and imagined terrors that lurk in the dark shadows of every girlhood. Because they grow up without understanding the secure value of a masculine presence in their lives, they find it difficult to get along with men when they are older. They learn badly how to relate to men, remembering only that it was a man who loved and left. Fearing male rejection, many women who grow up without a father unconsciously seek male rejection as adults, and abandonment becomes a self-fulfilling (and usually repeating) prophecy.

Increasing numbers of divorces indicate the degree to which we have moved from a child-centered society, in which each parent takes responsibility for raising the offspring, to one in which individual self-fulfillment, or "creative divorce" rather than family life, has become the standard by which we gauge adult experience.

Coinciding with the increased numbers of fathers abandoning families and leaving daughters to the care of single mothers, an increasing number of fathers have attempted to abandon the positive values of authority so long associated with fatherhood. Such a father becomes the weak man who cowers before responsibility, or evades it.

If there is one kind of father who is universally criticized by the women who talked to me, he is the Pusillanimous Patriarch, the weakling who hides behind his fears, who could not or would not stand up to his wife when the occasion demanded. The daughters of these men felt truly abandoned, robbed of sexual balance in their home, cheated of a male protector. Daughters of Dagwood, the comic-strip father who is afraid to confront his bullying boss and who is pursued by a nagging wife and disrespectful children, continue to see their fathers as figures of ridicule.

When Manhood Becomes Ma-hood

Comes now a new father of ridicule, creeping into the culture. At the extreme he is the father who wants to be a mother. Nature having failed him, he imitates and mocks the opposite sex, elevating such enterprise to virtue. He may start by becoming an active "participant" in the birth process, though his experience is by necessity somewhat different than his wife's.

Jonathan Gathorne-Hardy, in *Marriage, Love, Sex & Divorce,* describes how one Sensitive New Englishman, a student in prenatal classes conducted by the National Childbirth Trust of Great Britian, became so entralled with the birth of his child that he seemed to forget who it was who actually gave birth.

The perspiration was rolling off my head. Then the glorious moment when the little being was wholly released from the vagina. The nurses turned the baby round. "It's a girl, honey!" I shouted. "It's a girl honey, honey!" I was beside myself with joy! I had given birth along with my wife. I was exhausted. It was glorious, just glorious . . . ecstasy. . . .[2]

The actual mother's account was somewhat less vivid, rendered in a sentence or two. She no doubt remembered less. "It was very much a joint effort," she said. "Without John I'm afraid I never would have made it. He played the most important part."

Though this man is still an exaggerated example of the New Father, men who want to be mothers are familiar enough to trendspotters. *Ms.* magazine describes this surprise baby shower, given for an expectant father by his male friends: "With full stomachs and cold cans of beer, conversation became lively . . . but [there was not] a moment when every conversation in the room did not circle back to fathers and children, and Charlie [the expectant father]."[3]

Exhibiting this newly found maternal consciousness is even thought to be good politics. Toby Moffett, when a congressman from Connecticut, wrote a newspaper column about how he interrupted his preparations for a speech on national-defense policy to help his wife give birth to a daughter: "I catch a glimpse of the baby's head. A tiny bit of hair. I'm trying to concentrate on this and not on arms control. . . ."[4]

Many women enjoy the comforting presence of their husbands in childbirth classes and in the delivery room, and the tighter bonds of intimacy these intensely personal and private moments often encourage. But when a man makes these private moments public, the temptation becomes irresistible to say of this husband: "Methinks he doth protest too much."

The ritualistic participation in the birth of children may be indicative of other changes, some profound, taking place in many young men.

The heartthrob of the seventies was, without question, the New Sensitive Male: John Lennon, househusband, or Dustin Hoffman, "the maternal male par excellence," in the words of Erica Jong, the novelist, whose books usually describe different forms of male sex appeal. The heartthrob of the eighties, she speculates, will be

a man who "wishes perhaps that God had made him a woman."[5]
At the least, such a man seems to reverse the lament of Professor
Henry Higgins so that it becomes: "Why can't a man be more like
a woman?"

Hoffman himself suggests he sees himself as this new kind of
man. In a newspaper interview, he says he always felt nature
cheated him: "What I wanted to show [in *Kramer vs. Kramer*] was
something I'd always felt cheated on — that I simply couldn't be
a mother, that I couldn't carry a baby and give birth. I used to
have these conversations, and people would look at me like I was
crazy. I'd say, 'Don't you want to be a mother? Don't you miss
breast-feeding?' "[6]

Fathers who yearn to be honored on Mother's Day may be reflecting society's changing values. But such changes bode ill, not
only for daughters of such fathers, but for women who grow up
and marry such men to father their children.

Ray Lovett, a Washington, D.C., man who mothered his sons
for ten years, in a newspaper essay urges other men to emulate his
example: "Mothering has taught me the wisdom of silliness. The
masculine endeavors of deciding, competing, achieving, and making money sap the energy of men." Imitating maternity, on the
other hand, offers him "the value of dependency and passivity."[7]

Such parody of traditional womanly ways invites a backlash.
When a group of middle-class adolescent girls was asked to read
and comment on this father's feelings, they agreed that they
wanted their mothers and fathers to be different. Said one: "I
wouldn't marry a man like that because I want a man who has
some muscle." Said another: "If Daddy was like that I'd croak."
Said still another: "I definitely want a man who will help out with
the children, but not *that* much."

Marriage between men and women who both work outside the
home and seek an equality of parent roles is more and more frequent, and though this naturally demands a father to be more attentive to his family than in previous times, he will assume female
values and attitudes at peril to himself and his daughter's esteem.
What a daughter wants and needs most is a mother and a father,
neither two mothers, nor two fathers.

A young girl's security grows out of her knowing that her father is there to protect her with his male strength, stamina, and mettle that complement the female strength, example, and nurturance of her mother. If her father jettisons his manhood in pursuit of a higher feminine sensibility, he has little to give her, except more of what she already receives from her mother. At best he can offer only a parody of the real thing. One father, a chemist, who shares "parenting" on an equal basis with his wife, confides that he fears for his daughter's passivity: "I'm actually afraid she will grow up to be as passive as I am, and I'm working hard not to allow her to follow my example."

Many wives of such men, though pleased with some of the changes in their own lives, are nevertheless contemptuous of the changes in their husbands. Pierre Mornell, a psychiatrist in Marin County, California, where so many of the fashions of mellow America originate, recalls the complaint of one such wife: "My husband suffers from premature emasculation."

Men and women, says Dr. Mornell in his *Passive Men, Wild Women,* are on a collision course because a man's greater muscular strength no longer "defends him against a woman's greater emotional strength." The redefinition of male parenthood in the contemporary world robs the father of his psychological masculinity and he becomes like "a turtle without a shell . . . unprotected, exposed and vulnerable."[8]

When men pursue a feminine sensibility, women inevitably are shortchanged in their own fundamental psychic and sensual needs. "In my practice," says F. Joseph Whelan, a psychiatrist whose Washington practice includes many single women drawn to the Potomac power game, "I have noted that today's women want to have a placid, pliable man to deal with most of the time. However, they also want a virile, aggressive male when it comes to bedtime activities . . . a tiger in bed and a lamb in the living room. Such a creature is hard to find."[9]

The transition from tiger to lamb is a problem for fathers, too. Nurturing does not yet come naturally to them; they must *learn* what a woman *knows.* At the root of the sexual game of hide-and-seek may be this tiger-lamb tension, a man's fear of woman and of himself, a fear that grows out of his need to be aggressive sexually and to determine with absolute certainty the fatherhood of his off-spring.[10]

Men often connect violence and sex, and, as we have seen, daughters are occasionally the victims of their fathers' sexual violence. With a girl child, a man confronts the ultimate temptation of intimacy and the ultimate taboo of society. In most cases, of course, a father loves his daughter and he wants to help her grow and he will relinquish a great deal of freedom to see that she is nurtured well.

The Greening of Morality

Marriage is the institution that most successfully provides society with care for the young. Marriage is a contract for that care and requires a workable compromise of responsibilities. That there is a need for renewed sharing of responsibility between father and mother is clear to nearly everyone. But what the responsibility of each is, is not so clear.

We have moved beyond the father who thinks he demeans his male dignity by being seen holding his infant, or taking care of her routine needs, such as taking her to a pediatrician's waiting room populated only by mothers. Many of the ways attitudes have changed reflect a man's unabashed new pride in his fatherhood and of what his contribution can be, and this is all to the good. But he must be attentive to more than physical needs. Both men and women must now rediscover and redefine the moral center, an ethical core to be passed on to their children to replace the center and core lost with the breakdown of traditional paternal values.

When moral values have no place of honor within a home, and when parents accept no responsibility for shaping such values, their children are invariably cheated. And when children are cheated, those cheated most of all are their daughters, to whom is bequeathed the fire and breath of life itself. On this, there is growing agreement, forged at widely separated places on the political compass.

"We delight in the sophistication that tells us there are no absolutes, no moral authorities," observes William Raspberry, a black liberal columnist for the *Washington Post.* "And one result is that we confuse and frustrate our children, who keep telling us (though not usually in words) that they want rules: consistent, reliable guidelines for running their lives."[11] Ellen Goodman, a liberal feminist columnist for the *Boston Globe,* notes that "the rites of passage have been reduced to drinking, driving, and sex. The only value [young people] seem to have is as consumers. So they are being, quite literally, sold sex along with their deodorant and shampoo and eyeliner and movie stubs. . . . There is virtually no sex on television that isn't sniggering or exploitative, bumps or grinds."[12] Writes Dr. Ed Hindson, a professor of religion at Liberty Baptist College, in a quarterly published by the Rev. Dr. Jerry Falwell: "Men have led the headlong rush into hedonism, and therefore are often too guilt-ridden to deal with moral problems in their own home. Daddy, you cannot watch lewd television programs, laugh at dirty jokes, yell at your wife, read pornographic magazines, and expect your children to respect your leadership."[13]

All three, acknowledging the lack of moral guidelines for young people, strike grace notes on the theme of Christopher Lasch, whose *Culture of Narcissism* makes the point that parents who fail to serve as models of disciplined self-restraint, models of morality, parents who do not offer distinctions between right and wrong, court moral catastrophe. The collapse of parental authority, says Lasch, reflects the collapse of "ancient impulse controls": society has shifted from one system of beliefs in which the superego values of self-restraint were ascendant, to a system in which values of the id, values of self-indulgence, are raised to moral dominion. Abdication of parental authority inculcates the young with the traits of a corrupt, permissive, hedonistic culture, Lasch argues, and instead of holding the father as a symbol of parental authority, the culture encourages obeisance to an outside expert, a psychiatrist or guidance counselor or representative of the government.[14] Such outsiders may even occasionally help; but when all is said and done, the parent is robbed of responsibility for his young.

A daughter in particular feels robbed. She has looked to her father as a figure of all-protecting authority for all of her life, and now, as she sees him abdicating his responsibility to an outside authority, she may well see this as an abdication of his love as well; that by abandoning his responsibility he is abandoning her.

And Therapist Makes Three

In many middle-class families today there are three parents, Mom, Dad, and The Therapist. One father told me that when his teenage daughter turned sixteen, she wanted to see a psychiatrist. All her friends saw "shrinks," so why shouldn't she? She had problems she couldn't discuss with either parent. He agreed, but now regards that agreement as relinquishing personal responsibility in his daughter's life. Why the automatic therapist? "My wife wished that she had seen a therapist when she was that age, and I thought there are probably things I wasn't understanding about the female psyche that made that a good thing to do. But my daughter was having boyfriend problems. She had yielded her virginity and didn't know how to handle the complex issues of sexuality, and neither my wife nor I took on these issues with her. What did we know about this generation's sexual precociousness? I think now that we were part of the problem. We allowed a therapist to carry the values for us, and assist our daughter in her continuing alienation."

This father believes that in the years when his daughter was struggling toward adulthood, the teenage years when she needed to firmly establish her identity, he was not firm enough. He allowed cultural permissiveness to undercut his paternal authority. He let her be independent of him before she was ready. He wanted to impart tough-minded values along with strict curfews and docked allowances for broken rules, but was persuaded instead that his daughter needed only tender, loving care.

What she needed, he now believes, was a firm masculine authority, a father expressing his view of right and wrong about her everyday experiences. "I should have talked with her in those two hours she saw a therapist each week. I should have given her that private time for give-and-take with me in real life instead of letting a therapist, whose values I know nothing about, take charge of her secret life."

He thinks the therapy prolonged his daughter's rebellion. "Our daughter had an audience for playing out all the confidences she kept from us. My wife and I exchanged her dependency on us for one on an outsider."

It is impossible to know what a therapist actually accomplishes for an adolescent, of course, and the father's view may be harsh, but the readiness with which many families legitimize outside "expertise" is surely testimony to waning paternal authority.

Power to the Parents

At its best the father-daughter bond thrives in a family where mother and father provide a loving and respectful relationship that enables a child to see the problems as well as the pleasures in a male-female relationship. At its best the father-daughter bond uniquely joins male and female strengths. A father is singularly equipped to teach a young woman to understand and accept the differences between the sexes, to recognize the depths and flexibilities of those differences. He teaches her that an abiding love of opposites requires patient attention to the other's wants, needs, and personality.

Once mothers and fathers agree to assume responsibility for mutual obligations, affirming their belief in the values of raising their children in an intact family, they can find many ways to discharge these responsibilities. But a father's way of effectively preserving family values need not be a mother's ways.

The concept of self, as men have developed it, traditionally requires the exertion of power over others. This view does not fit the experience of most women. Most women feel a need to participate in and foster the development of others, to affirm their own sense of self worth. Women usually define power as the strength to care for others; female morality usually flows from this strength.[15]

From her father, a daughter can develop an understanding of power, an appreciation of the rewards and a recognition of the limitations of the traditional male approach to work. By modeling her nurturing ability on her mother, the example of the parent who nurtures best, she learns the delineation of another kind of power, which she can take both to the outside world of work and to the tender and intimate circle of the family.

In this better of all worlds, aspects of nurturing and independence flow from both parents, and a daughter can freely choose those qualities that she wishes to develop and emphasize. She will learn that a successful relationship with a man requires a workable compromise, that procreating a baby and raising it to a successful life with that man will require still greater compromise, either in the timing of children or timing of career or quantity of work outside the home. She can choose a father for her children who understands his contribution to this compromise, who accepts his responsibility for psychological, economic, and physical support.

By emphasizing natural incentives for family life, men and women can come to a realistic understanding of the values of honest compromise.

With the openness that would allow a new kind of father to prosper, a daughter would learn to her growing appreciation the potential for choosing many different paths to success, and once there, she could define the limits of success to suit herself. No longer would roles be written on stone, with a daughter learning that the role assigned to her was the role assigned the least value by men. Often the most formidable male obstacle was her father himself.

Because a father plays a crucial role in a daughter's perception of achievement, competence, and ambition, it is he who must show her that none of these qualities is incompatible with femininity — either her own view of it or male appreciation of it. The admiration of a feminized man, after all, cannot do much to enhance any woman's sense of her female self.

"We may find that we can keep certain cultural sex differences," writes Janet Radcliffe Richards, the English feminist, "once it is realized that it is only the ones which are degrading to women which are actually harmful."[16] She might also have acknowledged those that are degrading to men, too. Increased flexibility of sexual roles, with a forthright appreciation for difference, would be realistic family goals for both women and men.

As the father's hand is strengthened in the home, he may be encouraged to cut back his obsessive need to succeed at the office. He may assume greater responsibility for the psychological as well as the economic welfare of his children because he *wants* to. The division of labor would become more equitable, as he finds it easier to apply the firm and engaging assertiveness to family matters that he applies to his tasks on his job.

In time, he might even want to come out of his hiding place. He may become less afraid to be close to his daughter as he becomes less threatened by what is expected of him. When he discovers that he need not slavishly imitate his wife's behavior in a futile attempt to be a mother, he could learn to freely offer the things father knows best: paternal love, admiration of our femininity, and practical skill for working and protecting oneself in a world that is harsh and unforgiving.

Armed with an awareness of the electrical connection between a father and a daughter, a man has the special opportunity and the singular responsibility to light his daughter's way on her exploration of Freud's "dark continent of female sexuality." By developing her trust in an admiring opposite sex, he allows her to give full expression to her capacity to create a productive and fulfilling life.

She must learn from her father, as he himself was taught at the price of some pain, the futility of trying to achieve everything; that the notion that everything is possible is gossamer, and the energy expended in pursuing that notion is in the end wasted energy, destroying realistic possibilities and ultimately inviting frustration and despair.

So what will the father of the future be like? What will his daughter be like? How will the lessening influence of the father, so clearly visible to feminist and fundamentalist, misogynist and traditionalist, be made manifest as the male domination of our society continues to diminish? What is likely to replace his influence?

For better or worse, the responsibility for shaping the answers to these questions falls most heavily on women, and it is likely that women will continue to provide most of the answers. In doing so we must find a way to preserve and extend the strengths of strong men, while guarding against the delicious temptation to surrender to the security and warmth and the stunting constriction of an embrace of Daddy's Little Girl. Our heads tell us that the commonsense qualities of Rabbits, Colts, even Gremlins, are good for us, even as in our deepest hearts we raise a wistful sigh of fantasy for that time past, when Big Daddy climbed into the last of the big ragtops, pulled on his leather-suede gloves as soft as butter, and drove off into the night with the big whitewalls thrumming against the pavement to the tape-deck rhythms of Loretta Lynn's hymn to the fate of our fathers: *"They don't make 'em like my daddy any more."*

Notes

For complete publishing information, consult the bibliography.

Chapter 1: Daddies, Daughters, and Dilemmas

1. Steinem, "The Stage Is Set," *Ms.*, July/August 1982, p. 77.
2. Lamb, Owen, and Chase-Lansdale (1979), p. 89.
3. Lynn (1974), p. 105.
4. Napier with Whitaker (1978), pp. 67–68.
5. For a rundown of father-infant research, see Lamb and other essays in Pedersen (1980); and Parke (1981).
6. Freud (1925), pp. 27–38
7. Mitchell (1974), p. 117.
8. Klein and Tribich (1982), p. 18. On describing the symptoms of women suffering from hysteria, Freud wrote: "The astonishing thing was that in every case . . . blame was laid on perverse acts by the father . . . though it was hardly credible that perverted acts against children were so general." From his letter to Wilhelm Fliess, April 28, 1897. For further discussions of Freud's seduction theory see Sulloway (1979).
9. Statistics for incest are unreliable because of the extent of unreported cases. Blair Justice and Rita Justice (1979) discuss the dif-

ficulty of obtaining statistics, while providing some of their own. Jane Brody, in reviewing their book, cites one family in ten as the generally accepted figure in this country, in the *Baltimore Sun,* September 19, 1979.

10. Klein (1981), p. 191.
11. Letter to Fliess, May 31, 1897, quoted by Klein (1981), p. 197.
12. Freud (1933), p. 106. Freud wrote: "I was driven to recognize in the end that these reports [of paternal seduction] were untrue and so came to understand that the hysterical symptoms [were] derived from phantasies and not from real occurrences. . . . It was only later that I was able to recognize in this phantasy of being seduced by the father the expression of the typical Oedipus complex in women."
13. Erikson quoted in Sulloway (1979), p. 20.
14. Even in the celebrated "Dora case," in which a father offers his daughter Dora to his mistress's husband in exchange for his own sexual liaison, Freud places responsibility for the daughter's hysterical reaction to being bartered as *her* unconscious problem. Klein and Tribich (1979), p. 56.
15. Machtlinger (1976), p. 283.
16. Parsons (1949, 1955 [with Bales], 1964).
17. Based on 1980 census data report in *The New York Times* and *The Washington Post,* April 20, 1982. The number of children with mothers who work (31.8 million) is, for the first time in our history, larger than the number of children with mothers at home (26.3 million).
18. Erikson (1968), p. 96, identifies these challenges as crises, turning points that affect both parent and child.
19. Lamb (1980), pp. 21–42.
20. Hammer (1969), pp. 181–182.
21. Gaylin (1979), pp. 22–23.

Chapter 2: Daddy the Protector

1. Bettelheim (1970), p. 205.
2. ———, (1970), p. 206.
3. Alan Alda, "Dig Into the World," *Reader's Digest,* May 1981, p. 84.
4. Fromm (1947), p. 96.
5. Dr. John Bowlby (1973), the British psychologist, describes the effects of maternal deprivation in *Separation.*

6. Mahler, Pine, and Bergman (1975); Mahler and Gosliner (1955).
7. Lamb (1980), p. 37.
8. Elizabeth Hall, "Our Children Are Treated Like Idiots," *Psychology Today,* July 1981, p. 42.

Chapter 3: Daddy the Defector

1. Nin, Vol. I (1966), pp. 339–340.
2. Plath (1975), p. 25.
3. Alvarez (1970), p. 21.
4. Le Anne Schreiber, "The Journals of Sylvia Plath," *The New York Times,* April 21, 1982.
5. Alvarez (1970), p. 21.
6. Leonard (1966), pp. 325–334.
7. "Hers," *The New York Times,* August 20, 1981.
8. Sandy Rovner, "Judy Blume: Talking It Out," *The Washington Post,* November 3, 1981.
9. A discussion of Dr. Kaplan's work can be found in Nadine Brozan, "Bereaved Children Share Pain," *The New York Times,* December 14, 1981. Lisa and Amy's quotes are taken from this article.
10. Michaels (1981), p. 5.
11. Wolfenstein (1966), p. 106.
12. Goldberg (1981), p. 38.
13. Napier with Whitaker (1978), p. 113.
14. For personal accounts of problems for daughters of divorce see Laiken (1981).
15. Schnall (1981), pp. 173–184.
16. Hetherington (1972), pp. 313–326.
17. Lynn (1974), pp. 254–280.
18. Quote from paper delivered at Women in Crisis Conference, New York City, June 1981.
19. Quoted in Green (1976), p. 107.
20. Wallerstein and Kelly (1980), pp. 249–250. Many fathers disappear altogether, offering neither emotional nor financial support. In the first year after separation or divorce about 45 percent of fathers comply with court-ordered child support, but the majority do not. By the tenth year, 80 percent of fathers have failed to offer any support, either in time or money. (Mark K. Powelson and Marilee Strong, "Women at Work," *Focus,* July 1981.) According to the 1980 census, there are 5.8 million single-parent families in the United States and the vast majority of them are headed by women, a large percentage of whom are living in poverty.

21. This research is discussed in Carin Rubenstein, "The Children of Divorce as Adults," *Psychology Today,* January 1980. Despite these gloomy findings, it is estimated that one-third of the children in the United States will suffer their parents' divorce before they are eighteen years old.
22. Boszormenyi-Nagy and Spark (1973), pp. 151–166.
23. Jacqueline Kasun, "More on the New Sex Education," *The Public Interest,* Winter 1980.

Chapter 4: Rituals of Childhood: For Better and Worse

1. For the way little girls marry their fathers and eventually turn to their peers, see Nagera (1975), pp. 115–118.
2. Alice Miller (1981).
3. Mahler and Gosliner (1955), p. 209.
4. Bernard Gavzer, "The Lady Is a Tramp," *Parade,* February 7, 1982.
5. Hammer (1969), p. 182.
6. This quote and a discussion of this theory can be found in Abelin (1980), p. 152.
7. Gaylin (1976), p. 176.
8. This quote, and her discussion of infant research, is from "Women and Depression," *The New Republic,* July 5 & 12, 1980, pp. 25–29.
9. This discussion is based on Dr. Abelin's observations set forth in his unpublished manuscript (1978).
10. Freud (1933), p. 104.
11. A discussion of the Kleinian interpretation of femininity can be found in Barglow and Schaefer (1977).
12. For contributions from biology and genetics see Sherfey (1973), and Stoller (1968, 1976).
13. The peek-a-boo game, for example, has teasing overtones and is played differently between father and daughter than between mother and daughter. This game helps an infant master the anxiety of separation from both her parents by practicing separation in the formal structure of a game, but it can take on a distinctively exuberant and flirtatious playfulness when a father plays it with his daughter. See Kleeman (1967, 1973).
14. Mead (1935), p. 81. Encouraging little girls to learn coquetry, often thought to be a reflection of "macho culture," sometimes is

not. The Arapesh example is one such exception. The Arapesh father, more than fathers in most cultures, shares the responsibility for a baby's care. Dr. Mead tells of an outsider commenting to a group of Arapesh that one of the middle-aged men in the village is particularly handsome. An Arapesh parent answers solemnly, with no intent for irony: "Handsome? Yes. But you should have seen him before he bore all those children."

15. ———, (1935), p. 32. She describes the infanticide rite: "While the child is being delivered, the father waits within ear-shot until its sex is determined, when the midwives call it out to him. To this information he answers laconically, 'Wash it,' or 'Do not wash it.' In a few cases when the child is a girl and there are already several girl-children in the family, the child will not be saved, but left, unwashed, with the cord uncut, in the bark basin on which the delivery takes place. . . . If after one or two girls have been kept another is also preserved, the chances of having a son is much further postponed, and so, having no contraceptives, the Arapesh sometimes resort to infanticide."

16. It is perhaps no coincidence that young women from the Southern states, where Scarlett O'Hara is a patron saint and coquetry is an art form, invariably dominate the Top Ten. Mississippi has produced back-to-back Miss Americas, and in 1982, both Miss America and Miss USA were from Arkansas.

17. Lynn Darling, "Parade," *The Washington Post*, July 13, 1981.

18. For a view of different kinds of mother-father-daughter triangles, see Forest (1966).

19. Mead (1935), p. 179.

20. Herman (1981), pp. 109–125. Quoted material comes from p. 41.

21. Angelou (1970), pp. 62–63.

22. Mead (1949), p. 199.

Chapter 5: Mythologies from Childhood: Beyond the Shadow of a Dad

1. Lash (1979), pp. 57–97. Quoted material comes from pp. 57 and 97.

2. Dr. Block discussed her research on "The Pinks and the Blues," a public television program produced by *Nova*, September 1980.

3. Hennig and Jardim (1976), pp. 99–173.

4. This discussion is based on a personal interview with Paul Chodoff, plus three papers (1958 [with Lyons], 1978, 1982.)

5. Masters and Johnson, "Incest: The Ultimate Taboo," *Redbook,* April 1976.

6. Nin, Vol. I (1966), pp. 87–88.

7. Jung (1928), pp. 158–159.

8. Phyllis Naylor, "Strangers," *The Washington Post Magazine,* January 31, 1982.

9. In one study in which parents were interviewed and children were tested in second, third, and fourth grades, daughters who showed excellence in reading and math had fathers who often praised and rewarded their everyday efforts. See Crandall, Dewey, Katkovsky, and Preston (1964).

10. Amy Gross, "Were You Daddy's Girl or Mother's Daughter?" *Mademoiselle,* March 1974.

Chapter 6: Prelude to Adolescence: My Father and Me

1. D. W. Winnicott (1965), p. 92.

Chapter 7: Passing through Puberty: An Emotional Investment with Big Change

1. Blos (1962), p. 2.

2. Farber (1980), p. 48.

3. ———, p. 49.

4. May (1980) discusses the various ways young girls break the family ties, pp. 125–132.

5. Harrison (1980), p. 53.

6. Quoted in Joann Rodgers, "Sex Among the Bubble-Gum Set," *The Baltimore News American,* July 19, 1981.

7. Quoted in "Sexes," *Time,* November 9, 1981.

8. Jane Norman and Myron Harris, "The Private Lives of American Teenagers," *The Baltimore News American,* January 20, 1982.

9. Offer, Ostrov, and Howard (1981), pp. 98–101.

10. Bruch (1978). Quoted from p. 55.

11. Quoted in Maya Pines, "When Less Than Truth Is Better," *The New York Times,* May 10, 1982.

12. Hellman (1969), p. 39.

13. Quoted in James T. Yenckel, "Couples: What's in a Hug?" *The Washington Post,* February 2, 1981.

14. Ellen Goodman, "The Fear Grows with the Girl," *The Washington Post,* June 13, 1981.

Chapter 8: Sex and the Single Daughter

1. Farber (1980), pp. 44–47.
2. For a view of lost innocence in America today, see "What Became of Childhood Innocence?" by Marie Winn, *The New York Times Magazine,* January 25, 1981.
3. "Squealing on Teen-Agers," an editorial, *The New York Times,* February 5, 1982.
4. David Elkind, "Why Children Need Time," *Parade,* January 10, 1982.
5. "Ann Landers," *The Washington Post,* March 22, 1982.
6. Justice and Justice (1979), pp. 59–80.
7. For further reading on the incest taboo, see Freud, "Totem and Taboo" (1913); Parsons (1954); Levi-Strauss (1969).
8. Chesler (1974), p. 76.

Chapter 9: Messages and Models: Sugar Daddies, Sweet and Sour

1. The following discussion is based on Dr. Herman (1981), pp. 109–125. Quoted material comes from pp. 109 and 120, respectively.
2. Moulton (1973), p. 255.
3. Horney (1934), p. 185.
4. Mack and Hickler (1981).
5. Steinberg (1980), p. 120.
6. Dowling (1981), p. 120.
7. Cronen's work is discussed in J. C. Barden, "Relationships," *The New York Times,* April 26, 1982.
8. Hiroshi Wagatuma, "Some Aspects of the Contemporary Japanese Family: Once Confucian, Now Fatherless?" *Daedalus,* Spring 1977, p. 8.

Chapter 10: My Husband and Me

1. Dowling (1981), p. 31.
2. The word was *agape* in the original Greek text, and the word *charity* as it appears here is invariably interpreted as "love" in the spiritual sense.

Chapter 11: Father's Daughter/Husband's Wife

1. Dicks (1967), p. 5.
2. Levenson and Harris (1980), p. 270.
3. Peck (1978), p. 88.
4. Halpern (1982), p. 23.
5. Alvarez (1981), pp. 28–36.
6. Sheehy (1976), p. 17.
7. Jean Baker Miller (1973), p. 394.
8. Greer (1970), p. 326.
9. Dicks (1967), p. 31.
10. Halpern (1982), p. 53.
11. Tillich (1952), p. 123.

Chapter 12: Coming to Terms:
The Long Voyage Home

1. Mornell (1979), pp. 36–37.
2. David Reuben, "Older Women Can Give Birth Safely," *Parade,* January 17, 1982.
3. Gutmann (1976).
4. Langer and Avorn (1981) are two gerontological researchers at Harvard who take issue with the "tender loving care" approach to the aged because, they say, it communicates to them that they are unable to do things for themselves.
5. For a discussion of the concepts of generativity and stagnation, see Erikson (1963), pp. 266–268.
6. Kingston (1977), pp. 12–17.
7. Erikson (1963), p. 268.

Chapter 13: Goodbye, Big Daddy

1. Pogrebin (1980), p. 164.
2. Gathorne-Hardy (1981), p. 86.
3. Ned O'Malia, "Charlie's Shower — Celebrating the Expectant Father," *Ms.,* February 1982.
4. "Replying to the President Between Contractions," *The Washington Post,* April 25, 1982.
5. "Heartthrob," *Parade,* March 22, 1981.

6. Judith Weinraub, "The Lonely Perfection of Dustin Hoffman," *The Washington Star,* December 16, 1979. Karen Horney (1926) wrote of the intensity of male "envy of pregnancy, childbirth, and motherhood, as well as of breasts and the acts of sucking" (p. 207). Anthropologists have observed that many primitive tribes practice the *couvade,* whereby a man takes to his bed when a woman goes into labor, and he affects the labor pains of his wife. The couvade ritual has many interpretations, some of which include female identification, envy of woman, protection of woman against evil spirits (Zalk, 1981).

7. "Fathers: 'Will I Be Man Enough?' " *The Washington Post,* June 19, 1981.

8. The discussion is based on Mornell (1979). Quoted material comes from pp. 173, 37, and 39, respectively.

9. "Love," *The Washington Post Magazine,* April 11, 1982.

10. This point is made dramatically in a play, *The Father,* by the misogynist Swedish playwright, August Strindberg. A father suffers a stroke when his wife raises a doubt that their daughter is in fact his daughter. Though a man must take his paternity on trust, he says, his child is nevertheless his immortality. "Take that away and you wipe me out."

11. William Raspberry, "Have We Become Too Tolerant?" *The Washington Post,* November 26, 1980.

12. Ellen Goodman, "Indecency Is Legion," *The Washington Post,* September 20, 1980.

13. Ed Hindson, "How to Win the War Against the Family," *Faith Aflame,* Summer 1980.

14. Lasch (1979), pp. 304–305.

15. The idea for the different concepts of self as perceived by men and women draws on the work of Gilligan (1982), Jean Baker Miller (1981), and McClelland (1975).

16. Richards (1980), p. 287.

Selected Bibliography

Abelin, Ernest. 1971. "The Role of the Father in the Separation-Individuation Process." In *Separation-Individuation*. Edited by J. B. McDevitt and C. F. Settlage. New York: International Universities Press.

―――. 1978. *Self Image, Gender Identity and the Early Triangulations.* Unpublished.

―――. 1980. "Triangulation, the Role of the Father and the Origins of Core Gender Identity During the Rapproachement Subphase." In *Rapprochement.* Edited by Ruth F. Lax, Sheldon Bach, and J. Alexis Burland. New York: Jason Aronson.

Alvarez, A. 1970. *The Savage God: A Study of Suicide.* New York: Random House.

―――. 1981. *Life After Marriage.* New York: Simon & Schuster.

Angelou, Maya. 1970. *I Know Why the Caged Bird Sings.* New York: Random House; Bantam Books, 1971.

Appleton, William. 1981. *Fathers and Daughters.* Garden City, New York: Doubleday & Co.

Barglow, Peter, and Margaret Schaefer. 1977. "A New Female Psychology?" In *Female Psychology*. Edited by Harold P. Blum. New York: International Universities Press.

Bettelheim, Bruno. 1970. *The Uses of Enchantment*. New York: Random House; Vintage Books, 1977.

Bird, Caroline. 1979. *The Two-Paycheck Marriage*. New York: Rawson, Wade.

Bloom-Feshbach, Jonathan. 1979. *The Beginnings of Fatherhood*. Unpublished Ph.D. dissertation, Yale University.

Blos, Peter. 1962. *On Adolescence*. New York: The Free Press.

Boszormenyi-Nagy, Ivan, and Geraldine M. Spark. 1973. *Invisible Loyalties*. New York: Harper & Row.

Bowlby, John. 1973. *Separation*. New York: Basic Books.

Bruch, Hilde. 1978. *The Golden Cage: The Enigma of Anorexia Nervosa*. Cambridge, Mass.: Harvard University Press.

Chesler, Phyllis. 1974. "Rape and Psychotherapy." In *Rape: The First Sourcebook for Women*. Edited by Noreen Connell and Cassandra Wilson. New York: New American Library.

Chodoff, Paul. 1978. "Psychotherapy of the Hysterical Personality Disorder." *Journal of the American Academy of Psychoanalysis* 6, 4.

————. 1982. "Hysteria and Women." *The American Journal of Psychiatry* 139:5 (May).

Chodoff, Paul, and Henry Lyons. 1958. "Hysteria, the Hysterical Personality and 'Hysterical' Conversion." *The American Journal of Psychiatry* 1114 (February).

Crandall, V. J., R. Dewey, W. Katkovsky, and A. Preston. 1964. "Parents' Attitudes and Behaviors and Grade-school Children's Academic Achievement." *Journal of Genetic Psychology* 104 (March).

Dicks, Henry. 1967. *Marital Tensions*. New York: Basic Books.

Dinnerstein, Dorothy. 1977. *The Mermaid and the Minotaur*. New York: Harper & Row.

Dowling, Colette. 1981. *The Cinderella Complex*. New York: Summit Books.

Erikson, Erik H. 1963. *Childhood and Society*. New York: W. W. Norton & Co.

————. 1968. *Identity: Youth and Crisis*. New York: W. W. Norton & Co.

Farber, Barry. 1980. "Adolescence." In *On Love and Loving.* Edited by Kenneth S. Pope and Associates. San Francisco: Jossey-Bass.

Fisher, Seymour. 1973. *Understanding the Female Orgasm.* New York: Basic Books; Bantam Books, 1978

Forest, Tess. 1966. "Paternal Roots of Female Character Development." *Contemporary Psychoanalysis* 3 (Fall).

Freud, Sigmund. 1913. "Totem and Taboo." In *The Standard Edition of the Complete Psychological Works of Sigmund Freud.* Translated and edited by J. Strachey with others. London: Hogarth and Institute of Psycho-Analysis, 1966.

————. 1925. "Some Psychical Consequences of the Anatomical Distinction Between the Sexes." In *Women & Analysis.* Edited by Jean Strouse. New York: Grossman; Dell, 1975.

————. 1933. "Femininity." In *New Introductory Lectures on Psychoanalysis.* New York; W. W. Norton & Co., 1965.

Friedan, Betty. 1981. *The Second Stage.* New York: Summit Books

Fromm, Erich. 1947. *Man for Himself.* New York: Reinhart & Co.

Gath, Stanley, Alan R. Gurwitt, and John Munder Ross. 1982. *Father and Child.* Boston: Little, Brown & Co.

Gathorne-Hardy, Jonathan. 1981. *Marriage, Love, Sex & Divorce.* New York: Summit Books.

Gaylin, Willard. 1976. *Caring.* New York: Alfred A. Knopf; Avon Books, 1979.

————. 1979. *Feelings.* New York: Harper & Row.

Gilligan, Carol. 1982. *In a Different Voice: Psychological Theory and Women's Development.* Cambridge, Mass.: Harvard University Press.

Goldberg, Martin. 1981. "Current Thinking on Intimacy." *Medical Aspects of Sexuality* 15 (September)

Gordon, Mary. 1978. *Final Payments.* New York: Random House; Ballantine Books, 1979.

————. 1980. *The Company of Women.* New York: Random House.

Green, Maureen. 1976. *Fathering.* New York: McGraw-Hill.

Greer, Germaine. 1970. *The Female Eunuch.* New York: McGraw-Hill.

Gutmann, David. 1976. "Individual Adaptation in the Middle Years." *Journal of Geriatric Psychiatry* IX (November 1).

Halpern, Howard M. 1982. *How to Break Your Addiction to a Person.* New York: McGraw-Hill.

Hammer, Leon I. 1969. "Female Sexuality." In *Modern Woman: Her Psychology and Sexuality.* Edited by George Goldman and Donald Milman. Springfield, Ill.: Charles C. Thomas.

Harrison, Barbara Grizutti. 1980. *Off Center.* New York: The Dial Press.

Heilbrun, A. B. 1965. "Sex Differences in Identification." *Journal of Genetic Psychology* 106, 2.

Heilbrun, A. B., S. N. Harrell, and B. J. Gillard. 1967. "Perceived Childrearing Attitudes of Fathers and Cognitive Control in Daughters." *Journal of Genetic Psychology* 111, 1.

Heilbrun, Carolyn G. 1979. *Reinventing Womanhood.* New York: W. W. Norton & Co.

Heller, Joseph. 1974. *Something Happened.* New York: Alfred A. Knopf; Ballantine Books, 1978.

Hellman, Lillian. 1969. *An Unfinished Woman.* Boston: Little, Brown & Company; Bantam Books, 1970.

Hennig, Margaret, and Anne Jardim. 1976. *The Managerial Woman.* New York: Doubleday & Co.; Pocket Books, 1978.

Herman, Judith. 1981. *Father-Daughter Incest.* Cambridge, Mass.: Harvard University Press.

Hetherington, E. N. 1972. "The Effect of Father-absence on Personality Development in Adolescent Daughters." *Developmental Psychology* 7 (November).

Hobhouse, Jane. 1982. *Nellie Without Hugo.* New York: The Viking Press.

Horney, Karen. 1926. "The Flight from Womanhood: The Masculinity-complex in Women as Viewed by Men and by Women." In *Women & Analysis.* Edited by Jean Strouse. New York: Grossman; Dell, 1974.

———. 1934. "The Overvaluation of Love." In *Feminine Psychology: Previously Uncollected Essays.* Edited by Harold Kelman. New York: W. W. Norton & Co., 1967.

———. 1939. *New Ways in Psychoanalysis.* New York: W. W. Norton & Co.

Jung, C. G. 1928. *Two Essays on Analytical Psychology.* Princeton, N.J.: Princeton University Press; Bollington, 1972.

Justice, Blair, and Rita Justice. 1979. *The Broken Taboo.* New York: Human Sciences Press.

King, Florence. 1975. *Southern Ladies and Gentlemen.* New York: Stein & Day; Bantam Books, 1979.

————. 1977. *Wasp, Where Is Thy Sting?* New York: Stein & Day.

Kingston, Maxine Hong. 1977. *China Men.* New York: Alfred A. Knopf; Ballantine Books, 1980.

Kleeman, J. A. 1967. "The Peek-a-boo Game: Its Origins, Meanings and Related Phenomena in the First Year." *The Psychoanalytic Study of the Child.* New York: International Universities Press.

————. 1973. "The Peek-a-boo Game: Its Evolution and Associated Behavior, Especially Bye-bye and Shame Expression, During the Second Year." *Journal of American Academy of Child Psychiatry* 12 (January).

Klein, Milton. 1981. "Freud's Seduction Theory." *Bulletin of the Menninger Clinic* (November).

Klein, Milton, and David Tribich. 1979. "On Freud's 'Blindness.'" *Colloquium* 2, 2.

————. 1982. "Blame the Child." *The Sciences.* New York: New York Academy of Sciences (November).

Kübler-Ross, Elisabeth. 1970. *On Death and Dying.* New York: Macmillan.

Laiken, Deirdre S. 1981. *Daughters of Divorce.* New York: William Morrow & Co.

Lamb, Michael E., ed. 1976. *The Role of the Father in Child Development.* New York: John Wiley & Sons.

Lamb, Michael. 1980. "The Development of Parent-Infant Attachments in the First Two Years of Life." In *The Father-Infant Relationship.* Edited by Frank A. Pederson. New York: Praeger.

Lamb, Michael E., Margaret Tresch Owen, and Lindsay Chase-Landsdale. 1979. "The Father-Daughter Relationship: Past, Present, and Future." In *Becoming Female: Perspectives on Development.* Edited by Claire B. Kopp. New York: Plenum Press.

Langer, Ellen J., and Jerry Avorn. 1981. "The Psychosocial Environment of the Elderly: Some Behavioral Health Implications." In *Congregate Housing for Older People*. Edited by J. Seagle and R. Chellis. Lexington, Mass.: Lexington Books.

Lasch, Christopher. 1979. *The Culture of Narcissism*. New York: W. W. Norton & Co.; Warner Books, 1979.

Lash, Joseph P. 1971. *Eleanor and Franklin*. New York: W. W. Norton & Co.

Leonard, Marjorie R. 1966. "Fathers and Daughters: The Significance of 'Fathering' in the Psychosexual Development of the Girl." *International Journal of Psycho-Analysis* 47, 2–3.

Levenson, Harry, and Charles N. Harris. 1980. "Love and the Search for Identity." In *On Love and Loving*. Edited by Kenneth S. Pope and Associates. San Francisco: Jossey-Bass.

Levi-Strauss, Claude. 1969. *Elementary Structures of Kinship*. Boston: Beacon Press.

Lynn, David B. 1974. *The Father: His Role in Child Development*. Monterey, Calif.: Brooks/Cole.

Maccoby, E. E., and C. N. Jacklin. 1974. *The Psychology of Sex Differences*. Stanford, Calif.: Stanford University Press.

Machtlinger, Veronica. 1976. "Psychoanalytic Theory: Pre-oedipal and Oedipal Phases, with Special Reference to the Father." In *The Role of the Father in Child Development*. Edited by Michael E. Lamb. New York: John Wiley & Sons.

Mack, John E., and Holly Hickler. 1981. *Vivienne*. Boston: Little, Brown & Co.

Marcus, Maurice. 1982. "Toward a Better Understanding of Penis Envy." Unpublished.

Mahler, M. S., and B. J. Gosliner. 1955. "On Symbiotic Child Psychosis: Genetic, Dynamic and Restitutive Aspects." In *The Selected Papers of Margaret Mahler*, Vol. I. New York: Jason Aronson, 1979.

Mahler, M. S., F. Pine, and A. Bergman. 1975. *The Psychological Birth of the Human Infant*. New York: Basic Books.

May, Robert. 1980. *Sex and Fantasy*. New York: W. W. Norton & Co.; Wideview Books, 1981.

McClelland, David. 1975. *Power: The Inner Experience*. New York: John Wiley & Sons.

Mead, Margaret. 1935. *Sex and Temperament in Three Primitive Societies.* New York: William Morrow & Co., 1963.

———. 1949. *Male and Female.* New York: William Morrow & Co.

Meyer, Roslyn Milstein. *Parent-Daughter Relationships and Daughters' Sexual Self-Concept, Sexual Behavior, and Sexual Values.* Unpublished dissertation: Yale University, 1977.

Michaels, Carol S. 1981. "Summary of a Study of Father Fantasies of Preschool Children with Nonresident Fathers." Paper delivered at the American Psychological Association conference, Los Angeles, August.

Miller, Alice. 1981. *Prisoners of Childhood.* New York: Basic Books.

Miller, Jean Baker. 1973. "New Issues, New Approaches." In *Psychoanalysis and Women.* Edited by Jean Baker Miller. New York: Brunner/Mazel; Penguin, 1973.

———. 1981. "Visions and Realities." Paper delivered at dedication conference of Stone Center for Developmental Services and Studies, Wellesley College, October 24.

Mitchell, Juliet. 1974. *Psychoanalysis and Feminism.* New York: Random House; Vintage Books, 1975.

Money, John, and A. Ehrhardt. 1973. *Man and Woman, Boy and Girl.* Baltimore: Johns Hopkins University Press.

Mornell, Pierre. *Passive Men, Wild Women.* 1979. New York: Simon & Schuster.

Moulton, Ruth. 1973. "A Survey and Reevaluation of the Concept of Penis Envy." In *Psychoanalysis and Women.* Edited by Jean Baker Miller. New York: Brunner/Mazel; Penguin, 1973.

Nagera, Humberto. 1975. *Female Sexuality and the Oedipus Complex.* New York: Jason Aronson.

Napier, August Y., with Carl A. Whitaker. 1978. *The Family Crucible.* New York: Harper & Row; Bantam Books, 1980.

Neely, James C. 1981. *Gender: The Myth of Equality.* New York: Simon & Schuster.

Nin, Anaïs. 1966. *The Diary of Anaïs Nin,* Vol. I. New York: Harcourt Brace Jovanovich.

Offer, Daniel, Eric Ostrov, and Kenneth I. Howard. 1981. *A Psychological Self-Portrait.* New York: Basic Books.

Orthner, Dennis K., and Ken Lewis. 1979. "Evidence of Single-Father Competence in Childrearing." *Family Law Quarterly* (Spring).

Parke, Ross D. 1981. *Fathers.* Cambridge, Mass.: Harvard University Press.

Parsons, Talcott. 1949. "The Social Structure of the Family." In *The Family: Its Function and Destiny.* Edited by R. N. Anshen. New York: Harper & Row.

―――. 1954. "The Incest Taboo in Relation to Social Structure and the Socialization of the Child." *British Journal of Sociology* 5: 57–77.

―――. 1964. *Social Structure and Personality.* Glencoe, Ill.: Free Press.

Parsons, Talcott, and R. F. Bales. 1955. *Family, Socialization and Interaction Process.* Glencoe, Ill.: Free Press.

Peck, M. Scott. 1978. *The Road Less Traveled.* New York: Touchstone.

Pedersen, Frank A., ed. 1980. *The Father-Infant Relationship.* New York: Praeger.

Plath, Sylvia. 1971. *The Bell Jar.* New York: Harper & Row.

―――. 1975. *Letters Home: Correspondence 1950–1963.* Edited by Aurelia Schober Plath. New York: Harper & Row.

Pogrebin, Letty Cottin. 1980. *Growing Up Free.* New York: McGraw-Hill.

Richards, Janet Radcliffe. 1980. *The Sceptical Feminist.* Boston: Routledge & Kegan Paul.

Rivers, Caryl, Rosalind Barnett, and Grace Baruch. 1979. *Beyond Sugar & Spice.* New York: G. P. Putnam's Sons.

Romm, M. E. 1969. "Effects of the Mother-child Relationship and the Father-child Relationship on Psychosexual Development." *Medical Aspects of Human Sexuality* (February).

Rossi, Alice. 1977. "A Biosocial Perspective on Parenting." *Daedalus* (Spring).

Scarf, Maggie. 1980. *Unfinished Business.* Garden City, N.Y.: Doubleday & Co.

Schnall, Maxine. 1981. *Limits.* New York: Clarkson N. Potter.

Sheehy, Gail. 1976. *Passages.* New York: E. P. Dutton; Bantam Books, 1977.

Sherfey, Mary Jane. 1973. *The Nature and Evolution of Female Sexuality.* New York: Random House.

Spencer, Scott. 1979. *Endless Love.* New York: Alfred A. Knopf.

Steinberg, Laurence D. 1980. *Understanding Families with Young Adolescents.* Chapel Hill: Center for Early Adolescence at the University of North Carolina.

Stoller, R. J. 1968. *Sex and Gender.* New York: Science House.

———. 1976. "Primary Femininity." In *Female Psychology: Contemporary Psychoanalytic Views.* Edited by H. P. Blum. New York: International Universities Press, 1977.

Styron, William. 1951. *Lie Down in Darkness.* New York: The Bobbs-Merrill Co.

Sulloway, Frank J. 1979. *Freud, Biologist of the Mind: Beyond the Psychoanalytic Legend.* New York: Basic Books.

Thompson, Clara. 1941. "The Role of Women in This Culture." In *Women & Analysis.* Edited by Jean Strouse. New York: Grossman; Dell Publishing, 1973.

———. 1942. "Culture Pressures in the Psychology of Women." In *Psychoanalysis & Women.* Edited by Jean Baker Miller. New York: Brunner/Mazel; Penguin, 1973.

Tillich, Paul. 1952. *The Courage to Be.* New Haven, Conn.: Yale University Press.

Wallerstein, Judith S., and Joan B. Kelly. 1980. *Surviving the Break Up: How Children Actually Cope with Divorce.* New York: Basic Books.

Winnicott, D. W. 1965. *The Family and Individual Development.* New York: Basic Books.

———. 1971. *Playing and Reality.* New York: Basic Books.

Wolfenstein, Martha. 1966. "How Is Mourning Possible?" *Psychoanalytical Study of the Child* 21.

Zalk, Suzanne Rosenberg. 1981. "Transition from Son to Father: Unresolved Psycho-sexual Conflicts in Expectant Fathers." Paper presented at the American Psychological Association conference, Los Angeles, August.